Scarlet and Black

Scarlet and Black

Volume 2

Constructing Race and Gender at Rutgers, 1865–1945

EDITED BY KENDRA BOYD,
MARISA J. FUENTES, AND
DEBORAH GRAY WHITE

RUTGERS UNIVERSITY PRESS

NEW BRUNSWICK, CAMDEN, AND NEWARK, NEW JERSEY, AND LONDON

Library of Congress in Publication Control Number: 2016955389

ISBN 978-1-9788-1633-6 (cloth)
ISBN 978-1-9788-1302-1 (paper)
ISBN 978-1-9788-1303-8 (epub)

A British Cataloging-in-Publication record for this book is available from the British Library.

www.rutgersuniversitypress.org

Manufactured in the United States of America

CONTENTS

Epilogue: The Forerunner Generation   155
   DEBORAH GRAY WHITE

Scarlet and Black

Introduction

DEBORAH GRAY WHITE

Chair of the Committee on the Enslaved
and Disenfranchised in Rutgers History

> But they should not keep these prizes, I said; some, all, I would wrest
> from them. Just how I would do it, I could never decide: by reading
> law, by healing the sick, by telling the wonderful tales that swam in my
> head, –some way.
>
> Why did God make me an outcast and a stranger in mine own house?
>
> –W.E.B. Du Bois, *The Souls of Black Folk*

"How does it feel to be a problem?" At the dawn of the twentieth century, W.E.B. Du Bois, the preeminent African American intellectual, used this question to query white feelings about black people. Of course, he did not think black people were a problem. Rather, he thought that this probing question lurked in the minds of whites who found it hard to speak to him directly about race, who instead spoke circuitously of excellent colored people whose opportunities were thwarted, or about southern horrors too gruesome to fathom. Long before he indulged white people's duplicity as an adult, he had resolved to beat them at their own game: "I could beat my mates at examination-time, or beat them at a foot-race, or even beat their stringy heads."[1]

Though whites had reserved the best of everything for themselves and made him an outcast in his own land, Du Bois understood himself to be worthy of everything his American citizenship, intellect, and ability could achieve. To him, black people were not a problem; white people were. Indeed, he posed the issue differently and profoundly. "The problem of the twentieth century is the problem of the color line," he declared. Whether white people would erase it, and/or how black people would navigate it—that was the issue.[2] Du Bois, who earned two degrees from Harvard—a BA in 1890 and a PhD in 1895—resolved not to wait for whites to manage the color line, but to get an education so he could control his own destiny.

So did the twenty-five or so black men and women who attended Rutgers and the New Jersey College for Women before World War II.[3] They were an exceptional cohort, not only because they were among the tiny number of Americans, of any race, to earn the baccalaureate degree, but also because they were among the small percentage of blacks to earn the degree at a predominantly white institution. At the turn of the century, Rutgers, like its Ivy League peers, educated the children of the white elite and upper middle class.[4] Most African Americans who earned advanced degrees did so at segregated agricultural and industrial training institutions in the South, not because they did not want to attend better funded white institutions but because white administrators subscribed to the logic behind the 1896 *Plessy v. Ferguson* Supreme Court ruling that upheld the prevailing "scientifically" based notions that blacks were an inferior race that had to be separated from whites. Historically black colleges and universities (HBCUs) like Howard, Hampton, Fisk, Morehouse, Spelman, Tuskegee, Wilberforce, Lincoln, and Florida A&M, educated black America's talented youth and sent them forth to do uplift work for the race.[5] The small number of African Americans who daily braved the few white campuses that allowed them to matriculate were like W.E.B. Du Bois. Though the color of their skin outwardly marked them as outcasts, inside they carried a resolve that allowed them to wrest the prizes that came with an elite education. Early black Rutgers students were among those determined pioneers. As this volume demonstrates, though they were grudgingly, sometimes accidently, admitted, like Du Bois they would not be deterred.

The Rutgers that the pioneers encountered was not and had never been in the vanguard of institutions that practiced racial equalitarianism. Native Americans were dispossessed of the land on which Rutgers was built years before ground was broken on the college, but Rutgers never enrolled Native American converts to Christianity despite their desire to attend. As detailed in *Scarlet and Black*, Vol. 1: *Slavery and Dispossession in Rutgers History*, Rutgers, or Queens College, as it was known in the eighteenth century, was founded and sustained by slave traders and slaveholders. The family of Jacob Hardenburgh, the first president of Rutgers, owned the parents of Sojourner Truth, the renowned abolitionist and women's rights advocate. Old Queens, the first Rutgers building, was built by enslaved men whose masters were paid for their labor. In fact, Rutgers depended on the enslaved to build its campuses and serve its students; it depended on the sale of black people to fund its very existence. The faculty and curriculum at Rutgers reinforced the theological and scientific racism that provided the justification for the free labor of Africans, the absolute power of slave owners, and the separation of the races. Through their leadership of the state and regional boards of the American Colonization Society (ACS), men like John Henry Livingston (Rutgers president, 1810–1824), the Reverend Philip Milledoler (Rutgers president, 1824–1840), Henry Rutgers (trustee after whom the college is named), and Theodore Frelinghuysen (seventh president), agitated not to liberate African Americans from bondage but to colonize free blacks in Africa. Like Frelinghuysen they believed African Americans to be "a depressed and separate race" who were "licentious, ignorant, and irritated."[6] By 1892, the time James Dickson Carr became the first African American Rutgers graduate, the school had solidified its status as a land-grant school by receiving money from the sale of Indian lands in the West, land that was taken from Native Americans by force.[7] In short, nothing in its history had prepared Rutgers administrators, professors, or students to treat African Americans, much less African American students, equitably.

It was a miracle of sorts that any African Americans attended Rutgers in the late nineteenth century, the period in African American history known as the nadir. Because it was marked by white vigilante terror, peonage, lynchings, race riots, black codes, the convict lease system, disenfranchisement, and Jim Crow segregation, many scholars have questioned whether legal slavery ever really ended. Some have argued that the Thirteenth Amendment that ended slavery actually ushered in a period that was "worse than slavery," or "slavery by another name."[8] And the system of racial oppression that emerged after the Civil War was not a southern phenomenon, but national in scope. Although northern communities did not erect signs that separated blacks from whites, they nevertheless cordoned blacks off into everything that was least desirable. In the words of historian Thomas Sugrue,

> Public policy and the market confined blacks to declining neighborhoods; informal Jim Crow excluded them from restaurants, hotels, amusement parks, and swimming pools and relegated them to separate sections of theaters. All but a small number of northern blacks attended racially segregated and inferior schools. As adults, blacks faced formidable obstacles to economic security. They were excluded from whole sectors of the labor market. And as a result of the combined effects of segregation, discrimination and substandard education, they remained overrepresented in the ranks of the unemployed and poor.[9]

New Jersey was like other northern and western states. Although an 1881 law banned segregation in all public accommodations and schools, and outlawed segregation on juries, the law was inconsequential first because localities and merchants routinely ignored it, and second because the costs of fighting violations were prohibitive. Only two lawsuits were filed for violations of the law in the area of school segregation. Like the white citizens of Fairhaven, New Jersey, who in 1881 built a separate school for black children in

order to keep their schools white, New Jersey white citizens preferred segregation over integration.[10] Similarly, by 1896 blacks were barred from amusement
rides and beaches in Atlantic City and similar recreation areas along the Jersey Shore and in the Palisades. In Newark, blacks were barred from Olympic
Park, and everywhere housing was segregated and inadequate.[11] While blacks
were kept out of white neighborhoods by bankers who refused loans and white
homeowners who used vigilante justice and restrictive covenants, employers
used blacks as scabs to break strikes, and labor union hostility kept blacks in
the lowest paid jobs. Only six of twenty-two New Jersey labor organizations
opened their doors to blacks.[12] Part of what some historians call "Up South" or
the "Jim Crow North," New Jersey was not a haven from the heartless South.[13]

Still, it was the destination of thousands of African Americans who fled
the South in the late nineteenth and early twentieth centuries looking for
a better life. Black New Jersey's population tripled between 1870 and 1910.
In 1900 blacks made up 3.2 percent of the state's population; by 1930 they
were 5.2 percent, or 208,828. In 1940 New Jersey's black population was over
226,000.[14] New Brunswick's demographics also changed. Between 1870 and
1930, the city's black population grew from 577 to 2,086.[15] If African Americans in the state and the city of New Brunswick looked to Rutgers, their
state-supported university, to be a liberalizing force, they were sorely disappointed. Rutgers proved to be much like the rest of New Jersey in upholding
white supremacy. Though the black students who attended Rutgers before
World War II made the most of the opportunity to attend Rutgers, the school
adhered to policies and ideologies that made these pioneers outcasts and
strangers in their own school.

Scarlet and Black: Constructing Race and Gender at Rutgers, 1865–1945 charts
race and African Americans at Rutgers from shortly before the Civil War to
World War II. It begins with the stories of two African American men who
entered the New Brunswick Theological Seminary as the first black students of
that institution. Islay Walden and John Bergen attended NBTS in 1876, approximately a decade before Rutgers College admitted its first black graduate, James
Dickson Carr, in 1888. Although Bergen's presence as a student in the archives
remains fragmented and fleeting, Islay Walden's more substantial records tell
a remarkable story of an ex-slave with impaired vision who walked from North
Carolina to New Jersey seeking a formal education. His experience at Howard's Normal School and then NBTS as an older student exposes the contradictions in NBTS and Rutgers College philosophies on race, nation, and equal
education in the Rutgers intellectual tradition that championed white Protestantism. The chapter then examines Rutgers fraternities, literary societies,
and journals, demonstrating how both before and after black emancipation,
Rutgers professors and students argued the case for black and Native American inferiority. It also focuses on the school's foreign missionary work and its

essay contests as a way of showing how many Rutgers alumni spread the gospel of white supremacy abroad, making Rutgers a think tank for the ideological foundations of colonialism and imperialism. Chapter 2 expands our understanding of black life in the urban north from *Scarlet and Black*, Volume I, by continuing the study of African Americans in New Brunswick. This chapter follows a period of expanded African American migration north following the Civil War, and into the changing landscape of industrialized northern cities. African Americans would face both expanded labor opportunities not available in the postwar South as well as increased racial discrimination and surveillance typical of such northern migration. The chapter demonstrates that in response, African Americans focused on institution-building to support their growing communities threatened by white supremacy. The post–Civil War period was a time of extensive growth for Rutgers College as it established the Rutgers Scientific School as a land-grant school in 1864, built its own Geological Hall in 1872, opened its first residential dormitory in 1890, and founded the New Jersey College for Women in 1918. Paralleling the expansion of Rutgers, the African American community of New Brunswick grew by leaps and bounds. They eventually overlapped as Rutgers employed local African Americans as waiters, butlers, and housekeepers in their ever-expanding facilities. Close proximity, however, did not alter the racist ideology that oozed from the Rutgers intellectual tradition, nor did it alleviate the hardship that grew from New Brunswick's segregated schools, discriminatory labor market, or outright white terrorism. Chapter 2, therefore, looks closely at the black community that existed in the shadow of Rutgers—their struggles to establish quality education for their children and to build black businesses in the face of job and housing discrimination; their efforts to build institutions in reaction to white exclusion and terror; and the consequences of a demographic pattern that put black women in the majority.

Having established the on- and off-campus landscape that the first black students would have to navigate, Chapters 3 and 4 look at the first black men and women to matriculate at Rutgers and the racial and class projections imbedded in the meaning of "Rutgers Men and Women." Rutgers as an institution put forth images of students as future leaders of the American nation, embodying civic duty, honor, respectability, and social leadership. Thus, the first African American students, mostly from the black middle and upper classes, were self-possessed and intellectually stellar. However, despite their rightful presence and exceptionality at Rutgers, they were not fully embraced. Today they are duly celebrated as trailblazers but in the late nineteenth and early twentieth centuries, theirs was an isolated and lonely walk. Most could not and did not live in dormitories and though they joined some campus clubs, they were barred from other campus events. At Rutgers College, men like Paul Robeson, James Dickson Carr, and James Morrow strove to prove that black people not only deserved equal standing with their white counterparts but that they could achieve excellence and boost the reputation of the college. They pried open racially exclusive Rutgers doors and after graduation most went on to speak and work for black America. Similarly, at New Jersey College for Women (what would become Douglass College) the presence of young women of color, including Julia Baxter Bates, challenged racist representations still emanating from campus newspapers and student print culture circulating in the 1930s and 1940s. The last chapter of *Scarlet and Black* zeros in on two very light-skinned cousins, Julia and Malcolm Baxter, who were among the first African Americans to attend Rutgers. Julia was the first African American woman to graduate from the New Jersey College for Women, later to become Douglass College. Though both came from activist households, after graduation these two cousins' relationship to blackness diverged, and the chapter explores some of the reasons why Malcom Baxter may have chosen to "pass" as white while his cousin Julia spent her career fighting for black equality in New Jersey. The first black students at Rutgers faced many challenges to their right to an elite education. These chapters show how they persevered and opened the doors for future black students to thrive at Rutgers.

As is the case with Volume I of *Scarlet and Black*, this study of Rutgers and black Americans from the mid-nineteenth to the mid-twentieth century by no means exhausts this subject. It is still a beginning but part of an ongoing effort to recover Rutgers history with African Americans as a way of reconciling with it. This second volume is offered in the hope that it will provide insight on the past history of exclusion as a way to move forward with inclusion. Today the Rutgers student body is among the most diverse in the nation. One of its twenty-first-century mandates is to teach students of different cultures to work together for a productive future. The Rutgers motto is "Jersey Roots, Global Reach." *Scarlet and Black* offers this history in the belief that if Rutgers reckons with its roots, its reach will be broader and more meaningful.

1

All the World's a Classroom

The First Black Students Encounter the Racial, Religious, and Intellectual Life of the University

TRACEY JOHNSON, ERI KITADA,
MEAGAN WIERDA, AND JOSEPH WILLIAMS

Islay Walden, a child born from an enslaved woman and a white man, began his life enslaved in North Carolina. After witnessing the close of the Civil War and gaining his freedom, he, like many freed people, sought out employment and the right to an education (Figure 1.1). On an extraordinary journey to fulfill his dreams, Walden walked from North Carolina to Washington, DC, then to New Brunswick, New Jersey. He became one of the first two African American students admitted to the New Brunswick Theological Seminary. In the first decades after the Civil War, the New Brunswick Theological Seminary and its closely affiliated Rutgers College began their long and tenuous relationship with African American students pursuing higher education in the North. The seminary admitted two African American men, Islay Walden and John Bergen, in 1876, approximately a decade before Rutgers College admitted its first black graduate, James Dickson Carr, in 1888. Due to the close quarters of both institutions and their relatively small student bodies, Walden and Bergen represent the first black student presence on the Rutgers campus.

When the newly minted Rutgers College opened its doors for good in 1825, following what amounted to a series of fits and starts since the school's founding as Queen's College in 1766, the student body numbered all of eight people. For the next twenty years the student population hovered steadily around thirty students, until a substantial increase occurred during the 1850s. On the eve of the Civil War, approximately 125 students attended Rutgers College.

Largely made up of middle- and upper-class white men from the New Jersey, New York, and Pennsylvania area, a number of the students could also claim filiality to the college's founders, presidents, trustees, and donors. Many

FIGURE 1.1 "Islay Walden."

RCA Photos & Resources, http://rcaarchives.omeka.net/items
/show/26, Image courtesy of Special Collections and
University Archives, Rutgers University Libraries.

of these men were slave owners or the beneficiaries of the trade and toil of
enslaved men and women. Indeed, the history of Rutgers College had long
been entangled with the history of slavery.[1]

Given that the student body reflected a certain homogenous demographic—white, male, Protestant, and of relative means—it is not surprising
to learn that the college also fostered a related homogeneity in thought and
opinion during the first half of the nineteenth century. More often than not,
this particular worldview was characterized by a politics of moderation and an

aggressive policing of borders based on the dictates of race and religion. While these two tendencies—restraint and aggression—may appear at odds with one another, they nevertheless represent two sides of the same coin. After all, the first half of the nineteenth century was a moment wrought with incredible and widespread changes across the swiftly expanding nation. Though new markets and technologies such as canals and railroads began to crisscross and connect once distant places, some of the most consequential changes seemed to foretell a shake-up of the country's social order. With the specter of the abolition of slavery looming large and a significant number of immigrants reaching the country's shores, it was in the interest of white men to assert their racial and gendered power in order to preserve a status quo that recognized and rewarded their supremacy.

Many of the students of Rutgers College shared in the project of not only safeguarding but extending the prerogatives of white Protestantism, taking their cues from family and faculty along the way. During the first half of the nineteenth century, for example, a number of the college's educators and administrators were avid participants in missionary work among Native Americans as well as advocates for the forcible removal of African Americans beyond the borders of the United States. Though billed as reform efforts, evangelization and colonization were but thinly veiled attempts at creating a nation whose citizens were Christian and nonblack.

Efforts to disseminate this worldview both on and off campus were not limited to the antebellum period. Indeed, the white Protestant ethos animating these violent projects would find new life during the second half of the nineteenth and early twentieth centuries. With the abolition of slavery, many whites feared the loss of their once-sanctioned superiority and thus resorted to a number of legal and extralegal measures to further subjugate and terrorize African Americans. Even those who had opposed slavery found themselves questioning the ability of African Americans to self-govern and thrive. At the same time, white Americans struggled with nonwhite and non-Christian peoples beyond their borders owing to the brutal extension of their overseas empire.[2]

The students and faculty of Rutgers College, buttressed by a long-standing and homegrown intellectual tradition that privileged a white Protestant ideal, defended a particular vision of the American nation state at home and participated in missionary efforts to export it far and wide. By considering the intellectual production of some students, faculty members, and administrators at Rutgers College over nearly a century, alongside the stories of its first black students, this chapter will index the remarkable consistency with which people affiliated with Rutgers were able to justify the marginalization of racial and religious others both at home and abroad.

"That Ex-Slave at Rutgers": Islay Walden and New Brunswick Theological Seminary's Domestic Missionary Impulse

Throughout the nineteenth century, Christian missions were imperative to the students and faculty of the New Brunswick Theological Seminary (NBTS). Faculty minutes show an enthusiasm for the spread of Protestantism throughout the world.[3] Rutgers's foreign missions and the way they viewed nonwhite populations were influenced by the opinions they held of African Americans. After the Civil War ended and with the onset of southern Reconstruction, many northern whites sojourned south to evangelize among the newly freed people. Historian Eric Foner wrote that these northerners were not successful "partly because of their ill-disguised contempt for uneducated black ministers and their emotional services."[4] Missionaries to the South attempted to modify the behavior of black church services by repudiating the dancing, clapping, and call and response that they viewed as "heathenish." They aimed to raise a new class of black preachers trained in theology.[5] Faculty and students from the NBTS saw their institution's missionary work as essential to spreading the gospel nationally and internationally. Although there is no evidence to suggest NBTS students went south to conduct missions, the seminary carried out their own form of missions to the South's newly freed people.

Little is known about Walden's classmate, John Bergen. The seminary's biographical records list Bergen as a "blind Negro" who joined the Southern Presbyterian Church in Columbus, Georgia, after graduating in 1879. He passed away in 1893.[6] Walden, on the other hand, left a significant paper trail and lived quite an exceptional life. Born in slavery in North Carolina in 1843, Walden's status differed from his father, grandfather, and great-grandfather, who were all freemen. His father, William D. Walden, had a relationship with an enslaved woman named Ruth Gardner. Laws of the time stated that the status of Islay and other black children followed the condition of their mothers. Gardner passed away when Walden was only eight years of age.[7]

By all accounts Islay showed intellectual talents from a young age. One of his masters, so impressed by Islay's mathematical skills, would take the young boy into town and wager bets on how long it would take Islay to finish a complicated equation. Walden also acquired the gift of literacy through his master's wife, who taught him how to read by candlelight—despite the illegality of teaching slaves how to read. Perhaps seeing how bright young Islay was, or simply knowing the positive impact literacy could have on his life, his mistress decided to take the chance despite the potential consequences.[8] These skills enabled Walden to express his feelings through poetry—an art form in which he became quite skilled. One of his poems articulates his thoughts on the ending of the Civil War:

But now I see the war is ended,
And all thy anger is suspended;
Peace I think I hear thee crying,
As thou art to the Union Flying.

And Hallelujahs I am singing,
To see my race from bonds are springing,
For sure a better time is coming,
The insects whisper through their humming.

So now farewell to plough and hoeing,
For I to Yankee town am going;
No longer will I drive this wagon,
Nor under slavery's chains be swagging,

But Dixie, oh, the land of cotton,
Let slavery die and be forgotten;
And we will turn unto each nation
With greater zeal for education.[9]

This is an excerpt from his poem entitled "An Address to Dixie." It chronicles his own experiences witnessing the defeat of the Confederacy and the birth of freedom for himself and his enslaved brethren. On the day of Robert E. Lee's surrender in 1865, Islay worked in a gold mine in North Carolina. Freedom brought Walden the option to decide what he wanted to do with his life. He left the gold mine and the state on foot and made his way north to live out the "zeal for education" he wrote about.[10]

Walden arrived in Washington, DC, in 1867 where he hoped to attend Howard University, which was established in the same year. While in DC, Walden could not afford the tuition at Howard, so he yet again set off on foot northward to explore other opportunities. On his journey he made money by selling his poems. He eventually found his way to New Brunswick in 1870 and met George Atherton, professor of political science at Rutgers, who, through the Theological Seminary, pledged $150 per year for Walden's education at Howard under the agreement that he would return to New Brunswick and enter the theological seminary.[11]

Islay graduated with a bachelor of arts degree from Howard's Normal School Department in 1876. Not long after he made his way back to New Brunswick and enrolled in the seminary.[12] Faculty minutes from 1877 show that although Walden and Bergen took seminary courses, the Board of Superintendents did not officially sanction their attendance.[13] This is notable because seminary faculty essentially admitted Walden and Bergen provisionally, before asking permission from a higher authority. These two men were exceptions to the de facto segregation that governed the NBTS, Rutgers

College, and most mainstream educational institutions countrywide in the nineteenth century.[14] Perhaps Walden and Bergen were afforded this opportunity because, unlike most stereotypical depictions of black men, they were not seen as threat. Bergen was blind and Walden also struggled with his vision, they were both married, and Walden's considerable fame as a poet made him rather popular with students and faculty. It was in part because of Walden's rapport with students themselves that he was allowed to take classes among his white classmates.[15]

Walden's presence at the NBTS soon became known to those at other universities and stirred up a small controversy. During his first stay in New Brunswick in 1870, Yale College's student newspaper *The College Courant* wrote about Walden in their "College Gossip" column. It simply stated, "An ex-slave . . . thirty-five years of age, has entered Rutgers College where he will be maintained by the Second Reformed Church of New Brunswick."[16] In January 1871 Rutgers's student newspaper, *The Targum*, published a blistering rebuttal entitled "That Ex-Slave at Rutgers." The author, only known as Bayard, suggested that the Yale article was tasteless and written only to disparage the name of Rutgers, as the column did not include all of the facts on Walden's relationship with Rutgers and the seminary. Bayard wrote that Yale's column was "a little spicy, nutshelly line" that led to "outrage perpetrated on the name of [Rutgers]."[17] Bayard chronicles the events that led to Walden's relationship with Rutgers and seminary faculty, stating that after one conversation with Islay, Professor Atherton "describe[d] [Walden] as a man of unusual intelligence and observing faculties—showing wisdom of men and events quite extraordinary."[18] Bayard suggested that Walden's affiliation with the seminary was justified not only due to his intelligence, but because Walden "manifested a great desire to work among his own people in North Carolina, and will probably be sent there, when educated, to organize churches, etc. Of course, any help the Second Reformed Church afforded him was perfectly appropriate under these circumstances."[19] Bayard's words highlight, again, that Walden was accepted because of his exceptional intellectual faculties and not for integration in the white religious community. Rather, he would be sent away in service of "his own people." Walden and Bergen alike would have been anomalies to student and staff at Rutgers whose public discourse on race painted black and brown people as inferior.

His emphasis on the fact that Walden would not stay at the NBTS or in New Jersey for too long is, indeed, curious. Scholars have thoroughly documented the fear white northerners held of black southerners who migrated north. Historians such as Kali N. Gross, Khalil Muhammad, and Cheryl Hicks highlight that southern blacks were seen as inherently criminal and as posing a threat to northern society.[20] In his influential monograph *The Condemnation of Blackness*, Muhammad highlights the discussions white thinkers had on the problem that black freedom posed to white society. Thinkers such as Nathaniel Shaler wrote articles on the "Negro Problem" which argued that African Americans were not fit for citizenship and characterized blacks as "savages" and "beasts."[21] These beliefs of black inferiority and criminality justified discrimination against black people. Conversely, this does not seem to be the case with Walden, though, as people continually touted him as exceptional due to his prowess in math and poetry. Additionally, throughout NBTS records, he is portrayed as unthreatening due to his vision impairment and the fact that his wife was in New Brunswick with him. Bayard's quote does hint at the disdain whites held for socially aspirant blacks such as Walden who were well educated and "respectable." The college and the city of New Brunswick, had long exercised social control over blacks, free and enslaved, since its establishment.[22] Walden's nonpermanent presence in New Brunswick comforted whites in the city who were used to blacks occupying occupations and attitudes of deference. In this instance, although whites considered Walden exceptional, his exceptionality did not exempt him from views held about race and black comportment deeply entrenched nationally.

Minutes from Rutgers College's Philoclean Society (a student literary society common in early colonial universities) indicate disinterest in the lives of newly freed people. In 1877, Walden's second year at the seminary, the society debated whether the Compromise Bill of 1877 should be adopted. They "decided in favor of the affirmative."[23] The Compromise Bill of 1877 effectively ended Reconstruction in the South when Republicans and moderate southern Democrats plotted together to settle the disputed 1876 presidential election. The Republican candidate Rutherford B. Hayes was instated under the condition that Republican governments in Louisiana and South Carolina were abandoned. Historian C. Vann Woodward said of the compromise that "the Southerners were abandoning the cause of [their candidate] in exchange for control over two states, and the Republicans were abandoning the cause of the Negro in exchange for the peaceful possession of the presidency."[24] There was much at stake that resulted in the creation of this bill that the Philoclean Society may have discussed, including the dismantling of Republican rule in the former Confederate South. The compromise proved that the newly rejoined nation could choose a president without force. However, despite their reasons for voting to affirm the compromise, members of the society would have known the effect this compromise could potentially have on the newly freed people of the South. Their vote for the Compromise Bill of 1877 highlights the lack of concern they had for the plight and future of black people.

Of course, this disinterest was not indicative of all students or faculty at the seminary or Rutgers College. Walden's relationship with Rutgers professor George W. Atherton, while undoubtedly paternalistic, came with perhaps the best intentions of all Walden's institutional ties. Atherton was connected to Rutgers College, not the seminary, and the missionary impulse that was so integral to the seminary may not have been at the forefront of Atherton's mind. Atherton, professor of history, political economy, and constitutional law, graduated from Yale in 1863 and arrived at Rutgers to teach in 1871. Between these years he served voluntarily for the Union Army.[25] Although Atherton and Walden were born into vastly different circumstances, they had many commonalities. For example, Atherton's father died and left nothing for the family, when Atherton was a young boy. Atherton was forced to toil in a mill to earn a living for himself and when he was seventeen, Atherton's zeal for education led him to work and save to obtain a college education.[26] Perhaps, upon meeting Walden and hearing his life story, Atherton empathized on a personal level. Atherton's efforts to secure Walden one hundred and fifty dollars a year for his schooling at Howard University—not a small amount—suggests Atherton held respect and a fondness for him.

Although Walden had a good rapport with faculty and students, he still faced many difficulties during his tenure at NBTS. In 1878 Walden penned a letter to Professor David D. Demarest who was a member of the NBTS faculty, asking for a reduction in his rent due to financial struggles. Demarest was on the Hertzog Hall Committee, which was in charge of the seminary building and dealt with numerous matters including financial obligations. Walden recognized the debt he owed to the Hertzog Hall Committee but justified it due to "having been born afflicted in [his] eyes," and stated that it was "a great disadvantage under which [he] labor[ed]." Next, Walden highlighted the particular burden he carried as an African American student, stating: "As we have no colored churches it is hardly natural for me to take my turn in preaching on the Sabbath."[27] Although New Brunswick's Mount Zion A.M.E. Church existed and served the African American community of the city, Walden's affiliation with the Dutch Reformed denomination could have prevented him from preaching there.[28]

Walden's letter is revealing for a number of reasons: the "we" in Walden's letter refers to the Dutch Reformed Church, not the African American church in New Brunswick, since the Mount Zion A.M.E. Church was well established in the city at this point. Walden's use of the adjective "we" was a light critique of the NBTS and the Protestant church—that although Walden, the exception, was taken in by the NBTS, they had not yet made strides to evangelize to the black community in New Brunswick. Walden continued on about the ways in which he filled this gap and made an impact on local African Americans. Walden wrote that he "established what is called the Student's Mission which consists of 60 odd scholars, most of which were gathered from the streets." Although his cause added to his experience in preaching and evangelizing, it actually cost him money to run. He notes that some of the members "were so poor and destitute that we were not only compelled to fix them up but in many cases I had to buy soap that the peculiar scavengers might be removed."[29] Walden's altruism was at the expense of his own well-being. The letter highlighted the impossibility of Walden's situation—his vision impairment limited how much he could accomplish, scholastically or financially, without assistance. He at least sought an understanding of his situation—his race restricted where he could preach, and his institutional affiliation with the NBTS presumably barred his ability to preach at the Mount Zion A.M.E. Church. These were all things that hindered his financial situation.

The Hertzog Hall Committee's decision on whether or not to reduce Walden's rent is unknown—no trace of it exists in the archive. Perhaps, they agreed to lessen Walden's burden. It cannot be understated that the choice of NBTS to admit Walden and Bergen was a progressive one in its day. During Walden's time at the seminary he encountered the charitable nature of a few professors and students. It must be remembered, though, that Walden's story, much like his presence on campus, was an exception. Students and faculty at NBTS and Rutgers continued to hold personal views of black people that were less generous. These men did not shy away from expressing their beliefs publicly.

Associational Life and the Prerogatives of White Protestantism

Some of the earliest vectors for—and vindicators of—Rutgers's ideological consensus were student groups on campus and, in particular, two rival literary societies formed in 1825: the Philoclean Society and the Peithessophian Society of Rutgers College. Though these were not the first literary societies founded at the college, they were by far the longest lasting and most influential, especially during the second quarter of the nineteenth century.[30] Precursors—and in many ways parallel—to fraternities, these literary societies were the preeminent student groups on campus. And, given how few people attended the college during the second quarter of the nineteenth century, nearly every student belonged to one.

Membership to either the Philoclean or Peithessophian Society not only complemented the classical education students received at Rutgers, but it also helped to reinforce a particular culture of inclusion and exclusion. As historian Nicholas L. Syrett argues, associational life was a means of creating and maintaining social divisions based on race, class, and gender. Indeed, groups like fraternities and literary societies were powerful agents of conformity.[31] However, with an all-white, all-male student body during much of the nineteenth century, this conformity might seem like a foregone conclusion. However, the members of the Philoclean and Peithessophian Societies did not simply reflect institutional prerogatives but rather actively—and at times even aggressively—cultivated a sense of belonging that was white and

Christian. Not only did these societies reflect an implicit understanding about who belonged on campus but its members actively defended this logic within the United States and abroad.

Both the Philoclean and Peithessophian Societies were heavily bureaucratized groups. They produced and revised constitutions and by-laws, recorded meeting minutes, logged membership rolls, exacted dues and fines, and established impressive private libraries. One of the key features of membership, however, was participation in the weekly debates. Not only were these debates meant to hone the oratory skills of aspiring lawyers and politicians, they also articulated a range of concerns governing the period. While a number of these concerns were somewhat pedestrian—for example, students wondered if matrimony was preferable to celibacy—others were much more contemplative, inspiring such questions as whether or not private feelings should be sacrificed to the public interest. Perhaps not surprisingly, though, the most pressing and frequently discussed subjects of debate were illustrative of two of the period's greatest sources of anxiety: Indian Removal and slavery.[32]

Following their respective foundings, the question of whether or not white Americans were justified in driving Indians from their land dominated the debates of both literary societies. The 1829 election of Andrew Jackson, who made Indian Removal one of the cornerstones of his presidency, no doubt gave weight to this urgent issue.[33] Within the Philoclean Society, a spate of questions between 1829 and 1831 confirms this point—"Were the Europeans justifiable in dispossessing [sic] the Aborigines of the [United States] of their native land[?]," "Is it just for the United States to drive the Indians beyond the Mississippi[?]," "Has the Government of the United States in any instance treated the Indians unjustly[?]," and "Would the forcible expulsion of the Cherokee from Georgia be justifiable[?]"[34]

The issue of slavery proved an even more enduring one. During the second quarter of the nineteenth century, the members of the Philoclean Society debated questions related to slavery or the status of African Americans on no less than a dozen occasions. Subjects of debate included whether or not slavery was justifiable, whether or not immediate or gradual emancipation was preferable, and whether abolition or colonization provided "the best means of doing justice for our colored population and of elevating their moral condition."[35] Unfortunately, the arguments made in favor of and against various claims were not recorded in the meeting minutes; only the outcomes of the debate were preserved. Still, we can draw a number of correspondences between the literary societies at Rutgers College and the fraught nature of political discourse during the antebellum period.

For example, we know that the nature of the debates on campus became increasingly impassioned as the Civil War approached, as a growing number of members were fined and censured for their disorderly behavior. On one occasion in the fall of 1855, the members of the Philoclean Society considered the following question: "Should an American obey the fugitive slave law[?]" The Fugitive Slave Law of 1850, an amplified version of its late-eighteenth-century predecessor, was an incredibly polarizing piece of legislation that pit aggrieved southern slave owners against enslaved runaways and their allies. This revised and robust law not only had the imprimatur of the American state but benefited from the latter's considerable resources, too. From capture to courthouse, alleged fugitive slaves were at the mercy of large bureaucratic apparatus that had the power to override state and local laws in order to enlist ordinary individuals in the capture of runaways. Indeed, average citizens could be deputized at will and forced to hunt down suspected fugitives or, conversely, fined and imprisoned for harboring or concealing them. Thus, when the question of obeying the Fugitive Slave Law was raised at a meeting of the Philoclean Society in October 1855, its members were forced to grapple with the very constitutionality of slavery in the United States. Moreover, the rowdy debate that ensued belies the idea that northerners were unanimous in their dislike of slavery.[36]

These debates also allow us to extrapolate some of the political sympathies and orientations of Rutgers students. We also know that certain topics, like colonization, resonated with the students more than others. The concept of colonization, or the belief in and practice of removing enslaved and free blacks from the United States to West Africa, was not an unfamiliar one to the denizens of Rutgers College. Many of the college's trustees and faculty members were enthusiastic members of the American Colonization Society (ACS), a self-proclaimed antislavery organization formed in 1816. While it is true that many members of the ACS opposed slavery, they nevertheless espoused a thinly veiled antiblackness that ultimately denied equality to individuals of African descent. For advocates of colonization, true freedom for African Americans could only be achieved outside of the United States. This deferred and ultimately conditional freedom embodied the kind of gradualist politics that defined the ACS.[37]

Given that the Rutgers community was relatively close-knit during the antebellum period, it is not surprising to learn that the gradualist politics of the administrators trickled down to the students, who entertained the idea of forming their very own auxiliary of the ACS. Indeed, the members of the Philoclean Society who debated the merits of colonization were the very same group energized by a rousing pro-colonizationist commencement address delivered by the college's fifth president, Philip Milledoler, in 1831.[38] Milledoler was a consummate antebellum reformer. Not only was he the vice president of New York state's auxiliary colonization society between 1824 and 1829, but he was also an ordained minister and member of the American Bible Society, the United Foreign Missionary Society, and a past participant in missionary work among the Osage in Missouri. It is not surprising, then, that Milledoler encouraged African Americans to seize the continent of their ancestors in order to "regenerate" it. For men like Milledoler, colonization served a double function: not only did it put an end to slavery, which he regarded as a legitimate sin, but it also allowed for the evangelization of the supposedly benighted people of West Africa. The desire to abolish slavery among colonizationists, then, could not be separated from an aggressive white evangelical chauvinism that disparaged West African culture and customs in order to justify American interventionism abroad.[39]

While we may have a clearer sense of the political and religious orientations of men like Philip Milledoler, whose work and deeds were largely unambiguous, we nevertheless have occasion to make certain claims about the intellectual climate of Rutgers College as well as its students at mid-century. From its deep-seated ties to slavery, both at home and abroad, its proven political gradualism, as well as its distinctive Protestant bent, the college seemed to foster a conservative ethos. This context undoubtedly shaped the political orientations of its students, who learned that their white Protestantism effectively ensured that they would always be the agents—not subjects—of debate.

Print and Prejudice at Rutgers College

In order to better understand the intellectual climate at Rutgers College, we can to turn to two short-lived yet insightful literary journals published by its students: the *Rutgers Literary Miscellany* (1842) and the *Rutgers College Quarterly* (1858–1861). Unlike the debates of the Philoclean Society, for example, these literary journals recorded students' viewpoints and allow us to gauge their attitude concerning a range of contemporary issues during the tense two decades before the Civil War. Indeed, if we think of both of these periodicals as barometers for the intellectual and political orientation of the student body, it is unmistakably one of a gradualist moderation coupled with the need to maintain the prerogatives and privileges of white Protestants. For these men, nothing less than the sanctity of the American political project was at stake.

The *Rutgers Literary Miscellany* lived up to its name. It contained editorial items, poetry, short stories, essays, local notices, commencement addresses, and much more. Some of the items were reprinted from previously published works; others were the original compositions of students and the occasional faculty member. Though it only lasted a year, the magazine found time to stoke the flames of patriotism, warn its readers about the "insinuation" of foreign manners within the United States, counseled readers on the virtues of prudence and conciliation, as well as decry the perceived increase in fanaticism.

In an article entitled "Ultraism," the anonymous author denounced those "who seem governed by no rule but the rule of extremes, and who uproot former systems and former usages without any regard to propriety."[40] While the author was speaking in more or less general terms about their perception of the rise of religious and philosophical extremism, transcendentalism included, the specter of radical abolitionism loomed large.

When this article first appeared in 1842, the country had long been roiling over the question of slavery. Defenders of the peculiar institution were made particularly uneasy by a series of slave revolts during the 1820s and 1830s, an outpouring of antislavery petitions in Congress, newspapers and pamphlets that advocated immediate—and sometimes even violent—abolition, and the prospect of racial "amalgamation," or interracial marriage or sex. If anyone was looking to "uproot former systems" it was abolitionists. Faced with these mounting threats, proponents of slavery not only instituted a "gag rule" in the House of Representatives, which automatically tabled all antislavery petitioning between 1836 and 1844, but many also participated in frenzied anti-abolitionist riots in New York (1834) and Philadelphia (1835).[41] In spite of countless deterrents, a number of abolitionists maintained a single-minded commitment to achieving racial justice, earning them such degrading labels as "fanatic" and "monomaniac."[42] The condemnation of the related "ultraism" in the previously cited piece, then, is entirely consistent with the gradualist moderation espoused by the affiliates of Rutgers College. Instead of advocating for the overthrow of a violent and static social order, the *Rutgers Literary Miscellany* preached, as in the original piece entitled "Prudence," "vigilance in conduct, discrimination in judgment, and the dissipation of fantastic and impracticable schemes for advancing the welfare of society."[43]

Many of these beliefs and ideas were reprised and sharpened in the *Rutgers College Quarterly*. Published well over a decade after the demise of the *Rutgers Literary Miscellany*—at the height of the sectional crisis—by the members of the Philoclean and Peithessophian Societies, the *College Quarterly* nevertheless considered itself its intellectual heir. This relative continuity in thought over successive generations of Rutgers College students suggests something important about the political and intellectual milieu it fostered. Indeed, if its forerunner merely hinted at the conservatism permeating the campus, the *College Quarterly* outright defended it.

In an 1858 article entitled "Old Fogyism," the anonymous author reflects upon the invective so often levied against conservatives by "would-be reformers." While the author concedes that clinging to a "blind conservatism" is problematic, he nevertheless takes issue with the widespread characterization of all traditionalists this way. He accuses reformers of employing catchwords like "practical education," "common sense religion," and "human equality" to garner support, while branding all others opposed to these tenets as "bigots" and "old fogies." Continuing, he wrote:

> Review the course of political strife for the last few years, and note those men who have stood by our constitution and the principles of the elder time; you will find that they all have received this title, and noisy politicians have re-echoed it in every corner of the land. What, then, is old fogyism? Is it adhering to those principles which have made our country the asylum of the oppressed—the home of the free? Is it refusing to worship at the shrine of human wisdom, instead of the altar of the living God? If it be, let the slab above my final resting-place have but that one word of eulogy. But if it be not this, modern agitators must be more careful in its application, or it will become a title more to be desired than royal honors.[44]

While this piece is, for the most part, vague in its condemnation of the efforts of "would-be reformers," the author's reference to "the course of political strife for the last few years" and his dismissal of "human equality" as nothing more than a catchword suggest he was likely referring to radical abolitionists.

By the time this article came out, the simmering political tensions of the 1830s and 1840s had reached a boiling point. The Compromise of 1850—a collection of bills that included the controversial Fugitive Slave Law—had barely eased the friction between slave and nonslaveholding states, as best evidenced by a series of violent and bloody clashes that erupted in Kansas in 1854 over the future of slavery in that state. The role played by radical white abolitionist John Brown in some of these confrontations was particularly troubling to slavery's defenders. Moreover, and perhaps with greater consequence, 1857 saw the United States Supreme Court rule in the case of *Dred Scott v. Sandford* that individuals of African descent—whether enslaved or free—were not and could never be citizens of the United States and that Congress could not ban slavery in the territories.[45] Political strife, it turns out, was an understatement. In response to the Dred Scott decision, abolitionist William Lloyd Garrison, a man who famously referred to the United States Constitution as a "covenant with death" and an "agreement with hell,"[46] argued that his home state of Massachusetts should continue to defy the dictates of the Fugitive Slave Law as well as refuse "a human being to be put on trial to decide whether he has a right to himself, or is the property of another."[47] In effect, Garrison was asking slavery's detractors to reject the Constitution because of the allowances it made for slavery as well as the extralegal and illegal measures demanded by the Fugitive Slave Law and the *Dred Scott* decision. For the author of the piece in the *Rutgers College Quarterly*, who likely "stood by" the Constitution, the position of Garrison and radical abolitionists like him was untenable. The kind of radicalism espoused by men and women like Garrison—individuals who fought for racial justice and rejected the country's political foundation—was disdainful. And if this is what made the author an "old fogy," then he welcomed the insinuation.

Several months later, another article charged likely the very same "hot-headed reformers" with unjustly and superciliously labeling "men of conservative principles and profound reverence for old truth" old fogies. "O tempora, O mores! that such titles should be awarded so liberally to men unworthy of the distinction," the author lamented, before then wishing for the multiplication of old fogies.[48] This rearguard defense of conservative views amplifies the gradualism on campus of the preceding decades. Indeed, it suggests that at least some of these students were traditionalists who felt threatened by reform efforts, and radical abolitionism most especially. As white Christian men of ease, the students of Rutgers College had a vested interest in preserving the status quo that guaranteed their supremacy.

Perhaps the clearest indication of their racial politics emerges in a two-part article entitled "A Trip to the Bahamas," which was more than likely written by one-time *Rutgers College Quarterly* editor, future professor, and vice president of Rutgers College, Theodore Sandford Doolittle. The first part of the article provides readers with a cursory tour of the picturesque island. The second part of the article, however, offers some unambiguous ideas about racial difference in the decades since the passage of the Slavery Abolition Act (1833), which outlawed slavery throughout the British Empire, including in the Bahamas. While Doolittle concedes that formerly enslaved people "justly" hated slavery, he nevertheless wonders "whether the negro has been elevated either in his physical or moral nature by emancipation," which was "the same old knotty question here as elsewhere."[49] Interestingly, his views echo those of the American Colonization Society, which doubted whether "elevation" was possible within the United States, thereby providing the justification for removal. Not surprisingly, then, while Doolittle agrees that in the abstract every "rational creature" has a right to freedom, he argues that in actuality, "the black is destitute by nature of capacity to attain the ends which make liberty of any worth."[50]

Going further, he argues that with few exceptions, "the negroes of the Bahamas are degraded and indolent in the extreme." Employing many antiblack tropes used to justify slavery, he maintains that black Bahamians—"Sambos" and "Dinahs"—were thoughtless and showed no foresight, lied, committed theft, behaved promiscuously, were untroubled by their poverty, and lacked the industry and initiative to reverse their fortunes. Even black Bahamians' manner of talking, which the author describes as "meagre," "rudimentary," and "barbarous," is chalked up to "their awful sloth, which will not allow even the organs of the voice to perform their natural functions."[51]

It is important to note that Doolittle *did not* believe that race stemmed from innate biological differences. Indeed, he writes "it is moonshine to argue that there is something inherent in the color inevitably opposed to progress and civilization."[52] Any differences between whites and blacks deemed racial or civilizational stemmed instead from the harrowing experience of bondage. Though hardly satisfying, attributing black inferiority to slavery rather than biology is a distinction worth teasing out. Indeed, the distinction calls to mind the reigning explanations for racial difference during the antebellum period: polygenesis and monogenesis. Polygenesis represented a radical interpretation of Creation, whereby the races had been created separately, endowed with different and unequal aptitudes, and evolved divergently. Monogenesis, on the other hand, maintained that all humans descended from a single ancestral pair and that any differences between them were environmental or cultural rather than biological.[53] By suggesting that "the shiftless condition of the native negro is due to the reäction [sic] following the hard bondage, in which he remembers to have suffered," Doolittle signals his monogenetic beliefs.[54] Still, subscribing to monogenesis does not rule out the espousal of virulent antiblack views, as demonstrated by his unchecked racism. Not surprisingly, these views would persist throughout the length of Doolittle's life. In many respects, then, we may view the *Rutgers College Quarterly* as a staging ground for the kind of enduring conservatism that would animate his intellectual production at Rutgers College and beyond.

Importantly, monogenesis was not the only explanation for racial difference circulating around Rutgers College. An inventory of the library holdings of the Philoclean Society reveals that it contained Louis Agassiz's coauthored *Principles of Zoology: Touching the Structure, Development, Distribution, and Natural Arrangement of the Races of Animals, Living and Extinct with Numerous Illustrations* (1848) and *Methods of Study in Natural History* (1863).[55] Likewise, a survey of the meeting minutes of the Natural History Society of Rutgers College, which was formed in 1857 at the behest of geology professor George H. Cook, reveal that a lecturer (possibly Cook himself) gave remarks on Agassiz's multivolume *Natural History of the United States* (1857–1862).[56] Agassiz was a Swiss-born naturalist and Harvard professor of zoology and geology who was perhaps the most well-known proponent of polygenesis within the United States. Indeed, for men like Agassiz, it was this idea of fundamental difference that both created the conditions for—as well as continuously justified—the enslavement of individuals of African descent. While the extent of the students' engagement with Agassiz's work is unclear, their exposure to it nevertheless seems certain. Moreover, the fact that the Philoclean, Peithessophian, and Natural History Societies would eventually share space in Van Nest Hall, following its construction in 1848, suggests something about the easy fraternity and circulation of ideas on campus. In all likelihood, college students throughout the North had greater exposure to polygenetic ideas than their southern counterparts, as many educators and students in the South shrunk from anything that might undermine the divinity of God and the authority of the Bible.[57]

Within this context, it is no wonder that the students of Rutgers College were invested in preserving the prerogatives of a white Christian masculinity or gripped by a determined gradualism during the second quarter of the nineteenth century. Not only were they politically aware, but perhaps more importantly, they were besieged traditionalists who actively looked to preserve the status quo both within and outside their ranks—then and in the ensuing decades.

Race, Religion, and Reform: The Rutgers Public Intellectual

In an 1888 editorial published in the *Christian at Work*, a magazine based out of New York, Doolittle, the entry's author and a professor of rhetoric, logic, and metaphysics at Rutgers College, boasted about the religious makeup of the Rutgers student body. He states, "There are only about 20 [of roughly 150 students], and perhaps less, who are not professing Christians."[58] Doolittle had spotlighted the students' piety to quell dismal views of society as increasingly profane. The Christian affiliations of the student population were evidence of humanity's firm uprightness. A Rutgers alumnus (1859), former editor of the *Rutgers College Quarterly*, member of the Philoclean Society, seminary graduate, and licensed minister in the Dutch Reformed Church, Doolittle embodied the ideal Rutgers man—white, Protestant, and erudite—that defined Rutgers in the late nineteenth and early twentieth centuries. His scholarship often reflected a bias toward Christianity as the ideal way of living. In his writings, he deemed the Christian profile of Rutgers students a "cause for rejoicing and hope. The destiny of our national future lies in the heads and hearts of our educated young men. Religion is now more diffused as a living experience and controlling force than ever before."[59] Only a Christian education would ensure students' success and equip them to lead the United States, which Doolittle characterized as a nation superior to other countries.[60] The professor concluded his editorial with an appeal to parents, urging them to enroll their children in strictly Christian colleges.[61]

The brand of Protestantism Theodore Doolittle embraced informed his pedagogy and reveals much about how one Rutgers professor theorized about race in the late nineteenth century. If "control" of students summarized the primary purpose of religion in higher education—in which colleges instill patriotic values and Christian ethics in young American men coming of age—then religion outside of the academy functioned to similarly reform societies and produce ideal citizens, especially African Americans, immigrants, and religious minorities. These groups Doolittle characterized using racist stereotypes that captured the dominant lens through which most Rutgers students approached race. The two projects—producing ideal students and reforming nonwhites—complemented one another, and the professor of religion ultimately encouraged domestic and foreign missionary work among Rutgers students to make the world anew.

Theodore Doolittle and the Embodiment of the Protestant Worldview at Rutgers

To understand Doolittle's pedagogy and racial ideology, and its connection to Rutgers in its early stage, we must first parse his religious views. The prolific scholar left few lectures behind, but his public sermons and publications in the *Christian at Work*—written in his capacity as a Rutgers professor—provide insight into his embrace of Protestantism as an absolute authority and blueprint for social reform. He considered the Bible a divinely inspired document and flouted philosophers—namely, Voltaire—who either used science to debunk Scripture or employed a purely scientific approach to explaining the sacred text. In "The Relation of the Bible to Science," Doolittle implored readers to understand divine omniscience in the development of science as a field of inquiry. The scientific method, he argued, was subjected to the Bible, because God, chief orchestrator of Scripture, had preordained the discipline. Divine foreknowledge about scientific inquiry enabled God to choose its bearers, and therefore God willed science on God's time.[62] To present-day readers, the rationale Doolittle used to refute the viability of the scientific discipline may lack sophistication, but the religious lens with which he approached various topics demonstrates his preference for Christianity as a departure point for cultural and academic criticism. In virtually all his examinations, Doolittle privileged divine authority. A similar hermeneutic, for example, surfaces in his ideas on marriage. Writing in one of his weekly columns, "The Sunday School," Doolittle invoked biblical passages that defined marriage as a covenant between one man and one woman with the husband ruling over his wife.[63] Not only did Doolittle rely on a hyperreligious framework to challenge scientific thought and define familial structures, but he opted for a Christian reading of historical events, especially the Revolutionary and Civil Wars.

On the eve of July 4, 1879, Doolittle penned an editorial for the *Christian at Work* in recognition of the upcoming holiday. "Fourth of July Reflections" recounted the series of events that resulted in American independence, and Doolittle began his account by tracing the British journey to North America in what he interpreted as a mission "to worship the God of the Bible in unrestrained freedom." The "principled" and "devout" men, argued Doolittle, symbolized divine ordination in the moments leading up to the Revolutionary War, a form of manifest destiny that ultimately led George Washington, amid dismal circumstances, to defeat the British at Valley Forge.[64] An earlier essay, "The Nation's Birthday" proposed a similar argument. While Doolittle included discussion of important events critical to contextualizing the rise of the United States as a sovereign nation—such as historical tensions with the British caused by the Stamp Act and furthered fueled by the Boston Massacre—he nevertheless concluded that the nation achieved independent status because "God led the people by a way they knew not. Collision between the redcoats and the patriots seemed accidental, but was Providential."[65] Doolittle framed the Declaration of Independence as a divinely inspired document, theological reasoning that failed to reconcile the notion of divine intervention and omnipotence with the circumscribed liberty of women and the enslaved status of African Americans at the time.

To be sure, the biblical scholar bemoaned slavery and criticized its supporters. When Thomas Carlyle died, for example, Doolittle praised the historian and famed cultural critic but rebuked his well-documented defense of the Confederate Army.[66] Yet, for the most part, Doolittle's emphasis on religion and embrace of nationalism clouded his reading of the antebellum period. On the heels of the ratification of the Thirteenth Amendment, Doolittle, then a recent graduate of Rutgers College and the NBTS, stood before the First Reformed Dutch Church in Schenectady, New York, and delivered a sermon that praised the United States for finally manumitting all slaves. Just one year into his position as a professor, the young scholar took to the pulpit and censured the nation for its long-standing support of black enslavement. "Indeed, owing to a false education, or to partisan prejudices, or to the desire for gain," he roared, "we had begun to maintain that slavery was a divine thing for some, whilst we all felt it was an abomination for ourselves." He continued: "In taking this ground we put ourselves square against Washington and Jefferson and Madison, and all the founders of the Republic. Yes, though it be said without bitterness, against God himself."[67] White embrace of slavery constituted a spiritual transgression and resulted in a misguided patriotism. Neither God nor the founding fathers, in Doolittle's estimation, had intended slavery. This hagiographic and revisionist portrayal of the nation's early leaders overlooked Thomas Jefferson's ownership of African people and the overall complacency with which he and his fellow statesmen approached slavery. His preference for religious zealousness and patriotic rhetoric defined, for him, the outcome of the Civil War. The outcome of the war, according to Doolittle, restored the country to economic prosperity: "Schools and colleges have been largely endowed. Church debts of immense magnitude, and by the score, have been paid off. The treasuries of the Sanitary and Christian Commissions had been made overflowing, and the Gospel carried to the soldier in the camp and hospital and on the march."[68] Combined with the drafting of the Thirteenth Amendment into law, these accomplishments convinced Doolittle that the United States had embarked upon a new era of "universal liberty" with an

abundance of labor opportunities for workers, "holy relationships" for families, accessible education "for the enlightenment of the mind," and the possibility of a more harmonious state of race relations.[69]

Doolittle's extremely misguided optimism speaks to a much earlier
embrace of jingoism and Protestantism in his public scholarship as a Rutgers
professor, a stance strengthened by his belief in white superiority. Despite an
ardent opposition to slavery, Doolittle's views on race remained problematic
over the course of his academic career and some racist ideology is detectable
in his 1865 homily. During his discussion of the prospect of black success, for
example, he suppressed the sanguine tone used to describe the nation's future
in the rest of the sermon and traded it for more chary rhetoric. Even if "the
black man may not attain to all these blessings," he cautioned the congregation, "yet ours will be the justice and glory of giving him a fair chance in the
race of life."[70] Low expectations for the black community's progress seemed
consistent with the professor's belief in black inferiority. Racial equality would
remain a far-fetched reality only if African Americans failed to pursue the
opportunities created by their newfound freedom. Doolittle, a devout Christian who approached most dilemmas with faith, held little hope that the newly
released bondsmen, in what he considered their degraded condition, would
fully leverage the watershed moment.

A later editorial in the *Christian at Work* elucidated his racist views more
explicitly. By the last quarter of the nineteenth century, the black population in the United States had rapidly swelled to large numbers. From 1870 to
1910, New Jersey's black population especially increased due to the influx of
southern migrants in search of employment opportunities created by the port
industry in areas like Atlantic City and the need for domestic labor in other
parts of the state.[71] Concerned with the growth, Doolittle questioned "what is
to become of the negro, and of this country with the negro in it?"[72] The level of
urgency reflected Doolittle's own anxieties about a changing racial landscape
with a burgeoning African American population. These concerns echoed a
similar anxiety over racial integration captured by white responses to the possibility of one of the first African American students, Islay Walden, living in
the seminary. Doolittle's writings and speeches demonstrated how the white
Protestant image that defined Rutgers was not limited to the student body.
Like the students, Doolittle appeared unsettled at the idea of an increasing
black presence—whether on campus, at the seminary, in New Brunswick, or in
the United States at large.

In the *Christian at Work*, he considered black growth a cause for panic
and "a great problem pressing to the front for solution—of tremendous and
political and moral forces lying under the surface of our communities, and
already to burst sometime into volcanic violence."[73] Mischaracterizations of
African Americans as degraded and in need of guidance was a mainstay of

white Protestant thought in the nineteenth century. Historian Leon Litwack observes how northern missionaries and educators "assumed that nothing short of a massive moral and religious transformation could liberate southern blacks from the remaining vestiges of slavery." While a strategy of both black and white reformers, moral regeneration and its intellectual framing held different meanings across racial lines. African Americans viewed moral uplift as a communal endeavor and exclusively their responsibility given, among other issues, the long-standing support of and complacency with enslavement by white Protestants. In the postbellum North, the Dutch Reform Church had long embraced paternalism and benevolence to reform blacks and Doolittle's characterization of African Americans as savages aligned with this view.[74] To address the issue of so-called black degradation, Doolittle recommended educational and religious reforms "to transform these growing multitudes of colored people into industrious, intelligent, thrifty, useful, and happy citizens"—descriptors typically reserved for whites.[75]

Two years later, Doolittle again targeted African Americans and equated black spiritual expressions with criminal behavior. In one opinion piece, "Morality Divorced from Religion," he described the vivacious music and uninhibited dancing characteristic of black Protestantism as "not at all inconsistent with the robbing of hen-roosts during the week, to say nothing more of serious offenses."[76] Doolittle then referred to the case of Chastine Cox, a black Christian from New York City convicted of robbery and the murder of Jane Lawrence De Forest Hull in 1879. Cox's case had received widespread media attention because he managed to flee the crime scene before law enforcement eventually captured and sentenced him to death by hanging. The episode sparked a national public discourse around criminal justice reform with one journalist questioning if Cox would receive a fair trial given the history of faulty murder convictions in the legal jurisdiction that oversaw his case.[77] Rumors spread that Frederick Douglass, the U.S. Marshall for the District of Columbia, would intercede on Cox's behalf, which forced the popular activist and former abolitionist to issue a response in support of the conviction.[78]

Doolittle had obviously concluded that the courts handled the case with justice, but he went one step further and exploited the Cox episode to prove that blacks were pathologically dangerous and running amok. Evident of a much larger problem, Cox, according to Doolittle, represented a host of black adherents to an uninhibited Christian faith in need of better restraint in the church and greater social control in the streets. While some black Christians simultaneously praise God and plot evil with malice, Doolittle contended, "in too many instances the guilty violators of human and Divine law imagine that attendance upon church, liberal gifts to benevolent objects, and official joining in public prayers and hymns somehow atone for the crimes committed in business."[79] Black Protestants, in Doolittle's estimation, lacked a sophisticated understanding of divine grace, seemed too carefree and undisciplined in their spirituality, and possessed too strong of an impulse for crime.[80] These attributes resulted in the black community's overall immorality and could be best addressed with the inculcation of a more conservative Protestantism and the "practical, unceasing, and successful application of religious principles to daily character."[81]

The racial ideology in "Morality Divorced from Religion" reflected a pattern in Doolittle's public scholarship that focused on the intersection of race, religion, and reform. Like his treatment of black Christians, the professor negatively characterized communities of color with large Muslim, Hindu, and Buddhist populations. Often, these mischaracterizations focused on religious minorities in other countries and allowed Doolittle to mask a belief in white nationalism with religious discourse. Because Japanese and Chinese citizens worshipped a deity not derived from the Judeo-Christian narrative, Doolittle reduced their customs to idol worship and labeled them immoral. So destructive was Asian religious culture that it created a depravity among the general population and Doolittle concluded that "actually many of them are as untruthful, treacherous, and bloodthirsty as sin can make them."[82] Charges of deceitfulness often accompanied Doolittle's racist rhetoric. After Charles William Eliot, the president of Harvard University, emphasized the importance of integrity in his 1888 address to Harvard's academic community, Doolittle commented on the speech in the *Christian at Work*. His editorial, "Thou Shalt Not Bear False Witness," reiterated Eliot's remarks but also recounted an instance in which Rutgers expelled a student for his dishonesty, a penalty that demonstrated how Americans and Christians treated acts of deceit with the utmost severity. By contrast, Doolittle argued, "among the East Indians, Chinese, and other heathen countries, lying is reduced to a fine art," enabled by their adherence to non-Christian religious traditions.[83]

The professor's negative portrayal of Chinese immigrants seemed consistent with white anxieties about racial minorities in the post-Reconstruction era. In his examination of white missionaries from the American Baptist Home Missionary Society, historian Derek Chang notes how Baptist missionaries "shared with advocates of segregation and exclusion a fear that Emancipation and immigration might result in the irreparable depredation of American society. . . . American Baptists worried that unconverted blacks and heathen Chinese threatened their monument to God."[84] Not limited to white Baptists, these concerns reflected the rhetoric of white ministers in the Dutch Reformed tradition as well. Terms like *heathen* and *barbaric* animated Doolittle's scholarship that focused on religious minorities, such as his editorial celebrating Thanksgiving, in which he offered a remarkably negative connotation of African religious culture,[85] or an essay that declared the Japanese a helpless, "poor, distressed creature that was once demoniac—once covered with all evil passions, such as cruelty, superstition, dark and dreadful vices, fondness for war and scenes of violence, horrid tyranny over the weak."[86] To justify this unambiguously racist delineation of racial and religious minorities, Doolittle cited problematic research widely considered authoritative and credible at the time, such as Charles Darwin's review of Japan published in *Natural History and Geology* and the work of Henry Morton Stanley, a social scientist and geographer regarded for his case studies of Central Africa.[87] Such scholarship attested to the white nationalist premise of Doolittle's intellectual orientation, despite his insistence that Darwin "never allowed his prejudices to disturb his clear vision of facts or of the influences that were energetically and nobly at work for the physical and moral elevation of mankind."[88] Doolittle's preference for this type of scholarship also reflected a period in which white intellectuals increasingly relied on scientific racism standardized and advanced through academic studies of white scientists and journalists like Nathaniel Southgate Shaler and Ray Stannard Baker.[89]

The casual nature with which Doolittle cast people of color and religious minorities as the savage, barbaric other advanced public discourses on humanity and civilization steeped in prowhite nationalist rationale. A prominent feature of the dialogue included a concern for the influx of immigrants into the nation, a potential demographic shift that caused as much panic for Doolittle as the growth of black communities in the North from migration. Comprising mostly godless "anarchists" and "socialists," he suggested, immigrants threatened the democratic ideals of the republic.[90] Those sympathetic to an American way of living nevertheless "come here with characters already morally wrecked" and engage in criminal behavior characteristic of foreign nations.[91] It was, therefore, incumbent upon the United States to outline and enforce conditions designed to measure an immigrant's suitability for life in the nation. These terms included the potential for economic stability, possession of a clear criminal record, evidence of stellar health, and, of course, an allegiance to "Divine law"—stipulations that, if implemented, would effectively ban the poor and working class, those deemed violent and unfit for society, the disease-stricken, and religious minorities.[92]

The Rutgers Mission in the World

Doolittle's selection of "scholarly" sources held content that mirrored the exclusionary intellectual culture fostered by the literary societies at Rutgers, in which religious minorities and people of color remained inferior to white Protestants. Like himself, Darwin had proposed a Christian model of regeneration for Japan, outsourced through a strict process of Christianization focused on religious education and proselytization in foreign countries.[93] In Doolittle's assessment, no institution seemed better positioned than Rutgers College—an offspring of the Dutch Reformed Church—to train the next generation of Christian missionaries. Indeed, the primary purpose of education, he argued, should involve rigorous religious instruction and cultivating a desire for conventional biblical principles. The editorial penned in 1888 was but a small, yet telling, introduction to Doolittle's educational philosophy. Bound up with his views on race and reform, Doolittle's pedagogy centered student missions as the hallmark of a classical curriculum. Intellectual discourse alone, however, could not achieve the level of religious rigor Doolittle sought for college students and, in fact, potentially compromised an unadulterated Protestant education.

In "College Students and Church Life," he critiqued the faculty and administration at Harvard and Cornell for encouraging a solely intellectual interaction with ministers and theologians. When devoid of practical knowledge, he argued, any scholarly engagement with theology created an unwitting urge among students "to compare one speaker with another, to discuss the particular style of composition and delivery belonging to each, and to praise and condemn according to standards of aesthetic refinement in art afforded in the books and the class-room [sic], rather than according to the simplicity and effectiveness of the Gospel."[94] Warning against this type of scholarly atmosphere, Doolittle advocated for a Protestant-based curriculum with more practical implications and, in The Christian at Work, he featured the story of Pom Kwan Soh, an immigrant with ties to the Dutch Reformed community, to illustrate his point. Soh had recently fled his native Korea to Japan after spearheading a failed insurgency against the government. Before leaving Japan, he met a U.S. missionary, forged a relationship with the minister, and converted to Christianity. His matriculation into Rutgers came after baptism and, as Doolittle tells it, through providential inspiration to reform his homeland. Soh's religious encounters in the United States attested to the effectiveness of Christian missions as an instrument of social regeneration. While scant on details, Doolittle's spotlight of Soh's transformation from Korean dissenter to diligent Christian student armed with Bible in hand also shored up his call for religious training in higher education.[95] Indeed, Soh reflected a large part and long-standing tradition of the Rutgers student body who had, in fact, displayed an interest in missionary work during their studies and in post-graduation pursuits.

As Doolittle saw the importance of foreign missions, so did Rutgers alumni, students, and faculty members. They lived in an age of missionary zeal, imagining foreign countries and indeed residing abroad. Overseas missions were a way of life at Rutgers College, as seen in alumni missionary engagement, the school's essay competition on American missionary work, and the YMCA chapter on campus. Seemingly isolated, the history of Christian foreign missions was and remains an integral component of U.S. history since the early nineteenth century. Religious activities that took place outside the country contributed to the formation of American ideas at home.[96] The history of Rutgers College, like that of the United States, was tied to foreign missions and we can see the Rutgers Man's missionary zeal from the 1830s to the early twentieth century.

According to Craig Steven Wilder's *Ebony and Ivy* (2013), a study of American universities' connections with slavery and with other events related to the U.S. history of racism and colonialism, "[f]oreign missions allowed white Christians to convert indigenous and colored peoples without strengthening the political and legal claims of nonwhite and non-Christian peoples upon the United States."[97] Christian missions to indigenous and nonwhite people elsewhere were tied to forces that preserved racism in the United States. Wilder's argument could be further developed to suggest that the cultures of foreign missions on campus mirrored contemporary U.S. society that denied full citizenship to African Americans and Native Americans while showing little interest in the rights of nonwhite, colonized people overseas, and often supporting U.S. government interventions into local struggles for independence. Educational institutions in an age of missionary zeal wittingly or unwittingly imposed particular worldviews on local people, stabilizing colonial conditions, and preserving racial and social hierarchies. How then, did religious service overseas and resulting discourses shape and reflect racial ideologies of the Rutgers Man?

The 1916 alumni catalogue of Rutgers College lists the birthplaces and postgraduate trajectories of all Rutgers alumni from 1766 until 1916 and offers crucial insight into the history of foreign missions at Rutgers. The catalogue suggests that at least 70 of 2,157 alumni from 1830 to 1909 had relations with the American foreign missionary enterprise.[98] Many missionary alumni listed in this catalogue proceeded to NBTS after completing their study at Rutgers College. Some, born overseas, had inherited their vocation from missionary parents. The first Rutgers alumni who became missionaries were Elbert Nevius (class of 1830), William Youngblood (class of 1832), and Elihu Doty (class of 1835). Nevius, Youngblood, and Doty also studied at NBTS, and on a mission organized by the Reformed Church in America (also referred to as the Dutch Reformed Church) in 1836, they were sent to Borneo, a former Dutch colony comprising part of present-day Indonesia.[99] The Reformed Church in America was responsible for sending out the majority of Rutgers missionary alumni, but other organizations, such as the American Board of Commissioners for Foreign Missions and the Lutherans, also supported similar missionary trips abroad.[100] Sons of missionaries, born abroad, start to appear in the catalogue from as early as the late 1840s. Both Samuel D. Scudder (class of 1847) and Joseph Scudder (class of 1848) were born in Ceylon, present-day Sri Lanka, to their well-known missionary parents, John and Harriet. Charles Ray (class of 1849) was born in Calcutta, India (present-day Kolkata), also as a son of missionary father Edward Ray.[101] Their birthplaces were not only well-known

destinations of American foreign missions, they were prominent British colonies. The evidence shows that of these early missionaries' sons at Rutgers,
Joseph Scudder got involved in evangelical work in India from 1851 to 1860.

Since the first half of the nineteenth century, Rutgers alumni were involved
in American Christian missionary work abroad. Their destinations were the
colonies or semi-colonies of the Dutch and British empires, as well as the U.S.
overseas empire, into the turn of the twentieth century. They worked in the
Dutch East Indies (present-day Indonesia), China, India, Hawai'i, Japan, Arabia
(what we now call the Middle East), and British East Africa.[102] The widespread
work of these alumni missionaries suggests that Rutgers foreign missions were
embedded in the imperial histories of Europe and the United States.

The human flows between Rutgers College and the locations of foreign
missions continued at a moderate pace throughout the nineteenth century
and into the early twentieth century. The alumni moved globally between
sites of religious work overseas and their home country. Overseas-born missionaries' sons, likely white American citizens, returned to the United States
and studied in New Brunswick.[103]

The freedom of movement of Rutgers missionary students, their parents,
and alumni should be understood alongside discussions about immigration
to the United States. Through much of the nineteenth and twentieth centuries, the U.S. government and the public worked toward the regulation and
expulsion of specific immigrants through a series of immigrant acts, including the Chinese Exclusion Act of 1882. The history of immigration is a history
of nativism, including anti-Catholicism and anti-Asian sentiments, and American nationalism that worked in tandem with racism. Moreover, the work of
immigration restriction helped consolidate federal and municipal governments.[104] Rutgers foreign missions resonated with the asymmetry between the
restricted mobility of nonwhite immigrants and the unrestricted mobility of
white Rutgers missionaries.[105]

In addition to the alumni involvements in Christian service abroad, Rutgers College served as a site for the production of discourse on American missions by annually awarding two essay prizes. The Van Doren Prize was given to
student essays on missions in general, including foreign and domestic activities, in a competition conducted from around 1869 until 1914. Meanwhile,
from 1885 to 1914 the Van Vechten Prize was awarded to student essays on
foreign missions. Both awards were established through donations from William Halsey Van Doren and A.V.W. Van Vechten. Van Doren earned his BA at
Rutgers College in 1867, graduated from NBTS in 1871, and served as a clergy-
man of the Reformed Church in America.[106] Van Vechten founded the prize "in
honor of his mother, the late Louisa Van Vechten, and his father, Rev. Samuel
Van Vechten, D.D."[107] The donor's father completed his doctorate study at NBTS
in 1822, served as a clergymen of the Reformed Church in America, received an

honorary master's degree from Rutgers College in 1834, and died in 1882. The essay competitions were open to both seniors and juniors of Rutgers College and students of NBTS, and offered cash rewards of approximately twenty to sixty dollars. The submissions were judged by the faculty of the seminary.[108] Unfortunately we have no data on how many Rutgers students took seminary courses, but the combined reading of the Rutgers alumni catalogue and the biographical record of the seminary suggests that the two schools were quite close both physically and pedagogically. Not only did Rutgers students study at the seminary after their graduation from Rutgers College, but seminary students, like Frederick Kienhold Shield (alumnus of 1895), also took extra courses at Rutgers College and received "Bachelor of Divinity" degrees from the school in 1895.[109]

Many of the award winners became clergymen and a few became involved in foreign missions or were missionary sons. The Van Doren winner of 1886, William Isaac Chamberlain (class of 1882), was born in Madras, India (present-day Chennai), as a missionary son and became a member of the Reformed Church in America's mission to his country of birth. Similarly, Henry Johnstone Scudder (class of 1890), the 1896 winner of the same prize, was born in Coonoor, India, as a missionary son and served in the mission of the Reformed Church in America in Amoy, China.[110]

The award-winning essays can be read as collaborative products of student compositions and the seminary faculty's judgments, rather than simply the students' personal reflections. Although the information about these essay contests was not consistently recorded in the Rutgers College catalogue, a call for Van Doren Prize submissions—"Subject for 1896, essay limited to 3,000 words: 'Methods of City Mission Work'"—implies that the school, presumably the judges of the seminary faculty, decided the subjects of essays and encouraged students to read and think about specific topics which the school regarded as important.[111] Henry Johnstone Scudder, the Indian-born American missionary to China, won in the competition with his essay, entitled "Methods of City Missionary Work," a virtually identical title to the award prompt.[112] Other titles of prize-winning essays, including Philip Wilson Pitcher's "The Introduction of Missions in the Fiji Islands" (approximately 1885), Royal Arthur Stout's "Protestant Missions in Persia" (1910), and Charles Frederick Benjamin Jr.'s "The Present State of Mission Work in Africa" (1898), suggest that the Van Doren and the Van Vechten Prize essays reflected and shaped Rutgers alumni involvement in American Christian missions and, more broadly, cultures of Christian foreign missions at Rutgers.[113] Meanwhile, the award winners had few personal connections with the missionary destinations of their essay subjects, which the school selected. Their biased depictions of unfamiliar places, mirroring the prejudice of their own and Rutgers, produced an imaginative fantasy of the Rutgers Man.

The prize-winning essays serve as a window to look into the worldviews of the seminary faculty judges and into the racial ideas circulating within Rutgers College. The narratives in these essays can also be understood within histories of American Christian missions established in colonies and semi-colonies of European and American empires around the globe. Although the topics of prize-winning essays on American missions were broad and global, several essays on evangelical work in U.S. territories show how education at Rutgers College both reflected and legitimized U.S. imperial expansions.[114] Some essays were written in blatantly racist language that infantilized and exoticized locals. These essays celebrated American Protestant missionaries in various destinations, arguing that the Christian work civilized locals and brought progress to the world.

It should be noted that the missionary was not only an agent of God but also an agent of United States empire, a contested self-image but undeniable reality throughout the history of the nation. The concept of American exceptionalism, the idea that the United States is uniquely different from other European empires, has helped the country deny its imperial history.[115] Both Thomas Jefferson's term "empire of liberty" and the Louisiana Purchase of 1803 during his presidency accelerated westward settler colonialism and the expansion of slavery. The phrase "Manifest Destiny" was coined in 1845, just before the Mexican-American War, by newspaper editor John O'Sullivan, who supported the annexation of the Republic of Texas during the controversy. The idea of Manifest Destiny only gained greater popularity in the 1890s, helping to justify American expansions at the turn of the twentieth century, as epitomized in historian Frederick Jackson Turner's influential 1893 address, "The Significance of the Frontier in American History," in Chicago, during the World Columbian Exposition. Turner's thesis, insisting that the American frontier had closed, combined with the idea of Manifest Destiny to offer a political and intellectual legitimacy to the United States empire since 1898, when the government officially gained overseas territories, such as the Philippines, Puerto Rico, and Hawai'i.[116] Despite white American resistance to U.S. imperial expansions, like the 1898 foundation of the American Anti-Imperialist League, the worldviews of opponents of American empire and those of believers in Manifest Destiny were hardly oppositional: the former groups of people saw the United States empire as "accidental" and the latter asserted it as "inevitable."[117] Neither view fully considered the effects on the invaded populations.

The nation's long history of territorial expansion and the turn-of-the-century polarization over American empire resonated in Rutgers prize-winning essays in the early twentieth century on American missions to U.S. territories. Rutgers student George Edward Hagemann's "Missionary Work in the Philippines" (1912) argued that the American annexation of the Philippines was "accidental."[118] It noted, "As President McKinley said, fourteen years ago they [the Philippine Islands] 'dropped into our lap,' unexpectedly and not from any desire of our own for their possession."[119] In fact, the United States obtained overseas territories, including the Philippines, through the Spanish-American War of 1898. The United States engaged in the war under the rubric of liberating colonies from Spanish empire, but it also used military force against independence movements in the Philippines and Cuba. The subsequent Philippine-American War consolidated U.S. racial-imperial ideologies in tandem with domestic racial hierarchies in the United States.[120] While the U.S.'s active intervention against Filipino self-determination indicated its desire to possess the former Spanish colony, Hagemann argued that the Philippines became part of U.S. territory "unexpectedly and not from any desire of our own for their possession." Moreover, another Rutgers prize-winning essay, Simon Blocker's "Missions in the Philippines since the American Occupation" (1905), discussed the Filipino uprising of 1896 against Spain as "the fruits of an unspiritual religion and corrupt priesthood."[121] By emphasizing corruptions of Spanish and Catholics on the land and by omitting the Philippine-American War, Blocker naturalized the beginning of the American colonial period of the Philippines as "the dawn of a new era of political and religious freedom for the oppressed natives."[122] The essay reflected the view that the U.S. annexation of the former Spanish colony was "inevitable." We can see contemporaneous understandings of U.S. empire both as "accidental" and "inevitable" in these Rutgers students' essays. While the two essays did not see locals as "savages" or "children," they subjugated Filipinos by depicting them as in need of American Christian rescue and by erasing local struggles for decolonization.

Frederic Elmer Foertner's essay "Protestant Missions in Alaska" (1902) celebrated the efforts and success of missionaries in establishing religious and vocational schools in the territory. Alaska, the forty-ninth state, became American territory with its purchase from Russia in 1867 and experienced settler colonial immigration from the Klondike gold rush in the late 1890s.[123] Foertner argued that evangelical and industrial education brought benefits to indigenous peoples. Besides, he noted, "the inhabitants of Alaska, probably from the very fact that theirs is a cold country, are active and bright, and much more susceptible to mental education and a comprehension of the principles of a sound Christian doctrine than the inhabitants of a hot country are."[124] These ideas reflected climatic determinism, then a scientific idea that attributed human behavior, society, and the level of civilization to inhabitant climate. This knowledge, even if we can regard it today as pseudo-science, was used to legitimize imperialism and institutional racism.[125] Indigenous peoples in Alaska "are very ready to adopt the forms of civilization that are brought to them as in the dress, and also the arts and trades that are now being very effectually taught in the industrial schools."[126] While praising susceptibility to

Christianity and other "forms of civilization" of Alaskans in cold climates, the student essay suggested that people in tropical places, such as the Philippines, Hawai'i, or the U.S. South, were less susceptible to civilizing methods. People both in cold and hot places were taxonomized on the ladder of civilization, in which Rutgers students and faculty considered white Americans at the top.

Frank Stelle Booth's "The History of Missions in the Hawaiian Islands" (1902) shows imperialist and racist ideas more directly than the previous essays on the Philippines and Alaska. It began by arguing that "there is a Romance of Missions. In the strange corners of the earth, in the Islands of the sea, where dwell the dusky children of Nature it has ever produced its thrilling chapters."[127] Like other student writers, Booth wrote the history of missions as a romantic and harmonious story. To him and his readers, the Hawaiian archipelago was located at "the strange corners of the earth," somewhere peripheral in American, and perhaps Eurocentric, spatial imagination. Native Hawaiians were "the dusky children of Nature" and these infantilized people with nonwhite skin lived in a primitive world where they awaited an encounter with civilizing missionaries, or the "thrilling chapters" of the missionary saga. The essay despised vernacular religions, describing them as "idolatry" or "superstitions."[128] It offered a century-long history of missionary development in Hawai'i from Captain Cook's "discovery" of the islands in 1778 to the late nineteenth century. Since its foundation in 1795, the Kingdom of Hawai'i negotiated with European powers, such as Britain and France, and later the United States, to keep its independence. Merchants, missionaries, whalers, and, in the mid-nineteenth century, sugar plantation owners drew wealth from the indigenous land and intervened in the governance of the kingdom. However, this student essay does not tell us about the 1893 overthrow of the kingdom, the 1894 establishment of the Republic of Hawaii by white residents, and the U.S. annexation of the republic in 1898. Although the annexation may have affected Rutgers's decision on the essay subject, this student essay of 1902 ignores the contemporaneous situation, thus masking the U.S. military and economic expansion into Hawai'i in the shadow of Christian dissemination.[129]

Imperial and racist narratives are also evident in an essay on the U.S. South. After the Civil War, the South became the focus of reform and a subject of rescue, and was depicted in ways rhetorically linked to descriptions of other overseas territories of the United States empire, dwelling on backwardness, tropical climate, and the necessity of modernization.[130] Henry John Vyverberg's "Past and Present Mission Work among the Freedmen in the South" (1900) celebrated Christian missionary work for educating African Americans in the South since the Civil War. In this time period after the emancipation, African Americans were continuously discriminated against and criminalized by the federal government and American racism, evident in the beginning of Vyverberg's essay:

The negro problem in the South is continually assuming vaster and more alarming populations; the safety of the government is becoming more and more closely and vitally interlocked with the mental and material status of the freedmen. The rapid numerical expansion of the negro, his innate tendency to revert to his primeval African character and degradation, his present ignorance, stupidity, easy abandonment to crime hang as a menace of subversion over the heads of pure government and morality; for the negro, illiterate, credulous, feeble in judgement, weak in discrimination enjoys the highest prerogative of freedom in this free land—the right to vote.[131]

Like other students, Vyverberg, who was from Rochester, New York, and went to schools in the town before Rutgers College, likely never lived in the South.[132] Sharing anxieties about the "mental and material status of the freedmen" with the government and his white society, Vyverberg emphasized the intellectual inferiority of African Americans. He saw Africa, the ancestral land of the formerly enslaved people, as a barbaric place. He believed in the upsurge in the population of African Americans after the Civil War, a common racist trope. Further, his essay strongly rejected the idea of black suffrage. Regarding freedmen's voting rights, Vyverberg insisted that "this dangerous political factor must be eliminated."[133] Nonetheless, the essay won a prize, demonstrating that the students and faculty of Rutgers College and NBTS regarded political rights of African Americans as "dangerous" and believed these rights "must be eliminated." According to this racist rhetoric, freedmen in the South needed Christian education under the tutelage of white people from the North. The essay contended that "there is no hope for the negro except in Christian education" and relegated freed people to a single choice of Christianity.[134] By describing slavery negatively as "shackles," Vyverberg treated the system as an evil peculiar to the South.[135] The essay's "antislavery" narrative, however, masked the importance of the institution of slavery for Rutgers's establishment and development and the heated antebellum-era debates over the rightness or wrongness of slavery, as seen in discussions in Rutgers student bodies, like the Philoclean Society and the Peithessophian Society.

These award-winning essays argued that Christian missions benefited indigenous and nonwhite peoples, but the missionary projects they described actively reflected and reinforced colonial conditions and racial and social hierarchies that were embedded in the U.S. history of empire and race. Imperial modernization was never a unidirectional process from metropole to colony, or from missionary to the converted and locals.[136] Foreign missions also transformed the missionary organizations, along with their religious ideas and praxis. Meanwhile, many Rutgers student essays mirrored contemporaneous societal ideas of the necessity of white, Christian rescue of indigenous and nonwhite peoples and of the legitimacy of colonial and racially unequal conditions.[137] Many of the essays that were granted awards by Rutgers College defined peoples from elsewhere, as these, "Others," in order to maintain the identity of this predominantly white, Christian, male school in the U.S. North. The ideas and praxis of the foreign missions were constitutive of the Rutgers Man.

Conclusion

From its inception, Rutgers College inculcated in its predominantly white and Protestant student population a sense of racial and religious superiority that ultimately defined the institution in its nascent stage. Shared by multiple stakeholders—faculty, students, alumni, and administrators—the belief in the college's ability to implement social reform at home and abroad persisted throughout the nineteenth century and well into the twentieth century. On campus, students formed literary societies and participated in essay competitions that debated and reinforced the racial status quo. The few African Americans allowed at the school or its seminary affiliate reflected how whites only embraced blacks whom they considered harmless, upstanding, and unusually intelligent—attributes that belied the negative light in which they generally held most people of color. In the public sphere, professors proclaimed the gospel, urged extreme surveillance of the nation's borders, advanced Christian ideals, and favored biblically based education for a standard college curriculum. A critical component of this course of studies involved missionary work. Many alumni pursued overseas Christian evangelism in their professional lives, a testament to the pervasiveness and influence of white nationalist and Protestant thought on the student body. Through a strong emphasis on social reform, the Rutgers community essentially created a classroom out of the entire world, a project aimed at social regeneration for racial and religious minorities and reflective of the white nationalist ethos foundational to much of the discourses around race in the nineteenth and early twentieth centuries. Even the appearance of two African American students at the closely affiliated New Brunswick Theological Seminary during the immediate postbellum period did little to challenge the deeply ingrained worldview of Rutgers' students and members of the seminary.

2

In the Shadow of Old Queens

African American Life and Labors in New Brunswick from the End of Slavery to the Industrial Era

CAITLIN WIESNER, PAMELA WALKER,
BRENANN SUTTER, AND SHARI CUNNINGHAM

As the Civil War drew to a close, Rutgers College (or Rutgers University, as the institution would declare itself in 1925) embarked on a period of feverish growth that would persist well into the twentieth century. Rutgers College established the Rutgers Scientific School as a land-grant school in 1864, erected its own Geological Hall in 1872, opened its first residential dormitory in 1890, and, with the help of Mabel Smith Douglass, founded the New Jersey College for Women in 1918 (renamed Douglass College in 1955).[1] The expansion of Rutgers College in the late nineteenth and early twentieth centuries paralleled the growth of the local African American community that resided in New Brunswick. Of course, enslaved black people had accompanied the earliest settlers of New Brunswick in the late seventeenth century. They did not disappear when the passage of the Thirteenth Amendment finally obliterated the vestiges of slavery preserved in New Jersey's 1804 Act of Gradual Abolition.[2] Between 1870 and 1930, the city's black population swelled from 577 to 2,086.[3] New Brunswick's black population kept pace with the black population growth of Middlesex County as a whole, which nearly doubled from 1,625 in 1880 to 2,815 in 1920.[4] However, it lagged considerably behind the black population growth of the state of New Jersey, which surged from 38,835 in 1880 to 117,132 in 1920.[5] This growth was driven by the same forces of industrialization that catalyzed the expansion of Rutgers College. The promise of well-paying industrial jobs drew southern black migrants to New Brunswick at the turn of the century, although the modest pace of industrial development meant that "Hub City" offered far fewer industrial jobs than nearby metropolises like Philadelphia, Newark, or even Trenton.

Throughout the eighteenth and nineteenth centuries, the vast majority of New Brunswick's black residents merely lived adjacent to Rutgers College.[6] As Rutgers College and New Brunswick's black community grew, the two entities began to overlap. Rutgers College employed local African Americans as waiters, butlers, and housekeepers in their ever-expanding facilities. An exceptional few local blacks would breach the institution's long-standing ban on black students and enroll, as Alice Jennings Archibald did in 1938. The campus of Rutgers College would also serve as a backdrop for terrifying displays of racial hatred, as when local Klansmen erected a burning cross at the edge of the New Jersey College for Women in 1924.

Rutgers College began to more actively shape black life in New Brunswick in the late nineteenth and early twentieth centuries. Conversely, the changing contours of African American life in New Brunswick provide a crucial context for understanding the contested meaning of blackness within Rutgers College at the time. This chapter will, therefore, sketch the fluctuating conditions and meanings of blackness in New Brunswick from the end of slavery through the Industrial Era. Its argument is twofold. First, it contends that the end of slavery and the subsequent industrialization of New Brunswick were ambivalent victories for African Americans. While emancipation united the scattered black community of New Brunswick, racism continued to manifest in the city's segregated public schools, discriminatory labor market, and in the overt hostility of its white residents. The reorganization of New Brunswick's economy around factories redefined black presence in the city, from an unremarkable fact of life to a criminal social threat. Second, this chapter argues that the black community in New Brunswick responded to the unique challenges of an industrialized urban northern city with extensive institution-building. Organizations like the Rice Colored Industrial School, the Mt. Zion African Methodist-Episcopal Church, and various mutual aid societies empowered individuals like Ella Rice and Alice Jennings Archibald to improve the conditions of black life in New Brunswick and impart positive meaning to blackness by engaging in social uplift.

Due to the comparatively few industrial jobs available for black men and the rampant racial discrimination in the hiring practices of factories, New Brunswick's experience of the Great Migration departed from the generalized narrative applied to large northern cities. Black men's migration to New Brunswick was consistently outpaced by the influx of southern black women, who could find employment more easily as domestic servants. Federal census records confirm that black women consistently outnumbered black men in the city during this period.[7] The idiosyncrasies of New Brunswick's population provide a unique opportunity to explicate what historian Darlene Clark Hine has called the "gender dimension" of black migration and urban life at the turn of the century.[8] The comparatively greater number of black women than black men in the city allows us to foreground both women's experience and women's leadership in religious and civic organizations. In this respect, New Brunswick offers needed fresh perspectives on African American life in the era of industrialization.

African American New Brunswickers and the Fight for Education

The lives of African Americans in nineteenth-century New Jersey were complex, confounded by the ebb and flow of both social and legal allowances and restrictions enacted through federal, state, and local legislation. Although the state of New Jersey had passed the Act for the Gradual Abolition of Slavery in 1804, it was not until 1850 that the state finally abolished the last vestiges of the institution.[9] In 1850, there were still 236 enslaved African Americans accounted for in New Jersey, and of the 11 who remained in Middlesex County, all of them lived in New Brunswick.[10] In the wake of emancipation, however, "freedom" remained precarious and delimited for New Brunswick's black citizens as they continued to face restraints on their suffrage, education, and labors.

Since the late eighteenth century, the New Jersey State Constitution granted suffrage without regard to gender or race. For three decades, women and African Americans who met the age, wealth, and residence requirements routinely exercised their franchise, until the state legislature restricted the franchise to white male taxpayers in 1807. When black men finally regained the right to vote with the passage of the Fifteenth Amendment in 1870, black New Brunswickers held a large parade celebrating their newly solidified right.[11] Though the state could no longer deny African Americans the right to vote based on their race, New Brunswick counted only 130 registered black voters in 1870.[12] Yet by 1872, the *New Brunswick Daily Times* observed, "The colored voters of our lovely city" seemed to "never tire" as they attended weekly political meetings "with an earnestness and fire."[13]

As in their struggle for suffrage, African Americans in New Brunswick fought tirelessly for their children's right to quality education. In 1838, determined to educate themselves, the African American community of New Brunswick pooled their funds and started an educational society, but despite the sizable attendance of forty pupils the school closed after only nineteen months.[14] Their efforts seemed to be supported by the state legislature: in 1844, the New Jersey legislature established funds for free public education, acknowledging that an educated citizenry was essential to the productivity of the state. Since the earliest establishment of free public schooling, New Brunswick had placed great emphasis on the importance of educating its community.[15] One city document from 1855 described learning as a "beautiful Temple of Liberty."[16]

However, black residents' level of access to education proved to be uncertain. There was a full two-year gap between the establishment of the city's first public school on Bayard Street in 1852 and the New Brunswick Public School Board of Trustees' April 1854 declaration "to make educational provisions for educating the colored children" that established the French Street School.[17] In other words, black children had gone two years without schooling following the erection of the first school on Bayard Street. Within a year of the 1854 decision, the French Street School had a daily attendance of "sixty to seventy colored children of both sexes."[18] Yet, despite the establishment of a school for black students, education remained limited, as the French Street School only provided a primary education (the lowest level of the three tiers offered), while Bayard Street provided primary and grammar school for white students.[19] The black students were later moved in 1871 to a public school on Hale Street named the "Colored School" (later renamed the Hale Street School), which continued to only provide a basic primary education for black residents of New Brunswick.[20]

By 1875, the city had expanded their public school system to six locations. A map of New Brunswick (Figure 2.1) shows the six wards of the city and boundary lines indicated by roman numerals.[21] In addition, the original site of the A.M.E. Mt. Zion Church is indicated by the initials A.M.E. The six public schools are marked by letters and numbers where they existed in the 1870s, but it is important to note that the New Brunswick ward lines changed three or more times over the duration of the nineteenth century. Livingston Avenue School (L) was located on the corner of Livingston near Remond and Welton Streets and provided grammar and high school in Ward Five. Bayard Street (B) was located near the boundary lines of the third and fourth ward near George Street, which provided primary and grammar schooling. The French Street School (F) near Jersey Avenue served as a primary school in Ward Five, while a few blocks away on Hale Street stood the Colored School (C) (later renamed Hale Street School), also in Ward Five. The First Ward School (1st), in Ward One, also had their own primary school on the corner of Carman and Nielson Streets near Abeel Street. Lastly, the Guilden Street School (G) in Ward Six also provided primary school only.

With no advancement resolution in sight, the black residents of New Brunswick took their dissatisfaction with the limits of a primary education to their school board in 1879. The residents pleaded for the board to grant their children entrance into the Bayard Street School, asserting that their "children had long suffered . . . great injury and disadvantage" because of their inability to advance their education.[22] Unmoved, the board denied the request, stating that the injury claims were unfounded, since none of the children had exceeded the level of education "established and taught, nor had been refused the right to advance beyond these grades." In short, they suggested that the

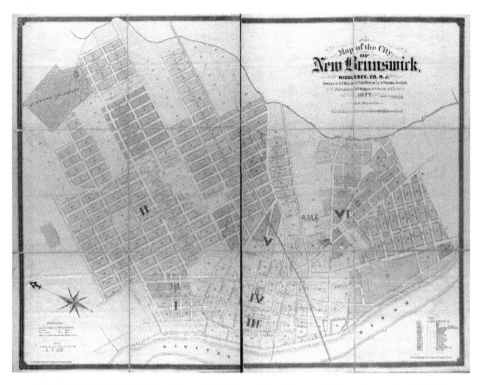

FIGURE 2.1 S. E. Weir Jr., *Map of the City of New Brunswick*, 200 to an inch (W. C. Dripps, 1877).

Image courtesy of Special Collections and University Archives, Rutgers University.

responsibility for moving beyond the primary school curriculum lay with the Colored School's teacher, Miss Jones, who was in charge of approximately sixty students ranging from ages five to eighteen.[23] By only providing black children with the minimum level of education required for state compliance and then attributing the continuance of segregation to a subjective standard of black intellectual achievement, New Brunswick education officials systematically denied black citizens an invaluable opportunity for social advancement.

The creation of separate schools for black children also mirrors major shifts occurring in black residential patterns emerging in the 1870s. While during slavery African Americans were diffused across the slaveholding households of New Brunswick, by 1870 discernible clusters of black residents emerged in the city, with the majority segregated into the Second and Sixth Wards.[24] Those in the Second Ward (in the area currently surrounding Feaster Park) made their homes in an area designated "Cream Ridge," which was widely considered to be "the headquarters of the colored population of this city."[25] Many also settled near the original Mt. Zion African Methodist Church, where the Fourth, Fifth, and Sixth Wards intersected (currently near Robert Wood Johnson Hospital), in an area which came to be disparagingly referred to by locals as "Nigger Hill."[26] The separation of black residents and the creation of separate schooling was reflective of other New Jersey cities like Newark, as well as cities nationwide.

Despite the conditions in which black residents lived, many sought autonomy and self-improvement through their labor. Ostracized from the city's higher paying manufacturing jobs, most black New Brunswickers found work as laborers. Some, however, did work as small business owners and educated professionals. Thomas Marsh, once a waiter, later became the owner of both the Temperance Restaurant and a local barber shop which he operated for over a decade; the restaurant changed locations twice, once at 42 Albany Street and later at 18 Hiram Street.[27] Other notable individuals include Charles Synder, an engineer, and William H. Johnson, who worked as a painter and owned his own paint dealership. Theodore Anderson owned both a barbershop and a ladies' hair salon, while John Bartley operated an ice cream garden at 102 Church Street for approximately a decade. James Bolan worked as a janitor for the theological seminary and lived on Seminary Place.[28] Men also found other forms of employment as drivers, coachmen, butchers, shoemakers, milkmen, bricklayers, and porters.

Black men and women also worked together in New Brunswick to establish their own privately owned black businesses. In the early 1900s, Walter and Etta Jackson owned the "only catering service in the city," a forerunner to the Bruns Catering Service as well as other successful catering services in the city. Yet exceptionally few black women became business owners in their own right. In some instances, they are mentioned as having held positions washing and ironing, as dressmakers, and in a few cases teachers. In fact, in one rare case in 1884, an African American woman by the name of Mrs. Phillips Treadwell was employed in an "intelligence office."[29] In the post–Civil War era, this office brokered deals between potential laborers and employers for the New Brunswick area.[30] These black men and women of New Brunswick were not merely gainfully employed but were symbols of engaged black citizenship, financial independence, and autonomy over the trajectory of one's life.

The labor shortages created by World War I also brought new labor opportunities in wartime industries for African American men. After the enactment of several federal European immigrant labor restrictions in 1917, African Americans flocked to the North in significant numbers to fill labor shortages in wartime industries vacated by European migrants. One of the largest industries in wartime New Brunswick was the Nixon Nitration Plant.[31] Sprawling some twelve miles throughout present-day Edison, Metuchen, Piscataway, and parts of New Brunswick, the Nixon Nitration Plant attracted men from across the nation, including a large number of black southern migrants to operate its machinery. One such migrant was Rodgers Capus Birt Sr., the father of class-of-1937 graduate Rodgers C. Birt Jr., who moved with his family from their hometown of Jacksonville, Florida, to Piscataway, New Jersey, sometime during 1917 or 1918 to work for the Nixon plant.[32] The Birt family joined the roughly 700,000 to 1,000,000 African Americans who left the South as a result of the First World War.[33] The Nixon Nitration Plant was one of the few industrial employment opportunities available to African Americans in New Brunswick prior to World War II. By contrast, the prominent Johnson & Johnson factory listed only one black employee in the early twentieth century: a wagon driver named Pelton Swann who delivered the company's goods to local customers and drugstores.[34]

The First Great Migration and
Black Women's Labor in New Brunswick

For those black New Brunswickers who were neither business owners nor educated professionals, the *New Brunswick Daily Home News* (hereafter the *Daily Home News*) provides a second avenue for understanding their lives and labors. For the first half of the nineteenth century, the city's newspapers were peppered with advertisements for female slaves that extolled their suitability for domestic service.[35] The end of legal slavery in New Jersey eradicated slave sale advertisements from New Brunswick's newspapers. In their place appeared "female help wanted" listings that advertised positions in the private households, restaurants, and hotels in New Brunswick. While an adjacent column advertised "male help wanted," the listings it contained were never so plentiful as those seeking women's labor. Although listings seeking a cook or housekeeper in late-nineteenth-century New Brunswick often did not specify a particular race, those that did habitually looked to the city's black women and girls to fill the positions.

In April 1887, the *Daily Home News* announced that "TWO GOOD COLORED GIRLS" could find employment as a cook and a nurse, respectively, by contacting the office of the *Daily Home News*, so long as they could provide the "best recommendations."[36] Such a listing was repeated hundreds of times within the "Help Wanted" section of the *Daily Home News* from its inaugural issues in 1880 through the 1930s. The ubiquity of these listings affirms one of the perennial features of African American life in the urban North in the nineteenth and twentieth centuries. African American women, barred from more profitable forms of employment, found themselves performing, for paltry wages, the same domestic service jobs that they had performed for no pay during slavery: washing clothes, cooking meals, scrubbing floors, and minding white children.[37] To be sure, African American women were not the only ones to supply New Brunswick with domestic labor. White women also held jobs as washerwomen and waitresses. Yet New Brunswickers did not automatically envision native-born white women as natural servants as easily as they did their black counterparts. In 1887, approximately 43 percent of the listings in the "female help wanted" section of the *Daily Home News* called for a "colored" domestic. By comparison, only 28 percent specifically requested a white servant, and the remainder did not specify a racial preference.[38]

During the 1880s and 1890s, the *Daily Home News* "Female Help Wanted" section indexed a lively domestic service market in the city that was both racialized and feminized, much like it was during slavery. However, this should not imply that black life remained static as New Brunswick absorbed its relatively tiny African American population into the free labor market. The *Daily Home News*'s salacious reports of crime in the city reinforced the cultural association of African American women with domestic labor while constructing a relatively new narrative: urban black criminality. The thieving black maid became a stock character in the crime reports of the *Daily Home News*. One typical report from 1887 described Maria Heimer as a local washerwoman and "ignorant negress . . . [who] caused considerable amusement by her efforts to clear herself" of the charge of petty theft of $16 from her white mistress before the court in New Brunswick.[39] When asked for her plea, Maria fumblingly replied "I ain't not guilty." Misreading her anxiety and confusion as stupidity, the report continued that Maria incriminated herself when she recalled finding the cash in the pocket of her mistresses' unwashed clothes and placing it beneath her tub.[40] Accusations of theft on the job were not limited to black women. In April 1894, the *New York Times* reported with a tone of bored annoyance that a Rutgers dormitory had been burglarized "for the fourth or fifth time since it was built."[41] Jon Van Dusser, a Rutgers College student hailing from Warwick, New York, accused William Watson, a "colored waiter," of stealing $135 dollars in cash, a diamond pin, and a suit of clothes.[42] New Brunswick was by no means unique in associating black domestic servants with crime in the late nineteenth century.[43] Nevertheless, New Brunswickers would simultaneously designate African American women a natural corps of domestic servants and an undesirable social element through the turn of the century.

The Great Migration, in which an estimated six million African Americans fled the grinding poverty and violent terror of the Jim Crow South for economic opportunity in northern cities in the early twentieth century, would not reach its apex until the First World War.[44] Even then, New Brunswick's modest factories like Johnson & Johnson and Nixon Nitration afforded far fewer jobs for black men than the factories of Philadelphia, Camden, Newark, and New York.[45] Blatant discrimination further limited industrial job opportunities for African Americans. In New Brunswick, the employment office of J. J. Creamer was exclusively interested in securing factory jobs for "white, sober, English-speaking men."[46] Still, by 1893 a sufficient number of southern black women had streamed into the domestic service market of New Brunswick to trigger a bitter editorial in the *Daily Home News*. The anonymous editorialist complained that the "irresponsible character of the untaught Southern negro is constantly illustrated in the conduct of those colored women that come North as servants."[47] They argued that southern black female migrants were lured to New Brunswick by the promise of "wages . . . treble what they are at home [in the South]." The inflated wages supposedly enabled unscrupulous black maids to hoard their earnings and "quit work and go to visit friends at home [in the South]," only to be immediately rehired by northern housewives upon their return.[48] According to this editorial, the crime of the black female domestic servant was not just alleged theft, as in the case of Maria Heimer. Black women were also accused of resisting the discipline of the northern industrial capitalist order that required workers to be consistently employed.

Despite vocal complaints about the supposed delinquency and shift-lessness of black female domestic servants, early twentieth-century New Brunswickers kept up a persistent demand for black housekeepers, cooks, and laundresses, especially those of southern origin. In May 1903, the *Daily Home News* announced that Martin & Co., a firm located in Richmond, Virginia, offered to furnish "Southern colored help," including "cooks, drivers, and farmhands."[49] Two months later, the *Daily Home News* reported that "50 COLORED GIRLS from Virginia" had arrived in New Brunswick. Their services could be engaged by writing or calling the Universal Employment Agency, located at 56 Somerset Street. New Brunswick was certainly not suffering from a shortage of female labor in 1903. European immigrant women from Germany, Hungary, Ireland, and Poland streamed into Northeastern cities like New Brunswick in the late nineteenth and early twentieth centuries, often competing with African Americans for domestic service jobs. Nevertheless, employment agencies turned a steady profit importing southern-born black domestics into New Brunswick. Intriguingly, the recruitment of black female domestics from the South took off just as the black percentage of New Brunswick's population was slipping to its lowest point since the abolition of slavery.[50] In light of these demographic shifts, the recruitment of black women, the traditional pool of domestic workers in the Northeast, may have served to reinforce a racial hierarchy that had been destabilized by emancipation and European immigration.[51] The presence of denigrated black labor within their homes reaffirmed the link between whiteness and superiority for wealthy New Brunswick families. Despite white New Brunswickers' reservations about the morality of southern black domestics, African Americans seeking situations in the city did not regard their southern origins as a liability on the job market. In some respects, it was a selling point. In March of 1904, a "YOUNG MAN (colored)" placed a listing in the *Daily Home News* seeking a position at general housework. He concluded his listing by informing the reader that he had "recently arrived from the South."[52] It seems counterintuitive that an individual would advertise his southern origins, given the vitriol in the New Brunswick newspaper toward southern black domestics. Perhaps the young man was attempting to signal his docility and deference toward whites, in contrast to African Americans born in the North.

While the black share of the city's population remained steady at the turn of the century, the proportion of European immigrants continued to grow.[53] New Brunswickers modified their enduring taste for low-wage black domestic labor accordingly, but this did little to unseat African Americans from the bottommost rung of the local labor market. In 1903, of all the "female help wanted" listings printed in the *Daily Home News* that specified a race, 39 percent preferred white domestics compared to the 40 percent requesting a "colored" domestic.[54] Among those specifying white help, a significant number stated preferences for particular strains of European immigrants—namely, Germans, Hungarians, and Poles. One-fifth of all employers seeking female domestic labor stated that they would gladly accept "white or colored" applicants. However, unlike their African American counterparts, white European immigrant women's tenure in the domestic service market would prove a temporary holdover. By 1903, New Brunswick's white European immigrant women followed the lead of their sisters in New York and took manufacturing jobs in the cigar, hosiery, and medical supply factories that lined Neilson Street.[55] For example, Hirschorn, Mack, & Co's cigar factory employed nearly a thousand white women between the ages of seventeen and twenty-one, a significant percentage of whom were Hungarian.[56] Hungarian cigar rollers, regarded by the forewoman as "excellent workers and . . . rather ambitious," earned twenty-five cents per hundred cigars rolled. An experienced hand could roll 700 cigars per day, prompting the same forewoman to conclude that "if a girl does not make one dollar a day after two months work the fault is her own laziness or stupidity."[57] These wages, while low compared to those earned by men in industrial positions, far exceeded the pay of domestic service, where one black maid reported earning "two dollars a week plus clothes when I asked for it."[58] While factory work offered some upward economic mobility for immigrant women, African American women were utterly excluded from these opportunities. Just as African American men were excluded from the well-paying industrial jobs at Johnson & Johnson and United States Rubber, New Brunswick's manufacturing factories were uninterested in hiring African American women in any notable capacity.[59] Instead, New Brunswickers continued to relegate African American women to their traditional positions in domestic service. In May of 1911, the Martin & Co firm of Richmond, Virginia, repeated their advertisement promising to send "Southern colored help" in the form of cooks and maids to white New Brunswick households.[60]

The African American population in New Brunswick nearly doubled from 690 in 1910 to 1,124 in 1920. The black share of the city's population continued to hover around 3 percent, its growth disguised by the continued influx of European immigrants.[61] This demographic shifting would destabilize black women's already precarious standing in the domestic labor market. By 1911, requests for a white domestic gained an appreciable majority among the racially specific "female help wanted" listings in the *Daily Home News*. That year, 54.5 percent of racially specific listings called for a white domestic, while only 36.3 percent preferred a black domestic. Racially ambivalent listings, in which the position was open to "white or colored" women, declined from 20 percent in 1903 to 9 percent in 1911.[62] The dramatic uptick in preference for white domestic servants may have been informed by the exodus of European immigrant women from the domestic service market as better paying factory jobs became available to them.[63] Crucially, the appreciable white preference in the New Brunswick domestic service market coincided with the expansive growth of the city's black population after a long period of relative dormancy. The timing of this development suggests that the increasingly pronounced presence of African Americans in New Brunswick may have elicited the resentment of white New Brunswickers whose ranks were swollen with assimilated European immigrants. One advertisement in the *Daily Home News* throws the emerging preference for white immigrant women within the New Brunswick domestic service market into especially sharp relief. The Burton Company of St. Joseph's, Michigan, sought a "colored woman desiring face bleach to use and sell."[64] Historian Tiffany Gill confirms that skin whitening agents were commonly marketed to African Americans in the early twentieth century.[65] However, the conspicuous placement of the advertisement in the "Female Help Wanted" section of the local New Brunswick newspaper, whose pages black women regularly combed in search of their next situation, alludes to a growing awareness that whiteness meant greater employability, even in a labor sector traditionally supplied by black women. Of course, the growing preference for white domestics to serve in the households of white New Brunswickers did not lead to black women's evacuation of the domestic service market after 1911. Listings that stated a preference for "colored" women or girls still appeared regularly in the "Female Help Wanted" section of the *Daily Home News*, but these listings generally did not direct interested applicants to the households of white New Brunswickers. Rather, the emergent preference for white household workers further dislocated African American women into an even less respectable sector of the domestic labor market. Spaces of public accommodation, like the Whitehall Hotel and the John Wells Hospital (the future Robert Wood Johnson Hospital), increasingly absorbed African American women for the onerous task of washing soiled linens.[66]

The historical experience of African American women in early twentieth century New Brunswick would seemingly confirm historian Jacqueline Jones's observation that "black women's work in the North was synonymous with domestic service."[67] However, black women gained a tiny, temporary foothold in local industry thanks to the labor shortages produced by the First World War. In the summer of 1918, the *Daily Home News* reported that "twenty-three sturdy colored women" had just arrived in New Brunswick from the South "ready to take up picks and shovels to do general track work on Division B, or the New York Division of the Pennsylvania Railroad."[68] Track work was dirty, dangerous, physically demanding, and, above all, a job traditionally performed by men. The fact that black women were designated as acceptable substitutes for male track workers speaks to the racialized and gendered imaginations of the white-owned-and-operated Pennsylvania Railroad and *Daily Home News.* Black women's racial status cast them outside the dominant notions of "womanhood" in the early twentieth century. Consequently, they were fit to take on the jobs that were deemed entirely inappropriate for their white counterparts. In spite of this, track work promised black women better wages than housework.[69] The *Daily Home News* predicted with a degree of apprehension that "it is probable that they will be a permanent addition to the permanent staff of railroad workers . . . largely to provide the labor for which there has been a great shortage." Their fears proved unfounded. As a writer for *World Outlook* observed in October 1919, "the colored woman is the marginal worker. She is the last to be hired and the first to go."[70] While some southern black migrants found work on the railroads, others, like one "NEAT colored girl from the South," continued to seek and find positions at "housework or chambermaid or waitress."[71] The statistics pertaining to racial preference in the domestic labor market reflect the labor shortage and fleeting economic mobility triggered by World War I. In 1918, listings that specifically requested a "colored" or "white" domestic servant broke even for the first time since 1905. Listings calling for a white servant and advertisements requesting a black servant, respectively, claimed 37.5 percent of the racially specific listings for that year. Racially ambivalent listings that welcomed "white or colored" applicants" trailed closely behind at 25 percent.[72]

The restrictions of an economy structured by race and gender also pressed some black women, either by choice or circumstance, to labor in New Brunswick's illicit sex trades. As historian Cynthia M. Blair notes, "sex work was a strategy for economic survival," wherein urban black women attempted "to negotiate both independence and a form of self-respect in an urban economy and social environment inhospitable to [their] financial and social aspirations."[73] Some black women in New Brunswick found relatively lucrative work and a greater sense of autonomy in soliciting on the streets, operating brothels, or renting rooms in disorderly houses. The brothels owned by black women tended to be comparatively small establishments, often with no more than four women paying around fifty cents to occupy a room each night. Illegal gambling and the sale of liquor served to bring owners more revenue, but they also drew a more volatile clientele and police inquiry. While brothel keepers made calculated business decisions to secure their own financial well-being, they also created opportunities for other black women to avoid or subsidize poorly paid domestic work. Other laboring women moved in and out of sex work whenever their personal circumstances required, as evidenced by the ill-fated Dora Miller. Miller moved from New York City to New Brunswick on a Friday, set to begin her new job as a domestic worker on Monday. She planned to take up work and lodging in a disorderly house just for the weekend, but before she could depart on Monday, she found herself caught in a Saturday night police raid.[74]

While prostitution itself was not considered a criminal offense prior to the Progressive Era, police officers regulated sex workers and their clients by pursuing charges of "lewdness," "vagrancy," or "maintaining a disorderly house" at their own discretion.[75] Such subjective law enforcement often disproportionately targeted black women, who endured racist stereotypes of their supposedly innate criminality and hypersexuality. And even though the majority of New Brunswick's brothels were concentrated near Burnet and Neilson Streets on the city's periphery, lively dancing, piano playing, and liquor consumption frequently provoked police raids and arrests. Black female sex workers also drew greater opprobrium than white sex workers because of the rampant social anxiety that disorderly houses were spaces where black women could often be "found carousing with white men."[76] Such a threat to the social order demanded harsh regulation, and the rise of Progressive Era politics in the early twentieth century only further increased police surveillance and repression on a trade already steeped in violence, exploitation, and disease. Women arrested for "maintaining a disorderly house" had bail set as high as $2,000, and those found guilty could expect a harsh sentence of six months in the county jail. New Brunswick also made swift and eager use of the 1918 Chamberlain-Kahn Act, a wartime measure which allowed health officials to arrest women suspected of carrying venereal disease, subject them to gynecological examinations, and detain them for an indefinite period of time.[77] Furthermore, passage of the Volstead Act in 1919 outlawed the sale of liquor, by which many black women earned an income, and provided police with new grounds to raid homes and prosecute women deemed immoral. For the black women who sought economic survival in illicit work, the risks could easily outweigh the rewards.

Whether the black female residents of New Brunswick remained in domestic service, secured better jobs, or tried their hand at the illicit economy, the end of World War I spelled the end of the wartime labor shortages that had afforded black women a degree of economic choice. By 1919, the domestic service market of New Brunswick overwhelmingly preferred white servants and would continue to do so well into the Great Depression. Between 1919 and 1932, the portion of job listings for white domestic servants hovered between 71 and 96 percent.[78] This full-throated preference for white help would lead to the depreciation of black female domestics' wages and working conditions, which were already paltry and squalid. Not surprisingly, the entrenchment of white preference in the domestic labor market continued to coincide with explosive growth in New Brunswick's black population. Once again, the African American population of New Brunswick nearly doubled in a single decade, surging from 1,124 in 1920 to 2,086 in 1930.[79] Unlike the first phase between 1910 and 1920, the growth spurt in the black population that followed the First World War significantly augmented the African American proportion of the city's population, from 3.4 percent in 1920 to 6 percent in 1930.[80] The corresponding drop in the white proportion of the population from 96.5 percent in 1920 to 93.9 percent in 1930 due to the restrictions placed on European immigration by the Johnson-Reed Immigration Act of 1924 rendered the African American community, flushed with southern migrants, hypervisible on the city's landscape.[81] In response, white New Brunswickers forcefully reasserted their racial superiority, which had been mildly challenged by the labor shortages of World War I. Few traces of the industrial opportunity afforded to black women during the war survived demobilization. In 1926, one listing in the *Daily Home News* sought out "experienced colored girls" to work as pressers at the Staten Island Dyework Company on Harvey Street in New Brunswick.[82] In 1928, another similar listing appeared seeking "colored pressers" for the dresses produced by the C&F Dress Company in South River, New Jersey.[83] While certainly a step above washing bed linens, these positions were ultimately an extension of the housework that white New Brunswickers had expected black women to perform since slavery. Moreover, listings of this nature were exceptionally few and far between in the years following World War I. Far more numerous were requests for housekeepers, cooks, laundresses, and waitresses, the typical occupations of black female southern migrants. In the same breath, white New Brunswickers made black women's livelihoods even more precarious by announcing that they would fill the positions with white women if they could.

After 1919, the expansion of Rutgers University created additional demand for domestic servants from New Brunswick. The founding of the New Jersey College for Women in 1918 (later Douglass Residential College of Rutgers University) and the College of Agriculture (later Cook College of Rutgers University) in 1921 both led to the construction of new academic and residential buildings. Naturally, these buildings required regular cleaning. The New Jersey College for Women placed an advertisement in the *Daily Home News* in search of a "reliable man as janitor" in 1920.[84] Another listing that year sought "at Women's College, a woman for general cleaning."[85] Additionally, as Rutgers University expanded it acquired droves of new students, male and female, who looked to New Brunswick's women to provide for their domestic needs. In March 1919, the *Daily Home News* included a request for a "woman to clean at fraternity house two mornings a week."[86] Similar listings in the 1920s sought cooks for fraternity houses on George Street and College Avenue and waitresses for the Cooper Dining Hall at the New Jersey College for Women.[87] Individuals connected to Rutgers College rarely specified a race for the domestic servants they hoped to find. When they did specify a race, their preference went to white women. In 1923, Jacob Goodale Lipman, professor of agricultural chemistry at Rutgers's recently acquired College of Agriculture, and director of the College Farm, placed an advertisement in the *Daily Home News* to find a "strong white woman as cook and general houseworker" for the facility.[88] The next year he resumed his search for a "competent white girl as cook."[89] Lipman's preference for a white servant demonstrates that the faculty and administration of Rutgers College were not immune to the racial ideology that gripped white locals in the 1920s.

The housekeeping positions offered by Rutgers College in the 1920s did little to compensate for the limited economic mobility local African American women had lost at the close of World War I. However, this should not suggest that black female domestic workers were utterly powerless before the racial stratification of the domestic service market in New Brunswick. Southern black female migrants who advertised their services as domestics in the "Situation Wanted" section of the *Daily Home News* conveyed a set of expectations regarding the conditions of their labor. With the exception of one self-described "real Southern mammy" who sought employment as a child-minder in 1931, few black women seeking domestic positions in the "Situation Wanted" section after 1919 mentioned their southern origins. Instead, black female jobseekers distinguished themselves with labels that spoke to the quality of their labor, not their docility. They described themselves as "very neat," "reliable," and "experienced."[90] In these listings, African American domestic workers deployed several strategies to control for their exploitation and retain a measure of independence from their employers. "Female Help Wanted" advertisements placed by white New Brunswickers most commonly requested a "general housekeeper" or "general houseworker." As opposed to a cook or laundress, "general housekeeper" was a generic term for a domestic servant that encapsulated all elements of household labor, from washing dishes to sweeping floors to minding children. Black New Brunswick women who sought situations at housework in the 1920s and 1930s often articulated their desired position as a specialized kind of domestic servant: an "experienced cook," or "chambermaid," or "laundry worker."[91] By limiting the domesetic tasks they were willing to perform, black female domestics in New Brunswick could prevent their white mistresses from treating them as all-purpose servants to use indiscriminately according to their whims.[92] Black female domestics in New Brunswick not only limited the tasks they were willing to perform but also the hours they were willing to work. Ethel Hush, who advertised her services as a houseworker in December 1930, stated upfront that she would not work Sundays.[93] By insisting upon "part-time work," "day's work," or "work by the week," New Brunswick's corps of black female domestics maintained flexible work schedules that allotted them leisure time with their friends and families.[94] Additionally, black female domestics in New Brunswick attempted to exert control over the location of their labor. To avoid the supervision of their white employers (which could easily lead to accusations of misconduct and theft, as Maria Heimer learned in 1887) and maximize time spent with their families, many African American women in New Brunswick chose to do laundry by the bundle out of their own homes.[95] For cooks and chambermaids, working outside the homes of their employers was a physical impossibility. Nevertheless, they resisted their exploitation within a discriminatory domestic labor market by refusing to "sleep in" the home of their employers. This demeaning practice was universally abhorred by domestic servants because it kept them at the beck and call of their employers at all hours of the night and robbed them of precious contact with their own families for days at a time.[96] Even in 1930, when the Great Depression was in full effect and "white preferred" advertisements claimed 85.7 percent of the racially specific listings in the *Daily Home News*, African American women seeking jobs as domestic servants in white New Brunswick households remained firm on their intention to "go home nights."[97]

African American Institution-Building and Education in New Brunswick

In addition to seeking autonomy through controlling the type and duration of their labor, many black New Brunswickers found refuge from the unrelenting labor market in the city's vibrant institutional culture. Beginning in the 1880s and accelerating throughout the 1920s, black New Brunswickers established numerous social clubs, mutual aid societies, and political groups. Largely segregated by gender, these organizations mobilized individuals and pooled resources to promote racial uplift; assist the sick, poor, and orphaned; and provide necessary social services to the local community. Black men founded local chapters of renowned fraternal organizations, including Raritan Lodge No. 2631 of the Grand United Order of Odd Fellows, Conklin Smith Post No. 108 of the American Legion, Progressive Lodge No. 17 of the Free and Accepted Masons, and Elks Superior Lodge No. 215 of the Benevolent and Protective Order of Elks. Membership in such fraternal orders offered black men leadership roles and a sense of "providership, production, and respectability," which helped to reinforce a middle-class masculine identity.[98] Many local black women joined the corresponding female auxiliaries of these groups, diligently organizing picnics, marches, parades, dances, concerts, charity balls, banquets, and lectures for the benefit of members as well as the community at large. During the 1910s and 1920s, as racial tensions escalated throughout the United States, black New Brunswickers also joined political organizations in droves, like the Men's Civic League, the Ladies Civic League, the Colored Women's Republican Club, and the Negro Uplift League, all with the intent of educating and protecting black voters. Meetings organized by black temperance organizations like the Colored Women's Christian Temperance Union and the Independent Order of Good Samaritans and Daughters of Samaria were also regularly said to have attracted "nearly all of the colored population of the city besides many white citizens," as many New Brunswickers looked to temperance reform to alleviate the social ills of poverty, violence, and vice.[99]

Yet while participation in all-black social clubs and volunteer organizations flourished across the country at the turn of the century, New Brunswick's black institutional life was made particularly exceptional by the existence of the Colored Industrial School, founded by Reverend W. A. Rice and his wife, Ella M. Rice, in 1897. Born into slavery in South Carolina in 1845, Walter Allen Simpson Rice joined the Union Army at age eighteen. After the war, he eventually returned to South Carolina where he worked as a Freedmen's Bureau public school teacher and a county court clerk. Gradually, Rice found life in South Carolina increasingly unbearable as his status as a beneficiary of Reconstruction-era policies subjected him to escalating racial hostilities and intimidations. Fearing for his life, he fled to New Jersey, where he embraced Christianity, received religious training, and ultimately became a minister for the African Methodist Episcopal (A.M.E.) Church. While at the Mt. Zion A.M.E. Church in Bordentown, Reverend Rice met and married Ella Mount, an organist for the church. During the 1870s, Reverend Rice became a critical member of a church-affiliated group that met in New Brunswick to discuss the creation of a private industrial school for black children.[100] Though New Jersey banned segregation in public schools in 1881, most blacks in early-twentieth-century New Jersey—including Reverend Rice—continued to believe that separate schools would better provide for and protect black children.[101] Finally in 1886, Reverend Rice succeeded in the achievement for which he is best known, founding the Manual Training and Industrial School in Bordentown, New Jersey. Informally modeled on Booker T. Washington's Tuskegee Institute in Alabama, the Bordentown School was initially intended to be a space for black students to receive trade-based instruction to assist in their integration into the paid labor force.[102] In just eight years, the number of students under Reverend Rice's tutelage grew exponentially, and though the school was gaining in reputation and prestige, he struggled to ensure adequate funding and facilities for the growing institution. Then in 1894, the state of New Jersey acquired the Bordentown School through a legislative act and turned over operations to state and county government officials.

Discharged from his duties as principal of the Bordentown School, Reverend Rice moved his family to New Brunswick, where he had previously served in the local Mt. Zion A.M.E. Church. The Rices soon began to focus their energies on founding another school for black children, and in September 1897, they opened the Colored Industrial School inside a leased property on the upper end of Livingston Avenue. By the next academic year, there were approximately thirty pupils in attendance and the Rices were able to relocate the school into a house they purchased at 110 Comstock Street. With Reverend Rice serving as principal and Mrs. Rice as an instructor, the Rices largely replicated the model which proved so successful at the Bordentown School. The Rice School was a coeducational boarding school, where students learned trade-based skills like sewing and cooking. Though the school had no official religious affiliation, Christian ethics served as the backbone of the curriculum. Yet unlike the Bordentown School, which eventually received state support, the Rice School struggled under the financial burdens of remaining a private institution. Reverend Rice repeatedly appealed to government officials and the local board of education for financial assistance, even seeking to incorporate the Rice School into the New Brunswick public school system, but to no avail.[103] Consequently, Reverend Rice sought out funds from a multitude of sources. Like many all-black schools, the Rice School frequently organized student-performed choral concerts as a reliable source of fundraising. Additionally, Reverend Rice also attempted to generate revenue by leasing out student labor. Identifying himself as the school's "manager," Reverend Rice advertised in the local newspaper that "persons wishing to secure capable and skilled girls as waitresses or other help to serve Thanksgiving dinners, or any other occasion, parties, etc., can do so by applying at the school."[104] While such a leasing program provided students with an opportunity to practice and refine their trade skills, the lines separating education and labor could easily and often did blur for young black students in turn-of-the-century New Brunswick.

The unexpected death of Reverend Rice in January 1899 triggered a reorientation of the school's mission and curriculum. Now principal, Mrs. Rice renamed her school the Colored Industrial and Literary Institute. The school's new name was not merely symbolic; it captured a growing sentiment in the early twentieth century that black students should not just receive industrial instruction, but a classical education as well.[105] The Rice School continued to teach trade-based courses like dressmaking and penmanship, but it now also offered students courses like "moral science" and "civil government." Though the school maintained a small full-time instructional staff, it employed a handful of part-time instructors, some of whom were students themselves at Rutgers College.[106] In addition to academics, the school flourished with extra-curricular offerings, including chorus, debate, and its own baseball team. The wealth of industrial, literary, and extracurricular opportunities made avail-able to students was particularly extraordinary given the sustained effort by the Rice School to admit orphaned and abandoned children. A 1913 newspa-per exposé noted the school's commitment in spite of the increased finan-cial strains: "If the orphan children have relatives to look after them board is asked, but where the children are worthy cases and there is no means of support, they are taken into the school and all possible done for them towards making them [the] right kind of men and women. At present there are 48 orphans at the school and a majority of these are without support."[107] While some enrolled students did have deceased parents, many were *situational orphans*, with parents alive but unable to provide for their children. Obliged to work within a discriminatory and temperamental labor market, many black parents were forced by economic desperation to forgo domestic stability as they searched for employment. The Rice School consequently received many students like Alfred Lloyd, whose parents enrolled him in order for them to leave New Brunswick and pursue seasonal work in New Jersey's seaside resorts.[108] The entrance of the United States into World War I also further trig-gered an influx of black children in need of guardianship. An additional fif-teen children entered the school in 1918 alone, all "children whose fathers and guardians were making the fight for democracy."[109] Thus, the Rice School not only provided for the well-being of black children, it also served as a critical resource to black parents and guardians as they navigated the demands of an unforgiving labor market.

As an all-black educational institution *and* a local charity, the contin-ued success of the Rice School truly became a community affair. In 1906, the school's Board of Trustees, an influential group of local churchmen and com-munity leaders, noted, "It is gratifying to note the great interest that the col-ored people of New Brunswick are beginning to take in this work."[110] As the school constantly struggled to pay its debts and taxes, its operations over-whelmingly depended upon the generous donations provided by New Bruns-wick's black community.[111] Individuals offered what they could—coal, clothing, shoes, meat, potatoes, fruit, candy, household goods, furniture, and bedding. Local organizations like the Mt. Zion A.M.E. Church, Ebenezer Baptist Church, Throop Avenue Chapel, Elks Lodge No. 215, and the Colored Women's Club of Middlesex County all helped raise funds for donation. Even local Jewish orga-nizations like Temple Anshe Emeth and the Hebrew Ladies Benevolent Soci-ety gave generously. The black and white club women who composed the Rice School's Ladies Auxiliary also worked together to organize appealing fund-raising events like picnics, pig roasts, and Easter festivals, where the entire

New Brunswick community was welcome to attend. Yet the highlight of the academic year was certainly the school's "closing exercises" held each June. Part fundraiser, part student performance, and part graduation ceremony, the event provided an opportunity for the school to showcase the achievements of its students to the community at large. Students presented essays and performed speeches, recitations, and musical numbers. Individuals affiliated with Rutgers College also occasionally assisted in the event, with graduates and faculty ceremoniously handing out certificates and prizes.[112] The event always attracted a large audience, and public reports frequently highlighted the high quality of the entertainment as well as the aptitude of the school's students, commenting that they "displayed excellent training" and "showed themselves to be very bright pupils."[113] Such public demonstrations of Rice students' erudition exemplified the school's success and further encouraged the local community to support the institution as best they could. Yet when a representative of the U.S. Bureau of Education visited the Rice School in May 1915, partly to assess "the advisability of giving outside help to the school," they concluded, "As a school with local support, it does not need to ask outside aid."[114] So even though the Rice School owed its continued existence to the contributions cobbled together by a black community stricken with its own financial hardships, the federal government cited such community involvement as justification for withholding desperately needed state funds.

On November 25, 1920, Ella Rice died suddenly after a brief battle with pneumonia. For nearly twenty-two years she served as principal of the Rice School, providing black children with an education, trade skills, and a safe place to eat and sleep each day. Recognition of her efforts extended well beyond New Brunswick—her death received mention in W.E.B. Du Bois's *The Crisis* magazine and the New Jersey State Federation of Colored Women's Clubs unanimously voted to establish the "Ella M. Rice Scholarship" in her memory.[115] At the time of her death, the school had grown to nearly seventy students and had just relocated to a larger property outside of New Brunswick on the northeastern border of Highland Park. In Mrs. Rice's place, the school's daily operations were taken over by two of her sons, Everett B. Rice and Walter Henry Rice, both of whom had previously taken summer courses at Rutgers College. Under the brothers' leadership, the school began a slow reorientation away from industrial and elementary education and toward "the training of children who seem backward in their studies and behavior."[116] Despite hosting a spate of fundraisers and benefit performances—including a talk on education by Rutgers alumnus Paul Robeson in November 1921—the Rice School continued to struggle financially.[117] Then in October 1925, a devastating fire destroyed the school building and an estimated $14,000 in industrial equipment.[118] Although the school made desperate efforts to remain open throughout the 1920s, it eventually closed under the weight of financial strain.

Though New Brunswick's black youth could still receive an education in the city's integrated public schools, the black community lost a vital institution of autonomy and self-determination with the closure of the Rice School. In 1922, when Rice student John McNeely was asked during a debate competition whether "'Mixed Schools' afford better educational advantages to colored students than colored schools," he asserted, "Mixed schools are not adapted to the negro's peculiar circumstances. They are founded and fostered to meet the needs, aspirations and ambitions of the most favored white youths."[119] As young McNeely argued, and surely observed, just because New Brunswick had integrated public schools did not ensure that black students received equal treatment or opportunities. In fact, it was at the segregated Rice School where students, parents, teachers, and the local black community at large found a space eager to protect and cultivate black "needs, aspirations and ambitions."[120]

The necessity and import of all-black institutions only grew as New Brunswick became increasingly complicit in the rising nativism, xenophobia, and racial intolerance sweeping the nation in the wake of World War I. Increasing immigration, black northern migration, postwar nationalism, industrialization, and urbanization all served to incite the resurgence of the Ku Klux Klan. Established near Atlanta, Georgia, in 1915, the "second Klan" would ultimately attract approximately 60,000 members in the state of New Jersey alone.[121] But while the Klan made its presence known in towns like Hoboken, Paterson, and Bayonne in the early 1920s, New Brunswick was comparatively slow to witness overt Klan activity.[122] Though reports of possible Klan activity circulated in this period, they were quickly dismissed by the white-owned press as jokes, hoaxes, or rumors.[123] New Brunswick's black residents, however, could not so easily deny an intensification of the city's already tense racial atmosphere. A palpable unease likely carried through the black community during incidents like "the gallant fight of the Klans" receiving hearty applause during a showing of D. W. Griffith's *The Birth of a Nation* at the New Brunswick Opera House.[124] Or when the Klan uniform became a popular outfit for costume parties in New Brunswick, with at least one man committing to the role by "glar[ing] threateningly at members of the colored race" present at the party.[125] Surely the individuals on the receiving end of that glare were unnerved—for how could one ever truly discern if a hooded man's threats were "in character" or real? Still, as late as February 1923, an editor for the *New Brunswick Daily Home News* said of the Klan, "If it exists here, it is so quiet that it is not worth considering."[126] Of course, to simply *not consider the Klan* was a privilege most black New Brunswickers could not afford.

Quite literally overnight, the presence of the Ku Klux Klan in New Brunswick became both overwhelming and undeniable. On the evening of May 2, 1923, the Klan organized a massive initiation ceremony on a private farm near

Middlebush, just five miles northwest of downtown New Brunswick. Figure 2.2 shows an undated photo of a Klan ceremony, although it is unclear if this is the incident that occurred on May 2nd. Believed at the time to be one of the largest Klan ceremonies to date on the East Coast, reporters on the scene estimated between 6,000 and 12,000 individuals in attendance, with over 1,000 receiving initiation rites.[127] Despite the Klan's reputed preference for conducting its affairs clandestinely, the event played out as a carefully orchestrated public spectacle. Klan organizers instructed all attendees to attach prominent white ribbons or handkerchiefs to their cars and to drive a designated route that cut directly through downtown New Brunswick. A *New York World* reporter observed, "There was never a time between 10 o'clock and midnight when the main streets of New Brunswick were not filled with the slow-moving processions," then adding, "There are many Negroes in New Brunswick's population. They vanished from the streets soon after 10 o'clock."[128] Unsurprisingly, black witnesses to this malevolent parade hid in the relative safety of their homes—perhaps sick with fear; perhaps halfheartedly attempting to distract themselves; perhaps even taking the opportunity to educate their children on racial violence. Overnight, the organization that had terrorized southern friends and family suddenly became frighteningly local. License plates indicated that the vast majority of attendees were from New Jersey and New York, but cars also arrived from Ohio, Georgia, and Florida—states with highly organized, highly violent Klan operations. This northern rendition of the Klan appeared equally comfortable deploying intimidation tactics, tightly surrounding the periphery of the ceremony site with guards wielding wooden clubs "from three to four feet long, often knotted, twisted and gnarled with the bark on."[129] The racist ideology driving the New Jersey Klan became explicit during the initiation ritual, when inductees were instructed to place their right hand over their hearts and pledge themselves to the maintenance of "white supremacy." To signal the close of the ceremony, Klansmen set fire to a sixty-two-foot cross that could reportedly be seen up to seven miles away.[130] The intended message of the event was abundantly clear. As one Klansmen chillingly remarked, "This is the real test of strength of the Ku Klux Klan."[131]

In the following days, Klan newspapers designated the New Brunswick ceremony "One of the Greatest Ku Klux Demonstrations" and claimed that "a new respect for the Klan has developed here since the public has seen visual evidence of the extent to which true Americans have rallied to its banner."[132] Indeed, the success of the May 1923 ceremony helped to unleash a period of sustained Klan activity in New Brunswick. Though members of the Middlesex County Klan largely managed to conduct their meetings and endeavors covertly, a series of prominent cross burnings throughout the city ensured that residents felt the Klan's presence. The Klan carefully selected locations that would attract the most attention and often carried special significance.

FIGURE 2.2 Undated Klan ceremony in New Brunswick.

Image courtesy of New Jersey Historical Society, Folder NJ Photo Collection Places, New Brunswick MG 1361 Ku Klux Klan 27/180.

Large fiery crosses were found on George Street at the Johnson & Johnson factory, as well as on Comstock Street near the Pennsylvania Railroad tracks.[133] On one particularly industrious night, the Klan set four crosses ablaze across New Brunswick. Two were placed near city entrances at Buccleuch Park and the Lincoln Highway, and two were placed in the Second Ward—one on Jones Avenue and one on Loretta [now Loretto] Street. The concentration of burning crosses in New Brunswick's majority-black Second Ward suggests a deliberate effort on behalf of the Klan to terrorize the city's black residents.[134] Yet *The Fiery Cross*, a Klan newspaper, reported that the Middlesex County Klan finally "came into its own" on February 2, 1924, when members burned a cross on James Neilson's property, a large tract of land that bordered the New Jersey College for Women.[135] A Rutgers alumnus as well as an influential member of the Board of Trustees, Neilson was one of Rutgers's most generous benefactors, ultimately donating much of the land that would comprise the Cook/Douglass campus. The Klan placed the cross at the top of a prominent hill on Neilson's property known as "lilac fields," which "commands a fine view of the Raritan and New Brunswick," as described in a 1915 edition of *New Brunswick Daily Home News*.[136] Left to burn against the dark night sky for over an hour, the fiery cross likely caught the eye of many in the city—from the young white students at the College for Women to the black residents of the Second Ward—yet the meaning of that symbol varied radically among the individuals who called New Brunswick home.

The rapid increase in the size and strength of the Middlesex County Klan ultimately led to its dissolution into smaller, city-based klans. On March 7, 1926, the national Klan headquarters in Atlanta granted New Brunswick its own independent charter in a ceremony presided over by New Jersey's Grand Dragon, Arthur H. Bell.[137] The chapter adopted the official title "Rutgers Klan, Number 44 of the Realm of New Jersey." Figure 2.3 shows an undated photo of the official Rutgers Klan Bond document. While other New Jersey chapters like those in Newark and Wildwood named their klans after prominent patriotic figures like George Washington and Theodore Roosevelt, respectively, the New Brunswick Klan paid tribute to its city's most prominent institution. Yet because the Klan closely guarded its membership rolls, it is difficult to ascertain which New Brunswick Klan members, if any, were also formally affiliated with Rutgers. The Rutgers Klan did, however, attract a sizable number of New Brunswick's white, native-born, Protestant community. The *Daily Home News* estimated that nearly 500 members attended the group's first outdoor meeting.[138] Along with its women's auxiliary, "Old Glory, Number 64," the Rutgers Klan wholeheartedly embraced the agenda advanced by the organization's state and national leadership, self-reporting that "Rutgers is going forward and is backing our Grand Dragon in everything he asks us to do."[139] Although there appears to be no record of members of the Rutgers Klan committing overt acts of physical violence, members did work to advance anti-immigration bills and elect pro-Klan officials into positions of local authority, with varying levels of success. And yet despite the malevolent and pernicious activities performed under the name "Rutgers," there appears to have been no sustained effort on behalf of Rutgers College's administration to either formally denounce the Klan or to disassociate its actions from the college. Without any such clarification from the college, many of New Brunswick's residents likely assumed strong ties between Rutgers and the Klan. And for the city's black population, the vast majority of whom had no personal interactions with the college and therefore no alternative frame of reference, the name "Rutgers" surely adopted new, frightening connotations.

The downfall of the "second Klan" began in the late 1920s as public scandals and leadership disputes undermined the organization and new immigration laws satisfied the nativist calls of many of the nation's white Protestants.[140] Yet despite the increasing marginality of the Klan in American public life, the Rutgers Klan managed to prolong its existence well into the 1930s before finally disbanding. An active presence in New Brunswick for nearly a decade, the Rutgers Klan shattered any illusions of the city as exempt from the terrors of southern-style racism.

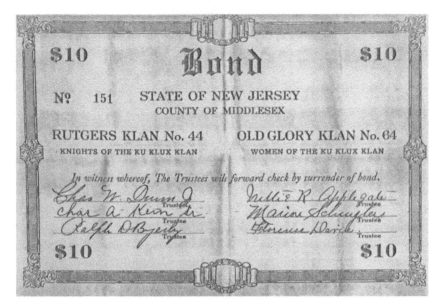

$10 $10

Bond

Nᵒ 151 STATE OF NEW JERSEY
COUNTY OF MIDDLESEX

RUTGERS KLAN No. 44 OLD GLORY KLAN No. 64
KNIGHTS OF THE KU KLUX KLAN WOMEN OF THE KU KLUX KLAN

In witness whereof, The Trustees will forward check by surrender of bond.

$10 $10

FIGURE 2.3 Klan bond.

Image courtesy of Special Collections and University Archives, Rutgers University. Bernard Bush Collection on the Ku Klux Klan in New Jersey (1915–1946), 1913–2010, Box 2, Folder 85.

New Brunswick and the Mt. Zion A.M.E. Church

In the face of white supremacist terror African Americans turned inward, creating their own institutions. However, the establishment of the Rice Colored Industrial School and other organizations would not have been possible without the ascent of the African Methodist Episcopal Church of the early nineteenth century. Eleven years after the founding of the first African Methodist Episcopal Church in Philadelphia, blacks on the banks of the Raritan defiantly followed the footsteps of their forerunners. In 1827, prominent black New Brunswickers Joseph and Joan Hoagland established what was likely the first black church in the city with the help of itinerant A.M.E. pastors in the area.[141] By December 12, 1829, the foundation of a church, which would resemble a "little red schoolhouse," was laid on Division Street, a road that runs perpendicular to one of the city's main arteries.[142] While Mt. Zion was not the first autonomous African American organization in the city (the African Association of New Brunswick founded in 1817 holds that title), it is recognized as the longest running black institution in the city.[143] Indeed, the founders of Mt. Zion A.M.E. learned from the short-lived but influential African Association, whose complicated alliances with white trustees, Presbyterian pastors, and colonizationist power brokers allowed the semi-autonomous black space to be manipulated as a tool for white social control over blacks in the community rather than a fully independent and liberatory space.[144] Therefore, when a coterie of African Americans set out to found a new congregation of the African Methodist Episcopal Church in New Brunswick in 1827, just one year after the African Association of New Brunswick was disbanded, they inscribed a provision in its charter which etched a future of black autonomy in perpetuity, declaring, "None shall be eligible as Trustees except free men, descendants [sic] of Africans."[145]

Historians have long acknowledged the influence of the Christian church in the African American community. As early as the nineteenth century, the church served as a spiritual home as well as an institutional base for organizing for equal rights, engaging in public discourse, community-building, and leisure. This holds true for African American churches in New Brunswick as well. When Mt. Zion A.M.E. was constructed on Division Street in 1829, it became a public sphere for blacks to debate and negotiate the meanings of freedom, identity, and citizenship into the twentieth century. Moreover, as scholars Evelyn Brooks Higginbotham, Cheryl Townsend Gilkes, and Jualynne Dodson have noted, African American women's significant numerical presence was a catalyst for the depth and breadth of the church's influence. And though many women did not operate in formal leadership roles, skills acquired through fundraising, administrative, and mission work were repurposed through community-based activism and social justice initiatives.[146] Into the twentieth century, Mt. Zion was a crucial site for black women, particularly those with academic and college credentials but whose opportunities were circumscribed by a racially discriminatory labor market. They harnessed institutional power within the church to transform their local communities and open doors in employment and education that had long been closed.

Since the nineteenth century, black churches have been "sites of a public discourse critical of white supremacy and the American nation-state as well as the spaces for identity construction."[147] Starting with the African Association and later the Mt. Zion A.M.E., blacks in New Brunswick consistently organized to carve out autonomous black spaces to protest discrimination and advance the black community. As previously noted, education and technical training schools like the Rice School were a site of their organizing efforts in the latter part of the century. But prior to the Civil War, when no such spaces existed, Mt. Zion benefited from holding the deed to the church and the property upon which it was built. African American ownership of the gathering space was a critical advantage for the members of Mt. Zion and other blacks in the area. Where blacks would normally hold meetings in the homes of those in formal and informal leadership positions, possession of an organizational meeting space meant more expansive programming and greater legitimization as an institution.[148]

Because Mt. Zion had circuit and short-term pastors during its one hundred years of existence, the edifice of the church itself, rather than any one particular individual, became a community cornerstone. As early as the 1840s, Mt. Zion was the site of quarterly conference meetings and colored conventions. Colored conventions were sites where free and fugitive blacks convened to strategize social justice initiatives in the areas of labor, education, and civil rights.[149] After the Civil War, the church was a significant site for meetings and lectures held by the Equal Rights League of New Jersey, an organization tasked with educating ex-slaves and southern exiles of their rights in the period immediately following emancipation. Samuel G. Gould of the *Equal Rights League* addressed the congregation and other black New Brunswickers in September of 1865, informing them of the "Political Rights and necessities for our people, strongly urging them to action while times were propitious, and while the public mind is awake." In the immediate aftermath of the Union victory, which resulted in nearly four million freedmen, Gould "urged the importance of unity of action, of striving to assist each other, of morality, education, wealth, and, above all, such a deportment in the ordinary walks of life as will constrain even our enemies to respect us."[150] Mt. Zion pastor Benjamin Lynch provided this account for the *Christian Recorder*, noting that directly following their attentive engagement with the lecture, parishioners "at once formed themselves into an Equal Rights League auxiliary to the State League."[151]

While Mt. Zion was a pivotal site for public and equal rights organizing in and around New Brunswick, the church fought for its existence financially, much like the Rice School. The congregation and the regular rotation of pastors spent the better part of the nineteenth century trying to climb out of debt. The constant growth of the membership meant physical expansion was regularly on the table; however, the financial struggles reflected the meager wages of the church body, indicative of the labor limitations imposed on the black community. For example, in 1872 the church only collected $42 from its sixty-three members. Because the church could not generate enough income to meet the needs of its growing but economically strapped congregation, leaders from the church were forced to borrow funds.[152] For this reason, fundraisers and festivals were regularly hosted by the church to generate income to pay off debts. For instance, an 1863 festival raised $15 to pay for the roof "which had blown off last spring."[153] As the church grew, leaders held Sunday "rallies" in local parks and organized "Valentine entertainment" to accrue funds for expansion and relieve their debt. The Christmas fair held in 1892, raised $41.61 when the church had grown to 102 members.[154] It would be many years before the church would reach financial stability, and this delay is likely because the short pastoral tenures prevented leadership from seeing projects for economic stability through to completion.[155]

Indeed, the chief purpose of the festivals and fairs was to fundraise for the expansion of the church and pay off debts. However, the consequences of the discriminatory labor market and racial hostility of the late nineteenth and early twentieth century was not simply institution-building as economic racial advancement but institution-building for the sake of pleasure and relief. These events also became important sites of leisure, community-building, and solidarity within the black community of New Brunswick. In these areas, resolute churchgoing women were the primary organizers.[156] As early as the 1830s, groups of AME women like the "Daughters of the Conference" concerned themselves with the material and financial health of the church by mending the clothing and robes of ministers and holding "'preconference' teas, dinners, receptions, etc.'"[157] Into the late nineteenth and early twentieth century, black women through their organizing and numerical power were able to harness institutional power which reached beyond the walls of the church. In her book about women's organizational power in the A.M.E. Church, Jualynne E. Dodson argues that "AME women were not using power in terms of personal individual, interpersonal dominance" but rather for the benefit of the collective.[158] Black women in the A.M.E. church negotiated power within the triple constraints of their positionality to "construct a community of respectable black citizenry, . . . eradicate racial discrimination," and protest gender bias "in their own church."[159] This was also true of the institutional culture of the Mt. Zion A.M.E. Church in New Brunswick. The life of Alice Jennings Archibald offers a point of entry to examine the ways in which African American women negotiated power within the church and used their voice to call for social justice in their local communities (see figure 2.4). An examination of her life, particularly her childhood and early adult years, sheds light on the day-to-day experiences of working class and "better class" blacks in New Brunswick.[160] Her family's multigenerational ties to Mt. Zion had a formative impact on her experiences and relationship to New Brunswick and created educational opportunities inside and outside of the city.

Alice Jennings was born on February 8, 1906, in New Brunswick, New Jersey, in the family home on Handy Street.[161] She was the fourth daughter of James and Edith Jennings. In Alice Jennings's words, her parents were working-class people, a drugstore worker and a part-time laundress, respectively. They were "good Christian parents" and true "Jerseyites," tracing their lineage in the state back many generations.[162] Jennings was raised, however, by her great-uncle and aunt, Joseph and Gertrude (Pierce) Titus, who had no biological children and desired to relieve the Jenningses of financial strain by taking in young Alice. Mr. Titus was a chauffeur for a member of the Johnson & Johnson family and Gertrude was a former teacher and active member of Mt. Zion A.M.E. Jennings's aunt was of fair complexion and a member of an affluent family from Gouldtown, a town in Cumberland County, New Jersey, concerned with "higher things" like education and mutual aid societies.[163] Gertrude's interest in education and her active participation in clubs like the Red Cross and Mt. Zion A.M.E. had a profound influence on the trajectory of Jennings's life. It was her aunt who instilled in her "a love of books" and encouraged her to go to college to become a teacher.[164] Jennings's desire to teach in her home state would launch her career in activism.

Growing up on Handy Street and attending New Brunswick High School meant Jennings regularly encountered integrated spaces.[165] In an oral interview conducted in 1996, Jennings recalled growing up with Italian, Jewish, and Hungarian children, playing with them in her aunt's yard and inviting them over for dinner. Reflecting on her childhood, she evoked a blissful ignorance on the matters of race: "[W]e were the only Afro-American family [on our block], but we didn't know we were Afro-Americans, they didn't know they were Italians, Jews, Irish, Hungarians. We all grew up together, we ate together if company came."[166]

Jennings recovered relatively few memories of discrimination in New Brunswick even through her high school years. One of few black students at New Brunswick High School, Jennings excelled in academic and extracurricular activities and was the salutatorian of her 1923 midyear graduating class.[167] Her singular memory of discrimination at New Brunswick High School came from a teacher, not her peers. When a prejudiced instructor, "from the south," gave her a "C" instead of the grade she deserved, her aunt and her classmates protested until the grade was changed. Recalling early memories from her childhood and adolescence, Jennings generally held that more extreme cases of prejudice and racism occurred in the South, not New Jersey. While admitting that a cheaper movie theater, the Strand, was also "kind of prejudice[d]" because of their segregated seating, Jennings said she didn't "dwell on it" but "went on about [her] business." Jennings's remembered experiences demonstrate that in New Brunswick racial dominance was pervasive yet incomplete. And compared to the laundresses and domestic workers who made the rounds working for whites instead of socializing and learning with them, Jennings's "better class" status as a member of a privileged cohort of blacks may have colored her remembrances of life in the Hub City.

After a positive experience at New Brunswick High, Jennings attended Howard University, a historically black college in Washington, DC. Jennings says that she chose Howard over New Jersey College for Women because she had always attended "white schools" and sought a new environment and opportunities in the nation's capital.[168] While her experience in the South was the first time she remembered encountering explicit racism, her Howard years were a formative time in her life, exposing her to African Americans from various walks of life and economic backgrounds. Howard University, she stated, "was [her] first experience with negroes with real money." It was also where she realized that there "were opportunities where you could better yourself if you tried." During her college years, Jennings made friends from Louisiana to Colorado and was introduced to writings of black intellectuals like W.E.B. Du Bois, Booker T. Washington, and Marcus Garvey. While Jennings did not necessarily align herself with any of the ideologues of the era, and considered herself a negotiator rather than a radical, she did not denounce such strategies: "I'm not a radical person, I don't believe; I'm more of the Urban League type of person. I believe in sitting down with people and trying to work things out in a peaceful manner . . . but there's a place for the radicals."[169] Later in life, when jobs turned her away, she would show her resolve as a negotiator and "Urban League type" to shift the course of some of New Brunswick's staple institutions.

After graduating from Howard University with a bachelor of arts degree in 1927 and obtaining an education degree from the University of Cincinnati in 1928, Jennings pursued a teaching career. Her home state of New Jersey, however, did not welcome her back. Jennings was denied employment for every teaching position she applied to because she was African American. The experience left her feeling disparaged and perhaps with a sense that the discrimination in the North and the South were two sides of the same coin. After much persistence and with the help of the American Missionary Association, she did find work, a teaching position in the South. Deeply grateful for the opportunity to work in her field, she still harbored some resentment and frustration regarding the outcome of her job search. "I had to go away from home, whether I wanted or not," recalled Jennings, "when one of my [white] classmates who wasn't as good as a student as I was, was teaching in one of the schools [in New Brunswick]." Though she took advantage of the teaching positions offered in North Carolina, at Parmele Training School and later at Brick Junior College, the experience of job discrimination in her home state, supposedly milder in racism than the South, led to a profound realization that self-determination alone would not lead to ground breaking racial advancement.[170] The structure of institutions, corporations, sites of education had to be transformed for there to be more broad-reaching change.

After teaching in North Carolina for about ten years, Jennings returned to New Brunswick, where she began a career as an activist and community organizer. Still unable to obtain a teaching position in New Brunswick, even after becoming the first African American woman to obtain a graduate degree from Rutgers in 1938 (the same year that the first African American woman matriculated through the New Jersey College for Women), Jennings took on clerical work to get by financially but poured her energy into Mt. Zion A.M.E.'s Willing Workers Club and the Urban League.[171]

As a member of the Willing Workers Club she committed herself to planning local social events, like plays, pageants, and teas, for members of the church and the black community. A brief sketch of the organization written by Jennings in the early 1990s revealed "dramatic readings," dance recitals, concerts, and "many, many projects too numerous to mention." Over the more than sixty-year life of the club, she assisted in planning national and international trips such as cruises to Bermuda, bus trips to Montreal, and vacations to Hawaii. Although these trips were not economically accessible to every member of the church, Jennings found it important to create opportunities for leisure and new cultural experiences for African Americans in a city where Klan activities were once highly visible and employment discrimination was the norm.[172]

Jennings's involvement in her church women's club was an avenue for her to pursue activism in New Brunswick. While Jennings described herself as diplomat rather than a radical, a letter she wrote to the editor of the *Daily Home News* in 1942 on behalf of the Willing Workers Club, an organization typically associated with teas and leisure, captured her pursuit of a more equitable community for blacks and whites in the city of New Brunswick.[173] The short piece, "What the Negro Wants," reads like a multipoint plan for achieving economic, educational, and social justice.[174] Among her requests were that white New Brunswickers treat African Americans "like any other loyal, well thinking, substantial American Citizen[s]" and that "more men and women . . . take firm stances against racial discrimination." She also insisted that the city "train [African Americans] for different phases of employment" and create "opportunities for school boys and girls to pick up jobs after school and on Saturdays."[175] Jennings also called for greater coverage in the *Daily Home News* of the "worthwhile things Negroes are doing" rather than the sharp focus on black crime. Jennings added quite plainly that white New Brunswickers should treat blacks like "human being[s]" who are "capable of making mistakes" not "super-human" stoic figures devoid of reactions and impulses. Her final request was a call for the New Brunswick of her childhood memories, for a "continuation of good comradeship" among children regardless of race and that there be more opportunities for interracial friendship and collaboration. This letter to the editor served as a catalyst for Jennings's involvement in the social justice programs and initiatives in the city of New Brunswick.

In 1944, the National Urban League granted a charter to the local Service Council in New Brunswick. The founding of the local league was initiated after a 1943 forum discussed the need for organizing efforts among the black community, particularly around the issue of residents' rights. Women of the League of Women Voters, the YWCA, and the Women's Auxiliary of the Jewish Community Center responded to the call to action by fundraising and garnering community support.[176] There are few details about the original organizational structure of the Urban League of New Brunswick, but Alice Jennings was a founding member. Her participation in the league helped to create

FIGURE 2.4 Anderson funeral service.

Image courtesy of New Brunswick Free Public Library. Anderson Funeral Service
(New Brunswick New Jersey), "Alice Gertrude Jennings Archibald Funeral Program,"
December 23, 2002, New Brunswick Men and Women, Folder A, New Brunswick Free
Public Library Collection, New Brunswick.

economic and educational opportunities that were denied to her in the 1920s and 1930s and to implement initiatives from her 1942 letter to the *Daily Home News* editor. Serving as the administrative assistant to two consecutive executive directors, she worked to get the first African Americans hired at Johnson & Johnson and the first teachers hired in New Brunswick Public Schools. "We established a lot of firsts," she recounts. Additionally, her work with the Urban League helped to change the culture of exclusion on the campus of Douglass College. While the first African American woman had been admitted in 1934, it was not until 1946 that the first black women, Emma (Andrews) Warren and Evelyn (Sermons) Field, were allowed to live on campus.[177] During her tenure as an administrative assistant, the Urban League achieved another first by prompting the construction of the first public housing complex in New Brunswick with Robeson Village.[178]

Jennings was a devoted and dedicated citizen of New Brunswick even when it failed her and other members of the black community. She was a bright and well-connected adolescent who excelled academically and had friends of many backgrounds and ethnicities. In adulthood, however, despite academic credentials and her relatively privileged class status, she faced a still circumscribed labor market for black women and was prevented employment as a teacher in New Brunswick public schools. This dissonance led Jennings to activist work in the 1930s and 1940s, striving for a New Brunswick that lived up to what she believed it could be. In the A.M.E. Church she worked to enrich the cultural experiences of everyday African Americans by creating opportunities for leisure and pleasure, while the Urban League allowed her to take a more confrontational stance toward economic and social justice, opening doors for others that had once been closed to her.

Nearly a century after the Civil War, African Americans in New Brunswick at all socioeconomic levels were still dealing with the consequences of the ambivalent victories of emancipation. The official end of slavery was not a panacea for white supremacist terror and hostility, nor did it create employment opportunities that looked vastly different from those available to blacks before the war. To be sure, turn-of-the-century industrialization redefined the condition and meaning of blackness, but it did little to curb the discriminatory labor market and segregation that was inherent in New Brunswick public schools and at Rutgers College. To counter the challenges of limited employment, institutional racism, and improvement of black life, the African American community established an extensive network of institutions and mutual aid societies, some still in existence today, that provided education, employment, and empowerment. The Colored Industrial School and Mt. Zion A.M.E. were spaces of leisure, refuge, and uplift and sites where everyday New Brunswickers harnessed institutional power that had once been foreclosed.

3

The Rutgers Race Man

Early Black Students at Rutgers College

BEATRICE J. ADAMS, SHAUN ARMSTEAD,
SHARI CUNNINGHAM, AND TRACEY JOHNSON

The first black men to attend Rutgers embodied contradictions. They were Rutgers Men and Race Men. The qualities central to both archetypes—civility, morality, thrift, intelligence—were similar. What made for incongruity was the fact that the Rutgers Man was originally raced white while the Race Man was unassailably black. This twoness could have presented irreconcilable problems for early black students. Yet they inserted themselves into Rutgers masculine culture and merged the two. This article will demonstrate how they did this. Though not an exhaustive study of Rutgers's first black men, this look at a few of them will demonstrate how they reconciled their identities and became Rutgers Race Men.

The Rutgers Man and the Race Man

The "Rutgers Man" was the archetype Rutgers students aspired to before they graduated from the college. Rutgers was often gendered as a nurturing mother figure who helped transform boys into true men by the time they graduated. Endowed in this collegiate representative were traits also associated with the institution itself: honor, civility, respectability, intelligence, social adeptness, confidence, competitiveness, athleticism, and attractiveness. The notion of the Rutgers Man developed while the college was still a men's-only institution and endured until Rutgers University became a coed institution in the 1970s. Though it was hardly ever stated explicitly, the Rutgers Man was presumed to be white. He was a credit not just to his family but to the American nation.

According to one student chronicling the history of his class, Rutgers Men were those who had triumphed in the metaphorical race for prosperity, satisfying academic requirements and ignoring the lure of "the fray or the festivity" the world offered.[1] Social Darwinian worldviews premised with the so-called survival of the fittest were pervasive in the twentieth century.[2] Men attending Rutgers learned to value life as a competition that they could win. One short story written in 1916 recounted a young man from a small rural town in New Jersey who arrived on campus a country bumpkin. Despite his allegedly backward environment, this white man, "living proof of the Darwinian Theory," proved able to apply himself and rise above his rural moorings.[3] He worked hard, and after immersing himself in the Rutgers customs and norms that dictated how to dress and act, he graduated a popular member of his class. The student-author concludes his story of "The Fable of the Guy Who Made Good" with grandeur and success. The country bumpkin from the "mosquito infested alfalfa fields of South Jersey" became president "of some five or six Railroad Corporations" and married an heiress.[4]

While they received their college education, Rutgers Men also learned masculine and social norms. Outside of the classroom, the Rutgers Man represented the ideal catch for respectable women of a similar or better socioeconomic class. Figure 3.1 illustrates the attractive qualities the Rutgers Man was expected to possess. As depicted, he is well dressed and exudes the manly confidence of someone who is socioeconomically successful. He is the center of young women's gazes. And he is white.[5]

Since the privileges afforded the Rutgers Man were not guaranteed to all students who attended the college, we can presume that the young man is also Anglo-Saxon. As historian Gail Bederman has demonstrated, all white-skinned men were not automatically granted the privileges of whiteness.[6] In the late nineteenth and early twentieth centuries, the United States experienced a wave of immigration that brought teeming numbers of people from Italy, Poland, and other countries. Individuals from these nations were not considered fully white, and thus experienced racialization as ethnic whites who were considered inferior to native white Americans and those from Western Europe.[7] Immigrant men, like black men, were thought to possess a rougher, less civilized type of manhood, one where physicality prevailed over intellect, and impulse and instinct trumped reason and deliberation. Over the course of the twentieth century, the category of whiteness would expand, but in early-twentieth-century America only Anglo-Saxon men represented the ideal.[8]

The experience of Alfred Gaipa, a 1914 Rutgers graduate, exemplified how race and manhood came together for immigrant whites at Rutgers in the first years of the twentieth century. Alfred Gaipa was born in Palermo, Italy, in 1890. His father worked as a glove cutter and his mother's occupation is unknown. He was a short man with dark hair and was on the gymnastics team

FIGURE 3.1 An image of a Rutgers student speaking with two women, this depiction is most likely a rendering of a college-sponsored social gathering.

Courtesy of Special Collections, Rutgers University.

when he attended Rutgers. His senior biography reveals a series of nicknames throughout his tenure at the institution. Gaipa was first known as "Mutt," then as "Jeff."[9] His first nickname suggests notions of racial impurity, and the nickname "Gip" (short for "gypsy") that appears with his picture in the 1914 yearbook was a derogatory term that described people of Romani descent as thieving and untrustworthy.[10] Yet, as the rhyme that accompanied his picture suggests, before he graduated, Gaipa became known as "Jeff," exposing a process of Anglicization—of becoming white—that he underwent while attending Rutgers. Gaipa's experience at Rutgers demonstrates that whiteness was a project that Rutgers was invested in producing. For Alfred Gaipa, an Italian immigrant, becoming a Rutgers Man meant becoming white.

But black men could not be reraced as white. Black men on white campuses during the Jim Crow era were an anomaly, if only because the logic of *Plessy v. Ferguson*, the 1896 Supreme Court decision that upheld separate but equal laws, presumed blacks to be so inherently inferior as to necessitate the separation of the races. As noted in chapter one, white Rutgers students and professors advanced ideas of scientific racism and social Darwinism. No matter how respectable and upstanding black men were, their journey to becoming Rutgers Men was obstructed by racism.

Moreover, black men entering Rutgers had other obligations. As part of what W.E.B. Du Bois called the "talented tenth," college-educated black men were expected to become Race Men. During the late nineteenth and early twentieth centuries, those considered to be Race Men often hailed from the elite of African American society. Many of the first black students at Rutgers came from families that were part of the "talented tenth," an exceptional group of black men and women who could serve as leaders for the race. Du Bois, the first African American to receive a PhD from Harvard University, popularized the notion of the "talented tenth" in 1903 when he wrote, "The Negro race, like all races, is going to be saved by its exceptional men. The problem of education, then, among Negroes must first of all deal with the Talented Tenth; it is the problem of developing the Best of this race that they may guide the Mass away from the contamination and death of the Worst, in their own and other races."[11] The talented tenth included black teachers and professors, ministers, business owners, and professionals such as physicians and lawyers. A black man attending college was obligated to care about his race and was expected to undertake the task of uplift. He had to embody "race consciousness, race pride, and race solidarity," and had to use his intellect, and the power and wealth that it produced, to elevate black people.[12]

Taking its first African American student in 1888, Rutgers was among the few American institutions of higher education to accept African Americans before the twentieth century. Part of a group of eighty-one institutions analyzed by W.E.B Du Bois in his 1901 publication *The College Bred Negro American*, Rutgers was, however, one of over two dozen institutions that had only produced one African American graduate by 1900. And while Princeton did not accept African Americans until after World War II, the University of Pennsylvania, Harvard, and Yale would all have over two dozen black graduates by 1909.[13] The unevenness of Rutgers's transition from an all-white space to one that included just a few African American male students is not only visible through statistical analysis but also by the lived experiences of its earliest black students.

These first black men were doubly pressured. They had to overcome the racism that obstructed their path to becoming Rutgers Men, and they had to be representative models of blackness. Somehow they had to merge the Rutgers Man and the Race Man. As the stories that follow demonstrate, it was easier for some than for others. One can imagine that it was harder for someone like Reuben McDaniel (class of 1928), the son of a Virginia sharecropper who migrated to New Jersey, than for Edward Lawson, whose father and older brother and sister were college educated. But as we will see, even economic privilege did not protect Lawson from the bite of racism. Admittedly, there are examples of black male students who found ways to gain acceptance as Rutgers Men by their classmates, Paul Robeson being a stunning example. But even Robeson had difficulty reconciling being a Rutgers Man and a Race Man at the same time.

One thing is for sure, however. The students covered in this article—James Dickson Carr, Edward Lawson, Paul Robeson, John Morrow, Edward Lawson Jr., James Hoggard, and Harry Hazelwood—upset the foundational principles of Jim Crow and broadened the definition of a Rutgers Man. They were living proof that the science of racism was bogus. Despite the omnipresent discrimination, they excelled in their studies, and by virtue of the education they received at Rutgers, they became part of the "talented tenth" and went on to fulfill their destinies as Race Men.[14] The brief biographies that follow provide insight on how African American men at Rutgers defeated the odds and reconciled their dual identities as Race Men and Rutgers Men.

James Dickson Carr (Class of 1892)

In 1888 James Dickson Carr entered Rutgers College, disrupting the institution's one-hundred-and-twenty-year tradition of excluding African Americans.[15] Just eighty years after an enslaved man named Will worked to lay the foundation of the Old Queens building and twenty-three years after the emancipation of enslaved blacks in the United States, Carr's presence on campus was pathbreaking.[16] Carr attended Rutgers at a time when few African Americans were allowed to attend elite American universities like Rutgers. Yet Carr was not only a pioneer in the realm of higher education; he would continue making inroads for African Americans long after he left the halls of Old Queens.

James Dickson Carr was born on September 28, 1868, to William T. Carr and Mary Louise Sprigg Carr in Baltimore, Maryland. William Carr's career as a Presbyterian minister took the family to New Jersey, where the younger Carr attended public school in Elizabeth. From 1886 to 1888, James Dickson Carr

FIGURE 3.2 Rutgers College Preparatory School where James Dickson Carr attended school prior to beginning his matriculation at Rutgers College in 1888.

Courtesy of Special Collections, Rutgers University.

finished his secondary education at the Rutgers College Preparatory School, commuting from Elizabeth (see Figure 3.2).[17] Carr received excellent grades, which were recorded by William H. S. Demarest, an instructor at Rutgers Preparatory School and future president of Rutgers College (1906–1924). Demarest gave Carr almost perfect scores in Latin. Perhaps Demarest's high opinion of Carr played a role in his admission to Rutgers College, as Carr was admitted to the Classical Section of Rutgers's freshmen class in 1888.[18]

During his time at Rutgers College, James Dickson Carr (Figure 3.3) seemed to embody many of the characteristics central to being a Rutgers Man. He was intelligent and agreeable. Henry Kimball Davis, who had known Carr since grammar school, reflected in 1920, that "the thing that impresses me . . . was the respect in which Carr was always held by his fellow students. This was due, I think, to his sincerity and his self-respect." He continued describing Carr as "a first class fellow, true as steel in his friendship without dissimulation and clean as a hound's tooth in speech and in his private life."[19] While Carr was not the best athlete (an accident early in his life left him without full sight in one eye), he still managed to fit in with most students at Rutgers.[20]

Archival records suggest that Carr was fairly well accepted by white students and faculty, even though he attended the college at a time when racial segregation was the norm. Legal scholar Peter Mazzei notes that almost every record the university has on Carr makes no reference to his race; Carr had a white roommate while staying at the Winants Hall dormitory, was given the

FIGURE 3.3 James Dickson Carr in 1892.

Courtesy of Special Collections, Rutgers University.

same attention as other students in the student yearbook, and was included in the class of 1892 photo. Additionally, James Dickson Carr participated in student organizations on campus, including the Rutgers Athletic Association, the Rutgers YMCA, the Rutgers Temperance Association, and was even elected as president of the Philoclean Literary Society.[21]

Yet there is some indication that not everyone was fully accepting and that Carr experienced racial discrimination while attending Rutgers. An 1892 *New York Times* article, notably titled "A Credit to His Race," reported that James Dickson Carr was "a colored man, whose admission to the institution four years ago was viewed with misgivings."[22] Carr's classmate Henry Kimball Davis noted, "He did not want to be patronized; and if any one was inclined to pass him by because of his color, Carr at least would not notice it."[23] Despite Davis's analysis that Carr "would not notice it," Carr certainly must have. What escaped Davis's attention was that as a "credit to his race," a Race Man, Carr had to hold his feelings in check. He was representing not only himself but his race. He could not get emotional but had to perform the intellectually calm demeanor of a Race Man. Davis also noted that Carr did not seem to be able to fully participate in the Rutgers male social community: "Probably outside of the informal meetings between classes, his social life in college was not wide, although everyone who called on him when he roomed on French street and later in Winants Hall always received a hearty welcome."[24] Again, as a Race Man, he was a different kind of Rutgers Man, one who was discriminated against on a daily basis. But as a cordial welcoming gentleman he embodied the elements of both.

Whatever obstacles James Dickson Carr faced, he did not let them prevent him from excelling academically. When Carr graduated from Rutgers College, he was inducted into Phi Beta Kappa, the oldest and most prestigious honor society in America, which recognizes excellence in the liberal arts and sciences. Carr also had a prominent role in the graduation ceremony for the Rutgers class of 1892. Carr stood before a large crowd in Kirkpatrick Chapel, where he delivered the "Ivy Oration." In this address, in which he placed himself firmly within the Rutgers Man tradition, he declared his devotion to Rutgers and implored the graduates of 1892 to love and be loyal to their alma mater. He exhorted, "May the boast of the mother of Gracchi, be the boast of our Alma Mater, that we, her sons, are her jewels, to be squared and polished as pillars of support and ornament. And may we stand upon the world's broad threshold . . . with manhood as the one immortal thing, act our part well."[25] Certainly, Carr felt a strong bond to the institution and no doubt considered himself to be a true Rutgers Man.

James Dickson Carr continued to be a pioneer after leaving Rutgers. He went on to become the first African American to graduate from the Columbia

University Law School, graduating in June 1896 and passing the New York Bar the same year.[26] He privately practiced law for a short time, before beginning a notable career in local politics. In the last years of the nineteenth century, Carr's political allegiance took a major turn when he was among the first African Americans to switch to the Democratic Party. The switch from being an ardent Republican (exemplified by his activities with the Republican Club at Rutgers) to a Democrat was significant because the vast majority of African Americans identified with the Republican Party during this time period. As the party of Abraham Lincoln, the Republican Party had played a key role in ending slavery in the United States. Even though the southern wing of the Democratic Party put their weight behind the legal system that enforced racial segregation, Carr joined Tammany Hall, the Democratic political machine of New York City, in 1897. This was the same year Tammany Hall created the all-black group "United Colored Democracy."[27]

James Dickson Carr's decision to join the Democratic Party was prompted by racial prejudice he experienced from New York Republicans. In the fraught 1896 presidential election, the Republic Party appealed to black voters by making promises to work for the advancement of African Americans. However, after black voters helped elect Republican candidate William McKinley, these promises proved to be largely empty. In New York City, the Republican district attorney, William M. K. Olcott, refused to appoint Carr as assistant district attorney although the job had been a pre-election promise.[28] According to Carr, "at the time I had the endorsement of the republican organization, and believed that I would be appointed, but Mr. Olcott refused to appoint me on the ground that I am a colored man."[29] Seeing this racism, some black leaders left the Republican Party for Tammany Hall. Richard Crocker, the head of Tammany Hall, promised fairer treatment for African Americans and to put "at least one colored man in every department of the city government."[30] In September 1899 James Dickson Carr became the first black assistant district attorney of New York County under Democrat Asa Bird Gardiner.[31]

Carr's appointment as an assistant district attorney was a source of race pride for black Americans living in the Jim Crow era. News of Carr's appointment made headlines across the nation, in states including Arkansas, Delaware, Florida, Louisiana, Nebraska, North Carolina, and Utah.[32] Carr was certainly making inroads for racial advancement, but not everyone was thrilled. For example, a North Carolina newspaper article suggested "the white man's [Democratic] party of North Carolina should send a protest to Tammany Hall at once for appointing a Negro to a responsible place. It's strictly against the edict of North Carolina Democracy, and its jurisdiction includes New York."[33] Additionally, a Florida newspaper printed news of the appointment directly below an article describing the castration of a black man by a white mob in South Carolina.[34] For all the praise Carr received, the harsh reality of what it meant to be a black man in the late-nineteenth-century United States remained inescapable.

Despite opposition, Carr continued in his political career and was appointed assistant corporate counsel of the New York City Law Department in 1904. He held this position until his death in 1920.[35] His success in the legal field was a source of pride for his alma mater. The Rutgers newspaper, the *Targum,* reported Carr's assistant corporate counsel appointment and the *Rutgers Alumni Quarterly* ran an article on his life achievements in 1920.[36] It seems Carr maintained an affiliation with Rutgers throughout his life. He submitted at least two alumni forms for the alumni catalogue to update the institution about his progress.[37] As the first African American graduate from Rutgers College, James Dickson Carr was not only a Rutgers Man but a Race Man as well. He likely served as a mentor to at least one other African American Rutgers student, Paul Robeson, in subsequent years.[38] James Dickson Carr lived in an era when many whites were against black equality and held racist ideas about African Americans' intellectual abilities. His excellent academic record at Rutgers and his successful career defied these ideas and set the mold for the Rutgers Race Man.

Edward H. Lawson Sr. (1904–1907)

Edward H. Lawson Sr. aspired to be a Rutgers Man long before he reached the halls of Old Queens in 1904. The son of Jesse and Rosetta Lawson of Washington, DC, Edward Lawson had spent his high school years using Rutgers's course requirements for incoming students to prepare for possible admission into the college. Lawson also wrote to Rutgers administrator Irving S. Upson requesting information on Rutgers's placement exams.[39] His hard work paid off, and Edward Lawson was accepted into Rutgers College. As September 1904 approached, Edward Lawson excitedly awaited the start of his first semester as a Rutgers Man. Yet no matter how much he had planned, Lawson could not foresee that he would never receive his degree from Rutgers College—not because of his own shortcomings but because of the shortcomings of others.

It seems both Edward Lawson and his father worked together to fashion an image of young Lawson that was attractive to Rutgers College. Jesse Lawson was himself a college graduate who worked for the federal government and founded the first sociological association in the United States, the National Sociological Society (NSS), in 1903.[40] Jesse Lawson wrote letters to Rutgers officials on NSS letterhead prior to Edward Lawson's admittance to the college and repeatedly referenced his son's qualifications, which included Edward's use of summer holidays for further academic improvement. But the senior Lawson did not solely rely on Edward's academic strengths to present him as a Rutgers-Man-in-the-making. He also pointed toward his elder son and daughter who were both finishing degrees at Howard University Medical School and Oberlin, respectively, to reveal the intellectual milieu from which Edward came. Further references to his own influential connections to New Jersey senator John Kean and representative Charles Fowler likely conveyed the Lawson family's respectability and social standing.[41] Neither father nor son revealed why they so earnestly wanted the Rutgers education. There was no alumni connection since Jesse Lawson had graduated from Howard University. It is possible that the family wanted Edward to attend Rutgers to prove that black Americans could thrive in white educational spaces. As one scholar explains, black Americans have historically relied on the "politics of respectability" to access rights and freedoms associated with U.S. citizenship.[42]

From September 1904 until November 1907, Edward Lawson made the most of his time at Rutgers. Yearbooks, faculty minutes, and the numerous letters Jesse Lawson sent to Irving S. Upson during this period reveal Edward Lawson's extensive efforts to fit the model of the Rutgers Man. During these years Lawson served as an associate editor of the *Targum* newspaper and was named an Honor Man, winning the Irving S. Upson prize for oration. He also joined the track team, the chess club, and helped plan his junior class banquet. In addition to his studies and extracurricular activities, he found time to work at the Library of Congress in Washington, DC, during the summer.[43]

Despite his father's testimony that Edward "ha[d] the college spirit, through and through," possessing a "devotion to Rutgers" that remained "unbounded," there is much that is troubling about Lawson's Rutgers experience.[44] It seems that he struggled to fit in with his white classmates and be fully embraced in Rutgers fraternal community. While he was certainly a part of the social fabric of Rutgers, Lawson did not live on campus until his senior year, and even then, he lived alone. These lodging arrangements suggest dynamics at Rutgers that may have been less than welcoming toward a black student.

More troubling were the circumstances of his dismissal in November of 1907. Seven months shy of graduation, Edward Lawson was accused of stealing from Winants Hall, the dormitory where he roomed. A package and letter belonging to Frank Dens, a white student, had gone missing from the mailroom, and the janitor, John Thomas, accused Lawson. Thomas's evidence was that Lawson "acted in a suspicious manner around the mail table."[45] Apparently, John Thomas had a history of chastising black people. In 1893 the *New Brunswick Daily Times* reported "one of the colored waiters at the dormitory was caught going upstairs this morning by Janitor John Thomas. This is against the rules of the dormitory and he was ordered down by Thomas." An altercation ensued, and the black worker was fired from his job.[46]

Picking up a dispatch from New Brunswick, the *Evening Star* reported that Edward Lawson, "a colored student at Rutgers College, was caught robbing the mails at Winants Hall dormitory Saturday afternoon, it is alleged, and had been dismissed from the institution."[47] Edward Lawson denied being the perpetrator and wrote to the *Evening Star* demanding a retraction. Lawson wrote: "I emphatically deny that I was 'caught robbing the mails at Winant's Hall dormitory,' or that I have been 'dismissed from the institution' as stated in that item. These statements are entirely misleading and erroneous." Lawson also claimed that, in fact, he was among the Rutgers students who had reported to federal authorities that his mail had gone missing in the past.[48]

Though there was no proof that Lawson had stolen the mail, the faculty voted and decided that the best course of action was to ask Lawson to withdraw from Rutgers College (though he really could not choose to stay). In other words, even though there appears to have been some doubt as to the veracity of Thomas's accusation (evidenced by the fact that the faculty did not vote to expel Lawson), they nevertheless took the word of a white janitor over a black male honor student, one who had tirelessly prepared himself to become a Rutgers Man and who was on track to become a Race Man.[49]

After the faculty members' vote in November 1907, it would seem that Edward Lawson lost his dream of graduating as a Rutgers Man. He transferred to his father's alma mater, Howard University, where he graduated in the spring of 1908.[50] Following Lawson's withdrawal from Rutgers, Jesse Lawson fought to protect his son's reputation and repeatedly expressed his frustration with the institution to administrators. In communications with Rutgers, the elder Lawson consistently noted when the college acted dishonorably. One notable incident concerned attempts to charge fees for his son's room after his departure. When Jesse Lawson noted in February 1908 that his son had not been registered since November 1907, Irving S. Upson responded that the college had been unable to rent the rooms because Edward's possessions were still there. Jesse Lawson reminded Upson that his son was barred from Winants Hall. Throwing the issue of integrity back on those who had disparaged his son, Jesse Lawson indicted Rutgers for violating its own Rutgers Man principles of honor: "To keep a man's money for something for which he has paid, and at the same time exclude him from the use of it is not agreeable to the code of ethics to which I subscribe, nor is it in keeping with the American sense of fair play."[51]

As a family that valued respectability, Jesse's efforts to clear Edward's name was underpinned by concern for the Lawson family's public image. On August 4, 1909, nearly two years after his dismissal from the institution, Edward H. Lawson wrote to Rutgers College Administrative Committee: "I have, throughout my life, no charges against me except those which through a well-organized and executed antagonism (for I can see it in no other light) came to me at Rutgers."[52] Lawson offered several character witnesses, one being Judge Robert H. Terrell, husband of famed African American activist Mary Church Terrell. On several occasions Lawson asked Rutgers to confer the degree that he should have obtained.[53] However, these efforts came to naught.

Not surprisingly, Edward Lawson never disavowed Rutgers and he continued to identify with the institution until his death in 1952. He had attended Rutgers for over three years, forged relationships with other students, and, though he lived off campus for most of his tenure, he had participated in the school's social life. Sources suggest that a few colleagues sought to maintain goodwill with Lawson after he left Rutgers College. One letter seems to indicate that one of the fraternities sent Lawson an invitation to join a year or two after he left Rutgers to convey that "some of us still trust and believe in you."[54] Similarly, in June 1908, following Lawson's graduation from Howard, Rutgers administrator Irving S. Upson wrote a reference letter for Lawson that made no mention of the Winants Hall controversy. Instead, he affirmed that Lawson "maintained a good scholarship standing and a good character throughout the Freshman, Sophomore, and Junior years in this institution."[55] Lawson's existing relationships could explain his enduring connection to the college, but not fully.

One way to understand Lawson's refusal to relinquish his identity as a Rutgers Man is to acknowledge that being a Rutgers Man was inextricably intertwined with being a Race Man. As a Race Man, Lawson was compelled to insist on equality and to fight injustice. He therefore had to maintain a relationship with the college and his classmates, if only to constantly remind them of his innocence and the discrimination he suffered. This duty was not always an easy task. While some of his Rutgers classmates wished to continue friendly relations, others rejected Lawson. In 1915, Edward Lawson declined attending an alumni event, explaining to one classmate that he had been figuratively "lynched" at a previous gathering of Rutgers Men.[56] In addition to fearing drunken references to his theft accusations, Edward believed it pointless to join other alumni who would treat him as inferior rather than their equal.

Edward Lawson found himself agonizing over the hypocrisy he saw in his fellow Rutgers Men. In a letter to D. J. Fisher (class of 1908), Lawson expressed his view that many Rutgers alumni did not adhere to their own principles of respectability:

I am studying you white people pretty closely—that is, endeavoring to find a community of you that exemplify the religion which you profess. I shall await your reply, therefore, with interest; and, if I do not hear from you I shall be even more keenly interested in you as a race and as a class, and as a group of college fellows who will grow into manhood one of these days and treat everybody white.[57]

By equating whiteness with negative characteristics, Lawson, the Race Man, unpaired the Rutgers Man from whiteness and suggested that his white "college fellows" could not be Rutgers Men because they had yet to treat everyone as an equal, something Lawson felt a Rutgers Man was compelled to do. In calling into question the institution's ethics, he criticized the existence of a Rutgers Man ideal premised upon the superiority of whiteness. In this way, his refusal to cast aside Rutgers as an alma mater enabled him to emphasize the superiority of the Rutgers Race Man, someone who was civil, moral, intelligent, industrious, *and* dedicated to the elimination of racial prejudice.

As a critic of the white Rutgers Man, Edward H. Lawson remained dedicated to the institution. He served as secretary-treasurer for the Washington, DC, chapter of the Rutgers Alumni Association and attended the fortieth reunion of the Rutgers class of 1908. Additionally, Lawson entrusted Rutgers with his eldest son, Edward Lawson Jr. (class of 1933), enrolling him during the lean years of the Great Depression. Of significance is the fact that Lawson Sr.'s insistence on claiming the status of a Rutgers Man was passed down from father to son. In a 1932 questionnaire, the younger Edward claimed that his father had *"graduated* [in] 1908."[58]

Paul Robeson (Class of 1919)

More than any other black Rutgers graduate, Paul Leroy Robeson exemplified the ideal Rutgers Man and Race Man. Still, while his life accomplishments were extraordinary, Robeson had much in common with other early black graduates. Like most of the black men who attended Rutgers in the late nineteenth and early twentieth centuries, he came from a privileged background. Born in Princeton, New Jersey, in 1898, Robeson came from a family that was educated. His father had escaped from slavery and managed to put himself through school at Lincoln University, where he received a theology degree. Paul Robeson's mother was a teacher and came from an old, distinguished Philadelphia family. His older siblings became physicians, teachers, and ministers.[59] Even though Robeson came from an educated family, his father's meager minister's salary forced the family to struggle financially. In fact, Paul Robeson was only able to attend Rutgers because he won a four-year scholarship by taking a statewide written exam in 1915.[60]

Robeson's success at Rutgers was foreshadowed by his high school years. The family moved from Princeton to Somerville, New Jersey, in 1910. He entered Somerville High in 1912 where he excelled academically and was an honors student. Under the influence of his minister father, Paul Robeson developed a passion for oratory at a young age. He participated in several oration contests prior to attending Rutgers, debating topics including women's suffrage.[61] In fact, as a senior at Somerville High, Robeson participated in a debating match held at Kirkpatrick Chapel.[62] His success in sports as a youth also foretold the illustrious athletic career he would have at Rutgers. In 1914 he took third place in the hundred-yard dash in the Somerville County track meet.[63] A local newspaper reported that Robeson was "one of the most feared men in scholastic athletics" during his senior year at Somerville High, where he played fullback on the football team, center on the basketball team, and was the catcher for the baseball team.[64] Soon, he would be the first African American to play for the Rutgers football team (see Figure 3.4).

But Robeson was not immediately welcomed at Rutgers. During the first weeks of practice his own teammates acted out their racial hostility and deliberately injured him, leaving him with a broken nose, sprained shoulder, and cuts and bruises.[65] Over time the initial racist reactions to his presence on the team faded and his teammates came to admire him because of his athleticism.[66] During his time at Rutgers, Robeson was touted as a "hero" and a "star" because of his contributions to Rutgers victories in football, track, basketball, and baseball.[67] The campus newspaper, the *Targum*, printed articles that endearingly referred to Robeson as "our own 'Roby'" and the "greatest player of all time."[68]

But Robeson was also reminded that he was not like other Rutgers Men. Some sports teams from other schools, including William and Mary and Georgia Tech, refused to compete against Rutgers because they had a black player on the team. Once, a white opponent on a West Virginia team threatened Robeson: "Don't so much as touch me, you black dog, or I'll cut your heart out." Spectators in the stands shouted "nigger" at Robeson.[69] Insult was added to injury when the Rutgers administration agreed to bench Robeson when they played against Washington and Lee University. This 1916 football game coincided with a celebration of Rutgers 150th anniversary and Rutgers did not want to cancel the game.[70]

When James Dickson Carr, now well established as a New York attorney and Race Man, learned of the Washington and Lee incident, he was outraged. Carr wrote a letter to William H. Demarest. At the time Demarest was the president of Rutgers College; previously he had been Carr's teacher at the Rutgers College Grammar School before he entered Rutgers College in 1888.[71] In the letter Carr wrote:

> You may imagine my deep chagrin and bitterness at the thought that my Alma Mater, ever proud of her glorious traditions, her unsullied honor, her high ideals, and her spiritual mission, prostituted her sacred principles, when brazenly challenged, and laid her convictions upon the alter of compromise. Is it possible that the honor of Rutgers is virile only when untested and unchallenged?[72]

FIGURE 3.4 Paul Robeson was the first African American to play for the Rutgers football team.

Courtesy of Special Collections, Rutgers University.

Carr posited that Rutgers was as much at fault as Washington and Lee, since it denied one of its students "equality of opportunity and privilege" solely on account of his color. He also implored Demarest to "disavow the actions of the athletic manager" who had dishonored the principles and traditions of Rutgers by keeping Robeson from playing in the football game.

In his admonition, James Dickson Carr drew upon the Rutgers Man ideal. He stated, "I am deeply moved at the injustice done to a student of Rutgers, in good and regular standing, of good moral character and splendid mental equipment—one of the best athletes ever developed at Rutgers."[73] In invoking the Rutgers Man ideal, Carr, like Edward Lawson had done eight years previously, was making a space for black men in the archetype. Indeed, as a Race Man himself, Carr knew all too well that white men had no lock on high morals and ideals and that Race Men embodied the same high character as Rutgers Men.

And Carr's activism on behalf of Robeson demonstrated just how well he embodied the two. In his letter to Demarest, Carr attempted to help the college's president understand that depriving Robeson of a chance to play meant depriving his race of a chance to be honored. Specifically, Carr stated that Paul Robeson "was robbed of the honor and glory of contending in an athletic contest for his college . . . not only he, individually, but his race as well, was deprived of the opportunity of showing its athletic ability, and, perhaps, its athletic superiority. His achievements on that day may have been handed down as traditions not only to honor his Alma Mater, but, also, to honor himself, individually, and his race, collectively."[74] Carr described Robeson as a "representative man." As a lawyer, Carr would have been familiar with the potent arguments that could be made to challenge racial hierarchy through the use of representative men and women who had obtained educational and professional success in America's racial caste system.[75] In fact, Carr himself was a "representative man" whose achievements refuted the claim that blacks could not handle the rights of citizenship. Demarest's reply to Carr sidestepped the issues Carr enumerated. Claiming that he did not particularly remember the incident, Demarest asserted that "Mr. Robeson has received in a very constant and prevailing way the highest regard from everyone in all relations as he deserved," an assumption the historical record proves false.[76]

In fact, Robeson continued to experience indignities on and off the field throughout his time at Rutgers. As a member of the Rutgers Glee Club Robeson was not allowed be a "traveling" member and could only participate in home concerts. At these concerts he was not allowed to attend the postconcert social functions. Similarly, Robeson was only partially accepted into the Philoclean Literary Society, unable to participate in all of the club's activities.[77] In

1916 Robeson won first prize in the Freshman Oratorical Contest at Rutgers. From the 180 freshmen the best 18 were selected to compete for the Barbour Prize in Public Speaking. Robeson's hometown newspaper printed a story about the contest under the headline "Elmer French Takes Prize at Rutgers." French was also from the area and had won second prize in the contest. The article talked primarily about Elmer French, with a brief mention of Robeson at the end, even though Robeson had won first place. Surely Robeson must have felt insulted. The newspaper's choice in printing this article gave a loud and clear message—that a white man was always considered superior, even if his abilities were not.[78]

But Robeson never believed he was inferior and continued to excel academically. He won oratorical contests throughout his time at Rutgers and was one of only four students inducted into Phi Beta Kappa when he graduated in 1919.[79] His success was no doubt made possible by support from other African Americans during his time at Rutgers. Robert Davenport, another black student, enrolled at Rutgers after Robeson's first year on campus. Davenport would become Robeson's good friend and roommate, making the experience of being a black man at Rutgers more enjoyable.[80] It is also likely that James Dickson Carr served as a mentor to Robeson and could have provided insight on navigating the racialized atmosphere at Rutgers. Robeson and Carr's relationship appears to have been fairly intimate; when James Dickson Carr died in 1920, just a year after Paul Robeson graduated from Rutgers, Robeson served as a pallbearer at Carr's funeral in Harlem.[81] Perhaps it was from Carr that Paul Robeson got the idea to pursue a law degree from Columbia University after he graduated from Rutgers (Carr had received his law degree from Columbia in 1896).[82]

It seems that some at the school recognized that Paul Robeson exemplified the Rutgers Man, even if he was subjected to second-class treatment (see Figure 3.5). When he graduated, the campus newspaper lamented, "With the departure of the Class of 1919 the Rutgers undergraduate body loses a man who has been for four years an active factor in its life. While on campus, Paul Robeson made a name and a record equaled by none, and now as he fares forth into the world we wish him the same success." The newspaper article praised his athletic career, but also his intellectual accomplishments: "Sad to say, most athletes are not students, but Robey starred in both. Each year an honor man, he was elected to the Phi Beta Kappa Society at the end of his third. A speaker of deep thought and marvelous ability in presentation, he won the class oratorical prize four years in succession and was on the varsity debating team." Finally, the article praised Robeson's honorable character when they wrote, "One may combine physical and mental ability and still lack the most important element in ones character, moral stamina. If such be the rule, Robeson is

FIGURE 3.5 Paul Robeson was inducted into the Rutgers Cap and Skull Society, which each year, since 1900, has recognized a few select students for achievements in the arts, academics, and athletics.

Courtesy of Special Collections, Rutgers University.

again the exception proving it."[83] From this description, we can see that Robeson had a reputation for embodying the ideals of the Rutgers Man.

The racist incidents Paul Robeson experienced at Rutgers no doubt affected him, and likely shaped the race work he would later become known for. While still at Rutgers, Robeson developed a reputation as a budding Race Man. The Rutgers 1919 graduating class prophesy expected that in the year 1940, "Paul Robeson is Governor of New Jersey. He has dimmed the fame of Booker T. Washington and is the leader of the colored race in America."[84] Robeson would not become New Jersey's governor, but he would go on to be a race leader.

After leaving Rutgers, Robeson moved to Harlem and pursued a law degree at Columbia University. Living in Harlem at the time of the New Negro movement had a profound impact on Robeson.[85] During this era black Americans became more assertive and militant in seeking equality and civil rights. The Harlem Renaissance saw an explosion of black artistic and cultural creativity, and much of the art and literature produced had racial and political themes. In 1920 Robeson was involved with the Amateur Players, a group of African Americans who banded together to produce plays "of their race." Robeson starred in *Simon the Cyrenian*, a drama about the black man who carried Jesus's cross, at the Harlem YMCA. Many more theatrical roles followed. He played in *Taboo*, a play about Voodoo, and was a member of the black quartet performing *Shuffle Along*. Since acting and singing had greater payoffs than working as a lawyer, where discrimination was rife, Robeson decided to pursue a career in theater.[86] Over the next decade, Paul Robeson's popularity skyrocketed, and he starred in plays including *The Emperor Jones*, *All God's Chillun Got Wings*, and *Show Boat*.[87] Ultimately, Paul Robeson became an internationally celebrated singer and actor.

Robeson used his celebrity platform to push audiences, black and white, to respect and recognize the refinement and lineage of black culture. In 1934 he wrote a piece in the *Spectator* entitled "The Culture of the Negro." Here he condemned those who downplayed the sophistication of black culture, particularly black spirituals. Robeson wrote, "When I first suggested singing negro spirituals for English audiences, a few years ago, I was laughed at. How could these utterly simple, indeed, almost savage songs interest the most sophisticated audience in the world? I was asked." But Robeson countered this kind of thinking: "These songs are to negro culture what the works of the great poets are to English culture: they are the soul of the race made manifest." In asserting that black culture was just as sophisticated as Western white culture, Robeson aimed to educate blacks about the cultural history of Africa and the diaspora, so that they could be proud of their culture and thrive in their creative abilities.[88]

An international celebrity, Robeson's travels not only exposed him to the racial discrimination and denial of human rights present in Africa, the Caribbean, and Asia, but also spawned his political activism which in turn made him a controversial figure.[89] In particular, he came under fire for his views on the Soviet Union and the way it handled the "minority question." Robeson had performed in Moscow in the 1930s and received a gracious welcome. There he met several black Americans living in the U.S.S.R. who had been drawn to the revolutionary ideas of the Soviet experiment and were enthusiastic about the prospects of socialism for racial equality. While Robeson did not join the Communist Party when he returned home to the states, he became known as a "fellow traveler."[90] In this he was like many other blacks who embraced communism because of its promise of racial equality and working-class empowerment. Working-class empowerment was a vital issue since the vast majority of African Americans at this time were working-class people.[91] Even if they did not join the Communist Party black Americans often respected the Communist Party's stance on racial equality and willingness to defend black clients in legal cases.[92]

However, following World War II, when tensions increased between the United States and the Soviet Union, developing into a "Cold War," Robeson and many other "sympathizers" were condemned as "subversives" because of their views on economic and racial justice. During what became known as the McCarthy Era, Robeson, and countless others, were accused of being communists, socialists, Marxists, and anarchists.[93] He was blacklisted and prevented from performing. He lost his passport in 1950.[94] People he had formally considered friends ostracized him and without the ability to travel abroad to perform, Robeson suffered financially.[95] He did not, however, retreat from being a Race Man. He argued that the revocation of his passport was directly linked to his race work. He claimed that the state department denied his right to travel because he was a spokesperson for African Americans' civil rights and had for years been active on behalf of independence for colonized people in Africa. Writing in 1958, Robeson defended himself: "Yes, I have been active for African freedom for many years and I will never cease that activity no matter what the state department or anybody else thinks about it. This is my right—as a Negro, as an American, as a man!"[96] In addition to condemning the hysteria of McCarthyism, Robeson also later refused to sign an affidavit stating that he was not a Communist.

In 1956 Paul Robeson was subpoenaed to testify before the House Un-American Activities Committee (HUAC), a committee that persecuted suspected subversives during the Red Scare. In this session Robeson defended the American citizen's rights to political freedom. He argued that the U.S. government asking individuals to sign a non-Communist affidavit was "a complete contradiction of the rights of American citizens." Robeson refused to answer questions concerning his political activities. When asked if he was a member of the Communist Party, Robeson replied: "What do you mean by the Communist Party? As far as I know it is a legal party like the Republican Party and the Democratic Party. Do you mean a party of people who have sacrificed for my people, and for all Americans and workers, that they can live in dignity? Do you mean that party?" When asked again if he was a member of the Communist Party Robeson replied sarcastically, "Would you like to come to the ballot box when I vote and take out the ballot and see?"[97]

Robeson called out the prejudice of the HUAC members interviewing him: "I am not being tried for whether I am a Communist, I am being tried for fighting for the rights of my people, who are still second-class citizens in this United States of America. . . . I stand here struggling for the rights of my people to be full citizens in this country. . . . You want to shut up every Negro who has the courage to stand up and fight for the rights of his people, for the rights of workers. . . . And that is why I am here today."[98] In his testimony, Robeson also refused to repudiate the Soviet cause and endorse anticommunism: "In Russia I felt for the first time like a full human being. No color prejudice like in Mississippi, no color prejudice like in Washington. It was the first time I felt like a human being. Where I did not feel the pressure of color as I feel [it] in this Committee today." When asked why he did not stay in Russia, Robeson shot back: "Because my father was a slave, and my people died to build this country, and I am going to stay here, and have a part of it just like you. And no Fascist-minded people will drive me from it."[99]

Throughout the interrogation Robeson truly displayed the characteristics of a Rutgers Race Man. He was confident and witty; his intelligent answers ensured his success in evading the coercive tactics of the committee members. Above all, Robeson displayed honor, standing firm in his conviction that one should not cave to injustice, simply because they were under pressure. He resisted political repression and stood up for democratic ideas that were supposedly at the core of American values—for citizens to have the right to choose who would represent them in politics. Throughout the Red Scare Paul Robeson remained steadfast to justice, equality, and freedom, even though it cost him his career, the ability to move about freely, and many friends and supporters. Whether in his role as scholar and an intellectual, as an all-star athlete, a charismatic artist, or as a warrior for justice, Paul Robeson was the ultimate Rutgers Race Man.

John H. Morrow (Class of 1931)

John H. Morrow had a long and distinctive career at Rutgers. Not only did he graduate as an honor student in 1931, he returned to the university as a faculty member after a career as a teacher and an ambassador. His French language training at Rutgers prepared him for his position as America's first ambassador to Guinea.[100] Yet Morrow thought Rutgers could have been more supportive. When he returned to Rutgers as a faculty member in 1964, he worked to create a more diverse student body and make the campus more welcoming to black students.

John Howard Morrow was born in 1910 in Hackensack, New Jersey, to a prominent family. His father, John Eugene Morrow, was a minister, and all his siblings set out to be leaders. Morrow's sister, Mellie K., was the first black schoolteacher in Hackensack; one brother, E. Frederick, attended Bowdoin College, was a varsity debater there, and would go on to become the first African American to hold an executive position at the White House; another brother, Eugene, also worked in government service.[101]

John H. Morrow was awarded a state-sponsored scholarship to attend Rutgers based on his scores on a competitive two-day examination. He intended to major in math but after hearing a lecture delivered in French, he decided he would like to become fluent in another language and soon switched his major to languages.[102] His decision seemed somewhat impractical at the time. In a period when black college graduates struggled to make a living that made use of their knowledge and skills, it seemed unlikely that Morrow would find work where his language skills would be of use.[103] Still, Morrow stuck with his dream to master foreign languages.

And he excelled scholastically. He was appointed to the honor school after the first term, and for the first three years held average marks above 94 percent. As a senior at Rutgers Morrow was elected to Phi Beta Kappa and was referred to as the "second edition of Paul Robeson"—for both his athletic and scholarly prowess. When he graduated in 1931, he could speak and write Latin and French fluently.[104]

Yet this "second edition" Robeson was similarly discriminated against. For example, one of Morrow's sociology professors asked him, "What can a black person ever do with a language like French?"[105] Like Robeson he was insulted by visiting athletic teams. He wanted to leave Rutgers when he was excluded from a wrestling match against Franklin and Marshall because his opponent would not wrestle a black person. His parents convinced him to stay by reminding him that his education was more important than sports, and that it was something no one could take from him.[106] He endured yet another indignity when New Brunswick High School refused to let him teach French to fulfill his practice teaching graduation requirement. Even though a professor attested to his excellence in languages, Morrow was forced to fulfill the requirement by teaching math at Middlesex County Vocational School. Both Morrow and his professor thought the rejection was motivated by racism.[107]

Discrimination followed Morrow into his postgraduate life. After finishing his bachelor's in 1931, he taught for several years before attending graduate school at the University of Pennsylvania, receiving a master's degree in 1942. He wanted to teach at the college level, and while teaching at a historically black college or university (HBCU) made sense, Morrow was reluctant to go South where most HBCUs were. Having been reared and educated in the North, the racial segregation of the South and the ritualized southern social order that called for black submission, gave him pause. Nevertheless, he could find no northern institution that would hire him as a college professor, including his alma mater, Rutgers. Since Morrow's wife thought moving to the South was in the best interest of his career, he began a ten-year journey of teaching at several HBCUs, including Clark College and North Carolina Central University. Along the way, Morrow continued his graduate studies, earning a PhD from the University of Pennsylvania in 1947.[108]

Despite his somewhat fraught relationship to Rutgers, John Morrow acknowledged that the language skills he gained at Rutgers laid the groundwork for a monumental change in his career. In 1959 he was chosen to be the U.S. ambassador to Guinea, a newly formed French-speaking nation in

Africa.[109] Morrow's language skills and research on French colonialism made him eminently qualified for the position. But it was also an appointment of political expediency. America was under pressure to demonstrate anticolonialism and racial egalitarianism and it was a good move to appoint an African American to a newly emerged African state.[110] Morrow served for only two years but his high-level appointment in foreign affairs was a source of pride for the African American community and for Rutgers University. It solidified his credentials as a Rutgers Race Man.

And as a Rutgers Race Man, Morrow fought to open Rutgers to African Americans. Upon returning to the United States, he worked for the State Department before accepting a faculty position at Rutgers in 1964. Although pleased at his appointment, he did not hold back his anger over the university's failure to give him a faculty appointment prior to his role as an ambassador:

> I wasn't good enough when I had the Ph.D.: the honor record didn't seem to matter: being a graduate influenced no one whatsoever, but I got called by President Eisenhower to go way across the world in another sphere, in another kind of work, had nothing to do with being a departmental chair of a foreign language department, and suddenly I am rediscovered by my alma mater.[111]

Moreover, Morrow compared his experience to that of a white male professor who had graduated from Rutgers around the same time as he did and who enjoyed a place at the university as a respected professor although he had not received a doctoral degree.[112] While not explicitly calling out the university for race-based prejudice, his comments point toward the larger structural racism that kept many accomplished African American academics from finding professorial jobs at predominantly white institutions prior to the student protests of the 1960s.[113] Still, in accepting the position Morrow seemed to feel some atonement in finally being able to become a faculty member at his alma mater.[114]

As a new faculty member Morrow pushed for more black representation on campus. He was disappointed to find that the racial climate on campus had changed little in the thirty years since he was a student and he voiced his dismay at seeing so few black faces on campus to administrators during his job interview. He was especially upset that there had been no black graduates from the university in the class of 1963. As professor of romance languages and chairman of the Department of Foreign Languages, and especially as chair of the Faculty Senate, Morrow fought for African American inclusion until he retired in 1978. He used this latter position to help make the campus more welcoming to black students.[115] His advocacy for more black students and professors helped Rutgers become more representative of the population of New Jersey.[116]

Throughout his academic career John H. Morrow worked for racial improvement, and in 1989 Rutgers University honored him by naming Morrow Hall on Busch Campus after him. As a pathbreaker in both his student and professorial careers at Rutgers, Morrow's connection to the university operated as a persistent challenge to institutional racism. He was a true Rutgers Race Man.

Edward Lawson Jr. (Class of 1933)

Edward Lawson Jr. was the son of Edward Lawson Sr., who attended Rutgers College but was asked to leave the institution in 1907 before graduating. Lawson Jr.'s graduation in 1933 in some ways was amends for the injustice experienced by his father. However, having graduated during the Great Depression, Lawson Jr. struggled to find work where he could make use of his education. Lawson first worked as a freelance writer, and then as an editorial assistant to *Parents Magazine*, which eventually stopped publication for financial reasons. The creation of the New Deal, a diverse array of federal programs enacted by President Franklin D. Roosevelt in response to the Great Depression, enabled Lawson Jr. to transition to the public sector. His appointment as special assistant in the Information Services of the Works Progress Administration (WPA) marked the beginning of a long career as a civil servant.[117]

The WPA was one of the largest New Deal programs. It sought to provide economic relief by employing as many people as possible, and it generated a diverse array of employment opportunities. WPA workers constructed buildings, collected oral histories, and administered after-school programs. However, the diversity of programs did not ensure equal treatment for those looking for work. Despite federal orders not to discriminate against African Americans, local WPA supervisors, especially in the South, often excluded black Americans from receiving their equal share of WPA benefits.[118] Nevertheless, the WPA did provide much-needed relief for African Americans, and its programs were part of a larger political New Deal agenda.

As an Information Service worker Edward Lawson Jr. did not just write about the WPA. He was a Race Man, and as such his articles pointedly showed African Americans how they could use the agency's benefits. In these articles, Lawson also revealed his racial consciousness and showed a clear desire to be an agent of African American uplift. For example, in an article he wrote for the *Crisis*, the official magazine of the NAACP, he focused on the WPA's Hot School Lunch Program, which provided 300,000 black schoolchildren with lunch. He emphasized the jobs provided by such programs, stating that thousands of black women were provided with jobs as cooks and dietitians for the programs.[119] In a fall 1937 article for *Opportunity* (where he would later serve as managing editor) Lawson described the progress being made by WPA recreation activities for black children. Highlighting the educational after-school care that kept African American children from participating in nefarious activities after school, Lawson also pointed out that these programs provided jobs to college-educated African Americans. Lawson noted that hundreds of unemployed educated "colored persons" had found jobs working as playground and recreation directors for WPA-sponsored youth programs.[120] These kinds of writings marked Lawson as a Race Man.

Fittingly, Lawson became a member of the Federal Council of Negro Affairs, known colloquially as the Black Cabinet. This was a group of high-ranking African American officeholders and race advisors to President Franklin Delano Roosevelt. The council was unique in that it marked the first time that the federal government officially recognized African Americans as an interest group and that racism and discrimination might demand federal intervention. All members of the Black Cabinet were considered part of the talented tenth.[121]

As World War II approached, Lawson shifted from working for the WPA to the President's Fair Employment Practices Committee (FEPC). This committee was created by Executive Order 8802, which prohibited racial discrimination in the national defense industry. The executive order and the creation of the FEPC were concessions granted by President Roosevelt after he was threatened with a mass demonstration during World War II by A. Philip Randolph, an African American socialist and labor activist.[122] In his role as the regional director for New York and New England, Lawson again played a formative role in challenging racial discrimination. He was tasked with visiting plants and factories making goods for the war and ensuring that they hired blacks and provided them with equal opportunities in the workplace.

A Race Man through and through, after the war Lawson began working for the newly formed United Nations Division of Human Rights. He believed that he was chosen because of the skill he had shown recruiting African Americans for jobs, not because he knew a lot about the emerging field of human rights.[123] Still, he undertook the work of fighting for people across the globe for over fifty years and as his career with the UN came to a close in the 1990s, he again put his writing skills to good use with the production of his *Encyclopedia of Human Rights*, a book based on his UN work and on study sessions he held across the globe.[124] In the opening to the book, Lawson wrote that the challenge of the decade was to realize "the full enjoyment by every living individual of his human rights and fundamental freedoms, guaranteed by a political order motivated by the conscience of the world."[125] The challenge Lawson extended in the 1990s was the same challenge he extended to himself throughout his career. This Rutgers Race Man had worked tirelessly to ensure that all people, including African Americans, could live in a world where they were free.

James C. Hoggard (Class of 1939)

James Clinton Hoggard graduated from Rutgers College in 1939, two decades after Paul Robeson. The two men's families were closely connected through their fathers, who were both A.M.E. pastors. Hoggard noted, "Father and Paul Robeson's father were members of the same Annual Conference of our church. When Revered Robeson died, my father gave the eulogy at his services."[126] Hoggard came from an exceptional family; both of his parents, Jeremiah and Symera Hoggard, graduated from college and the Hoggards were descendants of an African American man who fought for freedom during the Civil War. James was taught to read and write in German and French and was a talented organ player trained in German-style music.[127] In his late teenage years Hoggard and his family lived in an upper-middle-class, predominantly white neighborhood in Hackensack, New Jersey. He attended Hackensack High School where the demographics were like his neighborhood. He excelled in his studies and participated in the glee club, the band, the literary society, and served as an officer for the student council.[128] Hoggard's background made him a prime candidate to be transformed into a Rutgers Race Man.

Initially, Rutgers did not make it onto James Clinton Hoggard Jr.'s list of prospective colleges. Serendipity and a suggestion from a mentor led him to Rutgers in 1935. Hoggard wished to either attend Howard University or Lincoln University (both HBCUs), when a mentor suggested he attend Rutgers. Apprehensive, Hoggard believed it would be too expensive. He might have also wondered whether he would be welcomed at Rutgers. Nevertheless, he sent in an application, and upon his high school graduation, his father, an A.M.E. Zion bishop, moved their family to Somerville, New Jersey, to preach. This enabled Hoggard to stay home and commute to campus daily during his first year. Hoggard stated that while racial restrictions no longer existed for lodging, he lived at home "not only because [dormitories were] expensive, but also because racism was present."[129] The commute soon hindered Hoggard's studies and he and his family made the decision for him to move onto campus. Instead of living in Winants Hall, which he called the "inclusive dorm" because "all of the Jewish and minority students were in it," he chose to live in Hertzog Hall which belonged to the New Brunswick Theological Seminary (NBTS). There he found "fellowship with other students who contemplated a theological career."[130]

Hoggard experienced a more racially accepting Rutgers than did his family friend, Paul Robeson. Dormitories were no longer segregated in 1935 and segregation in extracurricular clubs had also waned. According to Hoggard, he was the first black student accepted into the college choir, a group Robeson, a noted singer, could not join.[131] Hoggard also held membership in the Rutgers Christian Association (RCA). Despite acceptance into these groups, Hoggard still faced discrimination but found respite in like-minded friends. One friend was a student, Alan Raffensperger, a white Christian. Hoggard and Raffensperger were comanagers of the choir and members of the RCA together. Hoggard explained that they shared very personal experiences about family, school, our society, and subtle racist practices. They remained close friends into their old age. Ties to a few fellow Rutgers Men after graduation helped Hoggard maintain a long relationship with, and affection for, Rutgers.

Hoggard's postgraduate application to Union Theological Seminary (UTS) tells us a lot about his Rutgers years. Most notable is the fact that Hoggard did not apply to NBTS. Although he credited his time at the NBTS dormitories as an experience fundamental to his religious career, Hoggard nevertheless felt that "the Reformed Church was a bit isolated and didn't know much about Black people."[132] That Islay Walden, the first African American to graduate from the seminary, had similar feelings nearly fifty years earlier speaks to the persistent difficulty black men had in being accepted as Rutgers Men.[133] The recommendation letter written by the dean of men at Rutgers, Fraser Metzger, to UTS is equally telling about inequalities at Rutgers. First, Metzger made sure to alert UTS that Hoggard was black. "He is colored, as you doubtless know," he wrote. He then went on to extol Hoggard's virtues: "He is a clean-cut fine type of boy; altruistic in the extreme." "Clean-cut" and "altruistic" were clearly qualities that met Rutgers Man standards, but the use of the word *boy* to describe a twenty-two-year-old man reveals the work black men had to do to be accepted as men, let alone Rutgers Men. There is, however, no doubt that Metzger felt Hoggard fit to be a Race Man, as demonstrated by a comment—"I believe that [Hoggard] would do excellent work among his own people if he succeeds in making himself eligible for a call to a church of his own race."[134] But it also suggests that Metzger felt comfortable circumscribing Hoggard's opportunities and restricting them to work among his own people. Given his background, this was probably Hoggard's ambition anyhow. But Metzger's letter unveils the racism at Rutgers's core, how it was spread through letters like Metzger's, how hard it was for black men to be happy at Rutgers, and just how much harder they had to work to be successful.

Hoggard was a success, and he managed to stay in touch with Rutgers professors he thought well of. After receiving his theology degree, in 1952 he was elected secretary-treasurer of foreign missions of one of the oldest black church denominations in America, the African Methodist Episcopal Zion church. The church had an extensive international network and sent many missionaries to South America, the Caribbean, and Africa. There they built schools and churches to spread the gospel. In a 1953 letter to Rutgers political science professor Edward Burns, Hoggard expressed interest in visiting the "Gold Coast and Nigerian and Liberian territories" in hopes of learning "more intimately about the revolutionary changes which are occurring in the colonial territories of British West Africa and South Africa."[135] Burns, who taught Hoggard in his Contemporary Civilizations class, wrote back to Hoggard and expressed his "envy" at the possibility of Hoggard visiting Africa during the revolutionary changes that were occurring there at the time.[136]

Indeed, it was a propitious time for an African American to work in Africa. During the 1950s through the 1970s, the world witnessed countries in Africa gaining their independence from European colonizers. African Americans widely supported and advocated decolonization, for many linked their struggle for freedom in the United States to the liberation of Africa from Europe. During his first term as secretary-treasurer of the A.M.E. Zion Church's department of foreign missions, Hoggard was sent to Liberia and Nigeria.[137] Although Hoggard, like his close friend and Council for African Affairs leader Paul Robeson, no doubt felt that African Americans and Africans were involved in a parallel struggle against white oppression, Hoggard remained relatively apolitical, certainly not as vocal as Robeson. Still, when Robeson passed away in 1976, Hoggard delivered the eulogy. He served as secretary-treasurer for twenty years and became a bishop of the African Methodist Episcopal Zion Church in 1972. For all of Dean Metzger's condescension, his prediction that James Clinton Hoggard would "do excellent work among his own people" proved true. Hoggard died a Rutgers Race Man in 2002. He was 85 years old.

Harry Hazelwood Jr. (Class of 1943)

Like all the Rutgers Race Men surveyed in this chapter Newark native Harry Hazelwood proved an exceptional student and leader. Also, like all those surveyed here, Hazelwood had to do more than demonstrate academic and extracurricular excellence to be accepted as a Rutgers Man. For them, becoming a Rutgers Man meant getting along with and pleasing their white contemporaries no matter how insensitive these more privileged men were toward blacks. Hazelwood did this well and went on to be a Rutgers Race Man par excellence.

Though not much is known about the racial climate that Hazelwood endured, there are some clues. To avoid racial insults Black students often lived off campus, at least for part of their Rutgers years. Hazelwood was no exception. From his hometown, Newark, he commuted to Rutgers before moving to New Brunswick to attend the college. Fraser Metzger, the dean of men who backhandedly complimented James Hoggard, also gives us insight into

Hazelwood's college days. He clearly thought Hazelwood's academics were superlative because in his letter of recommendation to Cornell University Law School he wrote that "even though he is colored I gave him an appointment as one of the preceptors, which is a highly selected group from our student body." Demonstrating that it was not enough for black men to be academically gifted Metzger went on to say that Hazelwood "had to deal with white students, who responded to his leadership without fail."[138] Indeed, Metzger felt Hazelwood exceptional because as a "young man . . . of the Negro race" he "established for himself an unusual place [at Rutgers]" where "he mingled freely with all our students."[139] This kind of "compliment" speaks to the extra hurdle that confronted black men who wanted to be accepted as Rutgers Men: white men had to demonstrate that they could lead men; black men had to prove they could lead *white* men. Given that most whites presumed themselves inherently superior to blacks, that they had rejected African American insistence on equality, and that white men had the cultural authority to arbitrarily accept or reject black leadership at will, this was a high hurdle indeed. That Metzger felt comfortable sending this letter of recommendation to Cornell, and probably to other law schools that Hazelwood applied to, speaks to the widespread acceptance of this "qualification." It also suggests that racial activists, those willing to persistently agitate for change, were unwelcome at Rutgers and universities across the nation. Black men who wanted to succeed had to know how to get along with, even placate whites.

Hazelwood's skill at this served him well. During his time at Cornell Law School he served as the president of the Cornell Law School Students Association, worked part time as an assistant librarian in the Cornell Law Library, and coauthored a publication in the *Cornell Law Review* with law professor George J. Thomas.[140] He was the first African American to graduate from Cornell Law School in 1945.[141]

Hazelwood's strong work ethic, intelligence, and charismatic demeanor led many to hold him in high regard; his ability to hold the respect of others, especially across racial lines, allowed him to access arenas not traditionally occupied by African Americans during this period. Upon completion of his law degree at Cornell Law School Hazelwood returned to Newark, New Jersey. He served as a law clerk for the Honorable Edward Gaulkin and after passing the New Jersey Bar in 1948 he subsequently opened his own law practice.[142] (Hazelwood's professional acceptance and success was not shared by all, as during this time the American Bar Association had refused to accept seven black New Jersey lawyers.) In 1949 he was among the lawyers who petitioned to have race removed from the American Bar Association application. Hazelwood was not only concerned about his own success but he stood up for the rights of other African American lawyers.[143]

Hazelwood's lifelong fight for racial equality proved not only that he was a Rutgers Man but a Race Man as well. With the endorsement of Newark mayor Leo P. Carlin and the Newark Citizen Committee on Municipal Government, he ran for councilman-at-large in 1954.[144] Although he did not win the election, he persisted in his community efforts. Just two years later he was hired as the first African American to serve on the legal staff of Essex County prosecutor Charles V. Webb as assistant prosecutor of Essex County.[145] Then in 1958, he was asked again by the Newark Citizens Committee on Municipal Government to run for public office, which Hazelwood humbly declined given his other responsibilities.[146]

During this same year, Hazelwood made national news in *Jet* magazine when he was appointed by Newark mayor Leo P. Carlin as the first African American judge in Newark's history. In July of 1962, the importance of his appointment to the African American community made national news as he was featured in *Ebony Magazine*.[147] This was of tremendous importance not only to the local African American community but the country at large. The 1960s were a turbulent time as African Americans like Judge Hazelwood challenged racial segregation and oppression. At the time, it was estimated that nationally there were somewhere between 5,500 to 8,180 judges, of which only 68 were African American, meaning that African Americans made up only 1 percent of the nation's judges.[148]

Although Hazelwood's race work was primarily local, what he did within his own community was felt outside of the boundaries of Newark. And although he saw himself as "just another magistrate" doing "whatever is necessary for the smooth running of Newark's Municipal Court" his devotion to Newark reached beyond city limits.[149] Making national news again Hazelwood was featured in *Jet* magazine where African Americans learned that it was predicted in Hazelwood's high school yearbook that he would one day become a judge.[150] In 1958 Hazelwood was appointed chief magistrate in Newark.[151]

Hazelwood was not only good at working across racial lines but he also worked for African Americans across religious and cultural lines. As a community organizer, Hazelwood was one of five, but the only African American of the Newark area, to be awarded the Brotherhood Award of the National Conference of Christian and Jews for northern New Jersey in 1968.[152] Besides having natural leadership skills, his ability to work across religious lines was nurtured by the community he grew up in—the southern part of the Third Ward of Newark, a section with a large Jewish community.[153]

As a Race Man, Harry Hazelwood was committed to Newark. He served as the president of the Newark branch of the NAACP from 1949 to 1952.[154] He also sat on several boards, including the Morton Street branch of the Newark Boys and Girls Club and the University of Medicine and Dentistry Executive Board, and also served as the neighborhood commissioner for the Newark-area Boy

Scouts of America.[155] At the height of his career in the late 1960s Hazelwood remained a Newark resident, during and after the city's racial and economic inequalities erupted into the five-day urban rebellion. Returning to the city, running for office, and serving as the city's first African American judge, he used his intellect to gain a political position where he could work to help the African American community of Newark.[156] As a Rutgers Race Man Hazelwood used his intellect and polished demeanor to strategically place himself in high-level positions where he could fill a void and be a voice for African American needs in Newark, New Jersey.

Conclusion

Although Rutgers accepted African Americans earlier than many educational institutions in the country, the climate on campus still reflected the race relations of the larger American society in the late nineteenth and early twentieth centuries. As time passed Rutgers became more tolerant of African Americans but tolerance was not a marker of social acceptance. Rutgers College had constructed what it meant to be a Rutgers Man: honorable, civil, respectable, intelligent, socially adept, confident, competitive, athletic, and attractive. But the Rutgers Man ideal also assumed whiteness. The experiences of the black students discussed here demonstrate that Rutgers historically maintained an investment in upholding racial hierarchies. Intolerance and injustice at Rutgers emerge in the stories of most of the college's early black graduates. Interestingly, these same men became racial leaders who fought for racial equality in their various careers, careers many of these men admitted were made possible by the knowledge and skills they acquired during their matriculation at Rutgers.

Decades before the student movements of the 1960s, the black students whose faces dotted the Rutgers campus had already begun to challenge the spaces and values associated with Rutgers University. James Dickson Carr, Edward Lawson Sr., Paul Robeson, John H. Morrow, Edward Lawson Jr., James C. Hoggard, and Harry Hazelwood called for racial equality and challenged the institution to live up to the ideals it seemed to embrace. As Race Men this was their duty but Rutgers University stumbled in answering their call. In both the material and epistemological sense, the institution remained the domain of the Rutgers Man, who was understood to be white. The earliest black students (see Table 3.1) grappled with this reality and despite Rutgers's institutional culture they reconciled their race leadership with the culture of the school. It would take decades more of challenges and generations of student activists for the institution to come face-to-face with the way whiteness was embedded in it. Rutgers's early black graduates—the Rutgers Race Men—were trailblazers who led the way for greater diversity and inclusion in higher education.

TABLE 3.1

African American Students at Rutgers, 1888–1943

Last Name	First Name	Residence	Housing	Degree	Graduation Year	Occupation
Carr	James D.	Elizabeth, NJ	WH	Bachelor's	1892	Lawyer
Lawson	Edward H. Sr.	Washington, DC	CA, CA, CA, WH	N/A	Left Rutgers	Teacher, Journalist
Robeson	Paul Leroy	Princeton, NJ	WH	Bachelor's	1919	Singer, Actor, Activist, Lawyer
Davenport	Robert R.	Orange, NJ	WH, WH, COM, WH	Bachelor of Science	1923	Professor of Romance Languages, Teacher
Lynch	Albert E. O.	Newark, NJ	COM	Bachelor's	1923	Medical Doctor
Allen	Vermont E.	Metuchen, NJ	COM	Bachelor's	1924	Teacher, Lawyer
Waxwood	Herbert B. Jr.	New York	CA	Bachelor's	1926	Principal
Winge	Daniel J.	East Orange, NJ	CA, FH, FH, CA	Bachelor's	1926	Colonel, United States Army
Howard	Weaver O.	Cape May, NJ	CA, BNB, BNB, BNB	Bachelor of Science	1928	Medical Doctor
McDaniel	Reuben R.	Vienna, VA	WH, WH, CA, CA	Bachelor of Science	1928	Professor of Mathematics
Eason	Charles R.	Elizabeth, NJ	COM	Bachelor's	1929	Professor
Morrow	John H.	Hackensack, NJ	BNB, CA, WH, BNB	Bachelor's	1931	Ambassador to Guinea
Boswell	James H.	Jersey City, NJ	CA, WH, BNB, WH	Bachelor of Science	1932	Retail Grocery Manager, College Instructor, High School Science Teacher, Coach
Hall	Egerton E.	Plainfield, NJ	COM	Doctorate in Education	1933	Reverend
Lawson	Edward H. Jr.	Washington, DC	BNB, FH, BNB, BNB	Bachelor's	1933	Writer
Dunlop	Archie W.	Irvington, NJ	BNB, CA, CA, CA	Bachelor's	1933	Sales Manager, Accountant

Last Name	First Name	Hometown	Residence	Degree	Year	Career
Brit	Rodgers C.	Piscataway, NJ	COM	Bachelor's	1937	Insurance Salesman, Teacher, Tax and Insurance Consultant, Office Manager, U.S. Postal Service
Chandler	John T.	Fanwood, NJ	COM	Bachelor's	1937	Semiskilled Metal Worker
McCarroll	Leon H.	Newark, NJ	COM	Bachelor's	1938	Welfare Case Worker, Post Office Clerk, U.S. Air Force Expert Marksman
Hoggard	James C.	Jersey City, NJ	HZ, HZ, HZ, COM	Bachelor's	1939	AME Bishop
Baxter	Ernest S. J.	East Orange, NJ	COM, COM, COM, CF	Bachelor's	1940	Lieutenant, United States Corps of Engineers
Moss	Simeon F.	Princeton, NJ	BNB, BNB, COM, COM	Bachelor in History	1941	Teacher, Assistant Superintendent of Newark Board of Education, Superintendent of Essex County
Johnson	Arthur M.	Atlantic City, NJ	BNB, COM, BNB, COM	Bachelor's	1943	Professor, Economic Analyst
Alexander	Walter G. II	Orange, NJ	COM	Bachelor's	1943	Dentist
Hazelwood	Harry Jr.	Newark, NJ	BNB, WH, COM, SU	Bachelor's	1943	Judge

Key:

- College Ave. = CA
- Winants Hall = WH
- Ford Hall = FH
- Commuter = COM
- Boarded in the New Brunswick Area = BNB
- Hertzog Hall = HZ
- College Farm = CF
- Student Union Building = SU

4

Profiles in Courage

Breaking the Color Line at Douglass College

MIYA CAREY AND PAMELA WALKER

If the fifty-four young white women of the 1918 inaugural class of the New Jersey College of Women had a time machine that transported them to the convocation of their school on its one-hundredth anniversary, they would have been transfixed by the changes that had taken place. They probably would have been pleased that their small women's school had been renamed in 1955 after its founder, Mabel Smith Douglass, but they might have been shocked that their numbers had grown to 2,600 undergraduates. Like many subsequent alumnae, they might also have expressed dismay that their beloved college had, over time, lost its college status and been transformed into a residential learning community of Rutgers University. But more than anything else they would probably have been awed, if not stunned, by the diversity of the ninety-seventh graduating class. From a small group of white, native-born, Anglo-Saxon women, who were being educated for narrowly proscribed female occupations, Douglass had transformed into a cosmopolitan universe of women of different colors, classes, ethnicities, religions, and nationalities, whose professional aspirations were unbounded. This chapter looks at some of the first steps taken toward the diversity our time travelers would have witnessed on the hundredth anniversary of their school's founding.

In the Beginning: New Jersey College Culture in Race and Gender

The New Jersey College for Women (NJC) was founded in 1918 after a long-fought statewide campaign for women's higher education initiated by Mabel Smith Douglass and the New Jersey Federation of Women's Clubs.[1] While liberal arts education was a central component of the curriculum, the founders of the college campaigned for NJC based on the principles of white republican motherhood, the image from which the ideal Douglass woman was created. In "nonthreatening vocational language," advocates argued that the college would create opportunities for women in a number of careers—"librarian, secretarial, nursing, domestic science, art, physical training, and social and civic betterment"—and would suit women to become "better citizens, better home makers, better club-women."[2] The constructions of this ideal were not simply gendered but racialized, as the campaign called for support and investment in "their daughters and their race." Thus, as initially constructed, the ideal NJC woman was a white mother whose background was Anglo-Saxon, Protestant, genteel, and middle class.[3]

Though the NJC woman was represented as white, Anglo-Saxon, and Protestant, "nonwhite" women began attending the college in the early 1920s.[4] Despite being excluded from this ideal, these women created their own image of the NJC/Douglass woman, as evidenced through their participation in mainstream campus culture. This section traces the representations of the NJC/Douglass woman in the *Red Book*, the *Quair*, and *Campus News*, print media published at the NJC, and the *Chanticleer*, a Rutgers College publication contributed to and consumed by NJC women. The image of the Douglass woman emerges from student- and faculty-produced media. Though students and administrators often clashed over what it meant to be an NJC woman, these publications help us consider the ways the college's administrators and students represented her and made clear their early expectations of the Douglass woman.

The *Red Book, Campus News, Chanticleer,* and *Quair*

Print media was the primary venue for the administration, faculty, and students to communicate rules and expectations, social events, and the latest news around campus and in the city of New Brunswick. The *Red Book* was the handbook for the women's college which stated the rules, regulations, and traditions for the women at the college, and *Campus News* was the campus newspaper run by student editors but funded by the college. These two publications were important sites for the construction of the Douglass woman, an image represented through prescriptive behavioral expectations.

More than simply laying out the rules, *Red Book*, which debuted in 1921, was the guidebook for new students, orienting them to campus life and the wider New Brunswick community. In addition to stating the "rigidly adhered to" hat tradition when off campus to maintain the "admiration of the townspeople by the orderliness of their appearance and refinement of manners," the *Red Book* also included a directory of approved restaurants that NJC women could patronize without chaperones and also listed New Brunswick churches.

Indeed, the earliest editions of the *Red Book* catered to the needs and expectations of white, Protestant women. Not until 1924 did the first synagogues and Roman Catholic churches appear in the directory. It would be thirteen years before a black church, Sharon Baptist Church, would appear in the pages of the *Red Book*.[5] The inclusion of a black church is most likely reflective of the fact that the first known black students were granted admission and began matriculating through the college in the mid-1930s. In general, though, there was not much attention to race, difference, or discrimination in the early years of the *Red Book*. Nonwhite women were not a focus of publications like the *Red Book*, suggesting that the authors did not consider nonwhite Douglass students within their constructed image of the Douglass woman.

Because of their gender, the movements of NJC's students were highly restricted. The 1921 edition of the *Red Book* stated, "At N.J.C. everything within reason and in the power of the college to do is done for the health and happiness of the students. Their mental, spiritual and physical growth is carefully watched and certain simple rules are laid down which are thought to assist in developing character in its threefold capacity."[6] The manual continued, "College is a place for training the mind, body and soul. It is not an excuse for pleasure-getting."[7] The rules that the college's administration included in the *Red Book*, such as the listing of restaurants that students could patronize without a chaperone, illustrated the kind of restrictions NJC women endured, restrictions that would have been doubly difficult for women whose color subjected them to the discriminatory practices of New Brunswick establishment owners.

Like the *Red Book*, *Campus News* generally did not focus on nonwhite women. This publication, which reported on campus social events, was an important site for discourse and criticism of the administration and traditions the editors deemed passé and old-fashioned. The 1920s, in particular, were marked by student unrest and the quest for female independence.[8] The image of the modern girl, with her short hair, lipstick, and a cigarette in hand (according to the *Red Book* smoking was banned at the college until 1930) appeared regularly in the pages of *Campus News*.[9] This visual representation of change and modernity during the interwar period was indicative of the culture clash taking place on the campus in the late 1920s and 1930s.

The relationship between *Campus News* and the administration became so combative that by the 1930s the future of the paper and its association with NJC was in jeopardy. *Campus News* editors, committed to free speech, desired independence even if it meant funding cuts. The administration, on the other hand, made their control clear. In 1940, after many attempts at negotiating a budget and the selection of editors, *Campus News* was abolished as the official undergraduate paper.[10] The short life span of the paper highlights the generation and culture clash between white women at the college, administrators and students alike. With discussions of race out of the picture, at stake was the preservation of a specific white womanhood which the modern girl threatened.

While the *Red Book* and *Campus News* were virtually devoid of conversations about race, the *Chanticleer*, a humor magazine published on the campus of Rutgers with Douglass women contributors, regularly featured people of color as punchlines in its pages. Named after the Rutgers mascot, a red rooster, the *Chanticleer* debuted in 1923 and ran for six years. It maintained a shared readership by men and women at both institutions during its existence.[11]

The magazine's curious editorials and drawings satirized popular elements of campus culture in the 1920s. It featured subjects like football, dating, freshman naiveté, youth in rebellion, and, of course, the modern girl—one of its most popular representations. The "straight and narrow" modern woman graced the pages of nearly every edition, exuding seductive, cigarette-smoking confidence.[12] One image, from the very first edition, captioned "The Snake Charmer," featured a sultry, flower-haired flapper, while a later illustration depicted a raven-haired, racially ambiguous woman in a revealing, one-shouldered dress with the description "A SPANISH LESS-ON" inscribed below it.[13] The racialized and sexualized images of the modern woman were consumed by both male and females subscribers of the magazine, as were the explicitly racist images of lynchings and sambo figures, often on the same page.[14]

Though offensive to African Americans, racist images were not uncommon in American culture. Blackface minstrelsy and performativity began in the 1830s and 1840s and ran well into the early twentieth century. Popularized images of the "mammy" and "sambo" were justifications for the institution of slavery and the later system of de jure and de facto segregation which emerged in the 1890s.[15] Numerous scholars have explicated the impact of the exaggerated, stereotyped images of blacks in American popular entertainment, especially in American cinema of the first four decades of the twentieth century.[16] More recently, scholar Tracey Owens Patton has examined the contemporary occurrences of blackface minstrelsy in white fraternities on southern campuses as a form of racial terrorism.[17] The dearth of scholarship on the relationship between blackface minstrelsy and campus print culture makes her article "Jim Crow on Fraternity Row" instructive for considering the implications of similar caricatures found in the *Chanticleer*. Patton argues that the "lack of overt action against racist performances in fraternities continues black marginalization in the White fraternal order and sanctions racial terrorism through the guise of humor."[18] While more work should be done on the prevalence of racist humor in campus magazines on northern campuses in the 1920s and 1930s, it is safe to argue that the pervasive image of caricatured black bodies marginalized minority communities on predominantly white college campuses. Furthermore, these "cartoons" and attempts at humor provide windows into the consciousness of white college students at northern colleges and universities.

The inaugural 1923 edition of the *Chanticleer* set the tenor of the types of humor that would be included in the "lighthearted" publication. In addition to short stories about schoolboys and college rivalries, it featured the image of a dark-haired man hanging from a tree branch by a rope, his feet tied with rope as three onlookers in checkered shirts, bandanas, and cowboy hats gazed from below. The caption reads "An Old-Fashioned Necking Party." This image appeared when the Ku Klux Klan was surging in interest in New Brunswick. In fact, the "Rutgers Klan" (with male and female auxiliaries) was chartered in the mid-1920s.[19] This was not the only lynching image featured in the *Chanticleer.* Three years later, the Lafayette number of the *Chanticleer* depicted the image of a man with the appearance of an immigrant laborer being lynched over an anonymous city with the caption "A High Strung Individual."[20] Mocking the terrifying act of lynching through puns and one-liners, these illustrations are perhaps two of the most perverse attempts at comedy in the magazine. In all probability, these violent images haunted students of color on and off campus. Indeed, the culture of Rutgers and NJC cannot be divorced from the racism of the greater New Brunswick community. The very existence of the Rutgers Klan evidences the challenges students of color faced in finding refuge and affirming space at NJC and Rutgers.

Less physically violent, but still insulting, images of African Americans were scattered throughout the pages of the *Chanticleer* for its six-year run. Even the *Chanticleer* rooster was commonly paired with a black-faced male figure as the lead image for some editorials.[21] Sambo and mammy caricatures hanging laundry, dancing the Charleston, or performing various types of labor made it into almost every edition, including the Girls' Numbers (the editions edited by NJC women). While poking fun at the wily adventures of life as a coed sneaking cigarettes behind the headmaster's back and staying out too late at fraternity parties, the editors of the Girls' Number for the 1926 edition included images of black-faced men, one in a striped shirt and straw hat facing forward, the other with a polka-dotted shirt, black vest, and hat. The men, "Say" and "Bo," are depicted as imbeciles who find their very existence humorous, seemingly giving the viewer permission to laugh too (see Figure 4.1).[22]

The limited images of black people also carried over to the yearbook, the *Quair.* In 1938, an image of the Sophomore Club showed its members being served by an African American male server.[23] One year later, the yearbook featured a photograph of the NJC Service League, a club that helped the needy people of New Brunswick. A black boy, presumably a target of their volunteer work, was included in the image.[24] Finally, in 1940, the *Quair* included a photograph of a Jumping Jive. The musician at the event, shown in the picture,

FIGURE 4.1 Cartoon from a Girls' Number edition of the *Chanticleer* (April 1926).

Courtesy of Special Collections and University Archives, Rutgers University.

was African American.[25] If the white women at NJC defined themselves as Douglass women against the blacks in the yearbook images, they would have seen the African Americans as entertainers, laborers, and welfare recipients, and themselves as the consumers of leisure and benevolent dispensers of aid. Indeed, as suggested by a photo in the 1941 edition of *Quair* they would have been at ease with the white tradition of blackface and not at all disturbed by the caricature of black women as Mammy (see Figure 4.2). These were the images that greeted some of the first African Americans to attend NJC.

Indeed, the first African American women at NJC met a culture that challenged traditional gender constructions while reifying racial stereotypes. *Campus News* and the *Red Book* broadcast the modern woman who transgressed traditional gender mores but still emanated a form of mainstream white womanhood. At the same time, however, campus print media also circulated demeaning or limited images of African Americans, images that undergirded

FIGURE 4.2 *Quair* (1941). Members of NJC's Junior class participating in Parents' Day 1941. Note the student dressed as a mammy in blackface.

Courtesy of Special Collections and University Archives, Rutgers University.

nationwide terrorism against blacks and helped to bolster racist and discriminatory thoughts in the minds of white students who already had little contact with students who were not white.

First Steps: International, Ethnic, and Nonwhite Women

Julia Feller Feist, a member of the NJC class of 1935, reflected on the demographics of the institution during her time as a student. She recalled, "When I was coming to school one of the rarities was a Jewish student. Black students were totally unknown."[26] Although NJC received federal funds from the Smith-Hughes Act, which supported home economics teacher training and which "prohibited any form of racial discrimination," the institution "remained an almost exclusively white institution until the 1970s."[27] The homogeneity of the campus meant that for the small number of nonwhite women who attended in the first thirty years of its existence, NJC could be a lonely, isolating, and unfamiliar place. However, women who were not seen as white saw themselves as NJC women too and they would be among the first to transform the school into the cosmopolitan institution our time travelers found in 2018.

Late 1920s–1930s: Emilia Caballero,
Carmen Martinez, and Catherine Kashiwa

Non-Anglo Saxon women who enrolled at NJC in the late 1920s and early 1930s were international students. Emilia Caballero of Caguas, Puerto Rico, was a member of the NJC class of 1930. As a student, Caballero was an active member of the student body. She was part of the French and Spanish clubs and the YWCA, and participated on campus event committees. Carmen Martinez, another student from Puerto Rico, entered NJC the same year as Caballero. Less is known about Martinez, but as evidenced by the *Quair*, both seemed to be welcomed by the student body.

Notwithstanding any lasting impact from the 1923 "Spanish Less-On" (which preceded these students), yearbook inscriptions offer insight into how students were viewed by their peers. Caballero's inscription says, "How glad we are Emilia/Came up here to N.J.C." Similarly, Martinez's inscription reads, "Since Carmen chose a college/From home so far away/We feel we are the luckiest/In all the U.S.A." Although the inscriptions were likely written by the *Quair* editorial staff, these brief, student-written yearbook excerpts, coupled with Caballero's involvement in the campus community (it does not appear that Martinez was involved in any activities), suggest that both students persevered through any discomfort they might have felt.

However, at least in the case of Caballero, being a student of color (a term not in use in the 1930's though one we use today) at NJC had its unique difficulties. Throughout the 1930s, NJC's administration kept personal history records and personnel cards for each student. The personal history records contained information about a student's place of birth and educational history, as well as the educational and occupational history of her parents and siblings. For example, Caballero's record lists her father as a businessman. The personnel cards feature several categories in which students were rated on a scale of 1 to 3. Students' academic, social, and personal lives were judged throughout their time at the college. Categories on the personnel card included appearance, leadership, "powers of comprehension," integrity, and "attitude towards men." They were also evaluated on the cleanliness of their rooms, mental health, and home environment. Finally, students received a "psychological rating," and their personnel cards noted whether they experienced any "emotional disturbances" or had any physical disabilities.

Caballero's personnel card reveals that she had problems adjusting as a student, at least initially. Under physical disabilities, the administrator noted that although Caballero had "the serious disability of comparative unfamiliarity with language, [she] has made great social and intellectual progress."[28] Interesting is the fact that NJC administrators perceived Caballero's difficulties with English as a physical disability rather than a cultural difference or language roadblock. We can only imagine the hurdles Caballero had to scale to assure administrators that she was a capable student. Caballero's complexion did not make it easy. Her personnel card is unique in that it includes an additional note stapled to the card. This note reads, "Emilia has been made unhappy in the past by the imputation of negro blood. (She is very dark). This is quite untrue, I believe. Her family are people of culture. She has come [out?] and up amazingly during the year."[29] According to this note, Caballero experienced unhappiness because her skin color led students to suspect her of being of African descent. The description of Caballero's unhappiness might have stemmed from her desire to have her Hispanic heritage acknowledged, or from her rejection of a black identity, or from her classmates' disdain of people of color. Whatever the cause, Caballero's melancholy, the administrator's equation of culture with whiteness, and the fact that the racist content of the 1920s *Chanticleer* was circulating during Caballero's time at NJC suggest that racial prejudice was not only alive and well but that it could be hurtful and burdensome.

That Caballero persevered and soldiered through is suggested by an additional note that she had "improved in happiness and ability and makes a good member of the community now."[30] Joining the Spanish and French clubs and other extracurricular activities likely helped her navigate racist incidents at NJC and develop friendships with other women who had similar interests. Still, it is likely that Caballero continued to navigate the campus as a racialized other. The two lines that preceded "How glad we are Emilia/Came up here to N.J.C." in Caballero's yearbook inscription say, "A Spanish Senorita/Is quite a rarity."[31] These two lines point to the ways in which Caballero's classmates exoticized her.

It might have been a small comfort to know that she was not the only women treated as "other." The racialization of students in the *Quair* is evident in other yearbook inscriptions, even for white students. Also a member of the class of 1930, Doris Cohn's yearbook inscription reads, "Do you know our Doris?/If you wish to—hark—/She has clothes aplenty,/Is small and very dark."[32] Eleanor Tilton and Phyllis Muriel Tracy, both of the class of 1944, were described as "tall and dark."[33] Jean Gordon, who graduated one year later, was "remember[ed] for her Arabian Nights' eyes."[34] Both Cohn and Gordon were Jewish.

Beyond the physical descriptions, the attributes white students attached to some nonwhite students were suspiciously couched in ethnic stereotypes. Important is the fact that Jewish and southern and eastern Europeans were, during the early twentieth century, not yet considered white, something that gradually changed after World War II.[35] The NJC woman, while raced white, was therefore perceived as Anglo-Saxon. She was decidedly not ethnic, and not "other." Ethnic stereotypes, however, were used in abundance when it came to non-Anglo-Saxon women. For example, Angeline Grace Maruca, whose surname originated in southern Italy, was described as a woman with "that Latin temperament with looks to match . . . 'Zoot' . . . dark and vivacious."[36] Barbara Louise Moreno of the class of 1946 was similarly described. The dramatic arts major was regarded as a "Spanish beauty" and "fiery."[37] Catherine Masaye Kashiwa, a Canadian citizen of Japanese descent who graduated from NJC in 1939, was described in the *Quair* as "one of the most understanding people in the world" and praised for her "agreeableness," which is "perfectly genuine and natural and not at all affected."[38] Just as Maruca and Moreno might actually have been as described, Kashiwa could very well have been passive and good natured. Still, although we do not know how these young women weathered the stereotypes that defined them to their classmates, there is no mistaking that they had to navigate ethnic tropes and that this has to be factored into how well they did or could do at Douglass.

A case in point involved Sara Ayala of Panama City, Panama, who matriculated at NJC between 1943 and 1945.[39] During her time as an exchange student, Ayala made a presentation to the New Brunswick Junior Chamber of Commerce. The group was studying Spanish and Latin-American relations and they wanted her to remark on her impression of the United States. The article reported that "the serious tempo of the night was interrupted by Miss Ayala's first remark: 'My first impression of America is that it's so c-h-e-e-l-i-n-g.'"[40] Perhaps the reporter expected a more cerebral response, but in ridiculing her accent he diminished the import of her remarks and her presence. While this did not happen on NJC's campus, incidents like this are indicative of the climate traversed by non-Anglo-Saxon women at NJC.

Maideh Mazda, an Iranian student and member of the class of 1947, made a similar presentation when she attended NJC. She was invited to speak at a conference held by the Junior Woman's Club of Bernardsville (the hometown of Julia Baxter) in 1945. There, she "told of life and customs in Persia."[41] Her presentation did not draw the same criticism as that of Ayala. The "attractive, curly-haired brunette with a winning smile and friendly black eyes that sparkle" was fluent in Russian and also spoke English, French, Turkish, and a bit of German. Mazda was slightly older than her classmates. She enrolled in NJC when she was twenty-two years old. Mazda graduated from the American Mission School in Tehran in 1940. It was there that Jane Elizabeth Doolittle, the principal of the school, told Mazda about NJC. It was Mazda's dream to study in America, and she was the first in her family to study in the United States. She remarked, "It is the one thing I've always wanted."[42]

Mazda resided on campus and was an active member of the community. Her extracurricular activities spanned the range of her interests. She volunteered at a children's home, sang in the choir, served on various event planning committees, and was a member of the Spanish and French clubs and the World Friendship Group.[43] In a student profile, Mazda is characterized as "A naturally friendly sort of girl [who] has been accepted wholeheartedly into the College community."[44]

Ayala and Mazda are examples of how international students could become ambassadors for NJC to the community at large. World War II brought about increased interest in international relations and other cultures. In addition to a handful of new courses, NJC also established an exchange program after 1939 with Latin America, which the New Jersey State Federation of Women's Clubs funded. The college instituted this program with countries in Latin America because travel to Europe was no longer an option after entrance into World War II.[45] The historical record does not illuminate anything else about Ayala's background or time at NJC, but considering what we know about Mazda, Ayala probably also helped NJC evolve into the cosmopolitan learning community on display in 2018.

Major Steps: African American Women, 1934–1949

As difficult as it was for non-Anglo-Saxon women to successfully navigate college life at Douglass, it was doubly hard for young black women. Unlike nonwhite or ethnic international students, African American students were not permitted to live on campus until 1946. Class also combined with race to influence their experiences. Whereas nonwhite and ethnic women came from middle- to upper-class backgrounds, with the exception of Julia Baxter, the first known black woman to enroll in NJC, the black women who attended NJC in these years came from working- to lower-middle-class homes. Some were the daughters of migrants from the U.S. South and Caribbean.

This class component not only differentiated them from other nonwhite students, but from other black women who attended northern women's colleges during the twentieth century. Historian Linda Perkins writes of the Seven Sister colleges, "These institutions offered African American women from prominent families not only intellectual growth and stimulation, but also entrance into a world of White power and privilege. Most of the Black women who attended the Seven Sisters between the 1890s and 1960s were from these educated, solidly upper- and middle-class families. Education was expected to endow them with the refinement and culture essential for entry into the highest stratum of African American society."[46] While most of the black women who attended NJC did not come from prominent families, their education at NJC did provide them with the opportunity for social mobility. After graduation, the women profiled in this chapter moved into the middle class with careers in fields of science and education.

The black women who were first attendees did not fit the original mold of the NJC woman, yet they inserted themselves into the college's culture. By involving themselves in campus activities and building relationships with students who were open to them, these early black enrollees helped redefine who and what the NJC/Douglass woman was, pushing the college toward the cosmopolitanism on display one hundred years after its founding.

Julia Baxter

Julia Baxter was the first black student to enroll in NJC. She was inadvertently admitted in 1934 when admissions officers misidentified her as white. Once aware of her race, school administrators tried to discourage her from registering. When she refused to withdraw, they informed her that she could enroll, but could not live on campus. In this, Douglass was like other women's colleges in the North. Of the Seven Sisters colleges only Wellesley allowed black students to live on campus and then only in segregated housing.[47] Had Baxter been allowed in on-campus housing, she would have lived in the cottages on the Gibbons or Douglass campus, where each cottage housed nine students, and each student had her own room. Or she would have stayed in the larger dormitories on Jameson campus, where two women shared one room.[48] As it was, because of her race Baxter was exiled to her home in North Jersey.

Baxter grew up in Bernardsville where there was only one other black family. Her father, Louis Baxter, was a veterinarian. While reflecting on her childhood, Baxter recalled, "I was raised in a white community. I never went to school when I had a black classmate. I knew I was black, but all my immediate friends were white."[49] Taking her background into consideration and Baxter's interactions with whites, attending NJC would not have necessarily been a culture shock for her. She was already accustomed to occupying spaces where she was the only black person. This did not mean that she was blissfully unaware of her blackness. Her father founded the Morristown Chapter of the National Association for the Advancement of Colored People (NAACP). This was the first chapter of the NAACP in that region. In addition to his political activities, he frequently reminded her of her racial identity, and urged her to take pride in it.[50]

Sources differ on whether the housing policy was the only instance of discrimination that she encountered during her time at NJC. In one article, Baxter recalled an incident involving an unfair grade. A professor from the South gave her a B-plus in his class, even though she received A's on all assignments and examinations. Baxter claimed that the professor gave her a lower grade "because she could not recite Chaucer with a southern accent, as he did."[51] The B-plus that she received in the course prevented her from getting her Phi Beta Kappa pin. Alma Geist, a white classmate who was also a member of the class of 1938, said that the faculty and administration at NJC were less accepting of Baxter than the student body.[52] If this was the case, Baxter herself chose not to fixate on it. In another source she recalled no bias. Baxter even remembered a friendly exchange between herself and Dean Margaret Corwin. "Her eyes twinkling," Dean Corwin, who was struggling with issues caused by the Depression, reminded her that they both "had a responsibility to 'break new ground.'"[53]

Whether or not Baxter experienced additional overt racism, her experience highlights the race-specific challenges faced by African Americans at predominantly white institutions. First, they had to worry about not being judged solely on merit or being held to an unreasonable standard. This is evidenced most clearly in Baxter's claim about receiving a lower grade than she deserved because she did not use a southern accent in her speech. Second, there was the pressure that came with being "the first" and, in later years, "the only" or "one of a handful." Even though Baxter and subsequent black students downplayed the weight of being the first to attend or to live on campus, the truth, as Corwin indicated, was that there was much at stake.

Although admissions officers discouraged Baxter from becoming a student at NJC, Baxter herself believed that Jewish students received harsher treatment. Indeed, Jewish students, both potential and enrolled, also faced discriminatory treatment in their interactions with the college. In fact, although applications from Jewish and Catholic women increased in the late 1920s, in an attempt to maintain the Protestant, middle-class image of the NJC woman, administrators, including Mabel Smith Douglass, attempted to limit the number of Jews and Catholics by recruiting in areas where they did not live, such as small towns and rural areas, and also by recruiting out-of-state students. These practices were not unique to NJC and, like the ethnic stereotypes cited earlier, were indicative of the anti-immigrant and anti-Semitic bent of American society in the prewar years.[54] During the early 1930s, Jewish community leaders in New Brunswick lodged complaints against the institution, and as a result, the percentage of Jewish students enrolled at NJC and Rutgers College rose throughout the decade. Still, Dean Corwin and the Trustees Committee capped the commuter population at 25 percent of the total student population, and this "effectively restricted the number of Jewish women."[55]

If Baxter did have it easier than Jewish students, it is probably because of her very light skin and her solidly middle-class background, which fit nicely within NJC's middle-class identity. Students seemed to accept her. In her acceptance speech for the 1996 Rutgers University Distinguished Alumni Award she remembered "the warmth with which so many of my classmates received and be friended [sic] me contributed a great deal to my success as a student."[56] Baxter's NJC information card indicates that she played soccer during her first year.[57] She did not talk about this activity in any other documents, and it is unclear why she played for only a year. Still, Baxter formed friendships on campus, and had relatively pleasant interactions with other NJC students. She commuted daily to New Brunswick from Newark, which she thought detracted from her positive experience at NJC. However, she claimed that she worked through it "by developing strong friendships with other day students who took the train to New Brunswick."[58] Her friends knew her as "Judy," and her fondest memory of NJC was the "lifelong friendships" she made.

Baxter arrived on campus during a period of increased radical politicization among the NJC student body. For example, a 1934 poll of NJC seniors showed that the majority of those polled were in favor of the Socialist Party. And by the end of the decade, when fascism in Europe took root and the threat of war was imminent, many women at NJC joined the peace movement.[59] The growing progressivism of the student body may have accounted for Baxter's ability to successfully navigate relationships with her peers. It is worth noting, however, that when Baxter was offered a room on campus during her last year, she turned it down, reportedly because she had grown accustomed to the train ride from Newark.[60] It would take nearly ten more years before black students lived in the dormitories at NJC.

The Early 1940s: Lydia Benning Moss, Veronica Henriksen, Constance V. Andrews, and Anna Carolyn Rice

Baxter's admission to NJC did not open a floodgate of black women students. During the 1940s, more black women were admitted, but there were only a handful who attended NJC throughout the entire decade. The 1940s were a critical time in the history of NJC. In addition to the entrance of the United States into World War II and a growing interest among students in international relations, there were also more pointed discussions about race and calls for more opportunities for black students—namely, the right to live on campus. Students in history, economics, and political science, formed the HEPS (History, Economics, and Political Science) club, and organized the Racial and Minorities Relations Committee in 1943. They declared that "our primary purpose is to better relations between racial and minority groups on campus, our secondary aim is to carry this program further into the community and the nation."[61] These calls for equality were happening at the same time that Americans across the United States were critiquing the discrepancy between America's rhetoric and claim to be the beacon of democracy for the world and its practice of racism and discrimination toward African Americans, other nonwhite groups, and white ethnics. HEPS brought these debates to NJC.

Histories of Douglass and its alumnae state that the next known black women to attend NJC after Baxter were Lydia Benning Moss (class of 1942) and Constance Virginia Andrews (class of 1945).[62] However, Veronica Henriksen (class of 1944) of Plainfield, was multiracial but identified as black, and she, not Constance Andrews, would have been the third black woman to enter Douglass. According to the 1930 federal census, Henriksen's paternal grandfather was born in Denmark and her paternal grandmother was born in the Danish West Indies. Her maternal grandfather was born in England, and her maternal grandmother was born in Brazil. In this census, Veronica Henriksen and both of her parents were identified as "Negro."[63] Henriksen is also identified as black in the U.S. Social Security Applications and Claims Index.[64] To be clear, census takers for the 1930 census were instructed to report citizens of black and white lineage as black, regardless of the percentage of black lineage.[65]

Notwithstanding federal policy, the Henriksen family self-identified as black. This is apparent from a 1940 Bridgewater *Courier-News* article about a concert held by the African American Trinity Male Chorus of Montclair. The proceeds of the concert went toward a scholarship for Henriksen.[66] It is also suggested by a 1948 article in the same newspaper which reported on a choral club recital sponsored by the E. Fifth St. branch of the local YWCA. The recital featured "compositions by classic and modern composers," adding that "traditional Negro spirituals will be sung."[67] Englehardt A. Henriksen was Veronica Henriksen's father and his wife, Mrs. Englehardt A. Henriksen, Veronica's mother, was a member of the choral club. Since the national Young Women's Christian Association (YWCA) branches were typically segregated into white and black divisions, Mrs. Henriksen's choral membership is additional evidence that the Henriksens self-identified as black.

Veronica Henriksen presents a perplexing yet revealing contrast to Baxter. If Henriksen and her family identified as black but secondary sources do not list her as the third black woman to enter NJC, it could mean that she passed as white while at Rutgers. Like Baxter, Henriksen was very light-skinned. Evelyn Sermons (class of 1949) mentioned in an oral history interview that "several years ago a story surfaced that someone knew of someone who lived here but was passing. And that is you know pretending to be white so that she could get in."[68] Henriksen lived off campus, so Sermons's anecdote might not have been about her. It does, however, demonstrate a consciousness about color and race among students and that rumors about passing were not absent from NJC lore. Even if Henriksen did not pass as white, but rather, a nonblack person of color, it still would have afforded her privileges and an ease not afforded known black students.

Whether or not she passed, Veronica Henriksen, known as "Ronnie" to her peers, was active on campus (see Figure 4.3). The sociology-economics major was an officer in the "Bees," the student group for commuters. Bees gathered in the "beehive," a space located in the science building where commuters could study and socialize with one another.[69] She was also a member of HEPS, Orchesis, and the Music Guild. Henriksen was known for her volunteerism and dependability. Her *Quair* description says, "'Ronnie,' who spends half the day commuting, is still able to find time for volunteer social service work in her major field . . . for holding important offices on campus. . . . Bees will stake their 'rep' on 'Ronnie' any day . . . she's just 'One of Those People.'"[70]

Like Henriksen, Douglass's black women were involved in a variety of on-campus activities. Mathematics major Constance "Connie" Andrews (see

FIGURE 4.3 *Quair* (1944). Photographed here are the Bees officers from the 1944 edition of the *Quair*. The Bees Club brought together commuters in an on-campus social setting. Veronica Henriksen is seated second from the right.

Courtesy of Special Collections and University Archives, Rutgers University.

Figure 4.4), who like Henricksen was from Plainfield, was a member of the mathematics club and was elected a senior class officer. Andrews' inscription read, "Mathematics . . . 'Connie' . . . tall and majestic . . . easy to like, friendly . . . placid, calm . . . commands attention . . . makes her own clothes, smooth and well-tailored . . . an accomplished organist . . . enjoys laughter . . . reliable, capable . . . always says the right thing at the right time—in that soft way of hers."[71] In an interview with Andrews about her time at NJC, she remembered the smallness of Douglass and how "everyone knew each other."[72] She also remembered the sense of healthy competition among her classmates who fought for a spot on the dean's list. Anna Carolyn Rice of Elizabeth, also a member of the class of 1945, was described as "a willing fourth at bridge . . . fortune teller . . . a new moron joke every day . . . distaste for first hours . . . that oh-so-slow way of talking . . . charming . . . likes comfortable clothes . . . friendly to all . . . enjoys a swift game of ping pong . . . deep love of poetry . . . pleasant smile."[73]

The evidence suggests that these black women not only were deeply involved in campus life but were well liked by their peers. They were able to find and make friends within their particular niches and also gain leadership positions in these spaces. Like Baxter, finding these social spaces was critical to their success as students, and also allowed them to assert themselves as Douglass women.

FIGURE 4.4 *Quair* (1945). Senior officers of the NJC class of 1945. Constance Andrews is seated.

Courtesy of Special Collections and University Archives, Rutgers University.

Some of these women reshaped what it meant to be an NJC woman by challenging the notion that NJC woman were women firmly planted in the middle class. The black women who graduated from NJC between 1938 and 1945 came from relatively diverse socioeconomic backgrounds which set them apart from black women who attended the Seven Sisters colleges. Unlike Baxter, Andrews came from a working-class household. Andrews's father, Charles, was born in Grenada and immigrated to the United States in 1911. As of 1940, he worked as a packer at the National Sugar Refining Company in Edgewater, New Jersey. Her mother, Clemmie, was a homemaker, and like her husband, not native to New Jersey. She was born in Alabama. Neither of Andrews's parents went to college. Charles Andrews did not go beyond high school, and Clemmie Andrews did not go past the sixth grade.[74] Lydia Moss of Princeton was also born to migrant parents. Her father, Simeon Moss, and mother, Mary Moss, were both born in Georgia. Moss's mother was a nurse, while her father worked as a janitor at a private school in Princeton.[75]

Baxter, Moss, Henricksen, Andrews, and Rice laid claim to the title of NJC woman through their conscious efforts to find their niche and become involved in campus life, but there were only a few black women who attended the college in the 1930s and early 1940s, and most did not attend at the same time. The second half of the 1940s would be a moment of major transformation for African American students at NJC and for the college itself. NJC alumna Cecilia Avon Rahner made the point this way: "In 1955 Rosa Parks got on a bus and sat down in the front of that bus and changed the history of the South forever. But before that in September of 1946, Emma Andrews and Evelyn Sermons, two African-American sophomore women of the class of 1949 entered their dormitory room at New Jersey College for Women and changed the history of N.J.C./Douglass forever."[76]

Emma Andrews and Evelyn Sermons

Emma Andrews followed in her older sister Constance "Connie" Andrews's footsteps and entered NJC in 1945. Emma Andrews claimed that when it was time to decide which college she would attend, she actually did not have much of a choice. She said, "Realizing the limited resources of my family, I decided that I would follow Connie."[77] In her discussion of her upbringing, Emma said that she and her siblings were raised in the "strict British Caribbean way," which included learning the "Queen's English."[78] Her parents emphasized that "education was the way to succeed economically and socially."[79] Emma Andrews carried her parents' lessons about the value of education with her to NJC. She described herself as laser-focused on her education and work.[80]

Evelyn Sermons's background was similar to that of the Andrews sisters. Like the Mosses, Sermons's parents, William and Mattie Sermons, were also from Georgia. Mr. Sermons served in World War I, and between the 1930s and

1940s worked as a house painter and as an operator at a city disposal plant. Mrs. Sermons was a homemaker. Both Mr. and Mrs. Sermons ended their formal education with elementary school.[81]

HEPS, the Urban League, and the NAACP were instrumental in calling for black students to be able to live on campus and the eventual desegregation of the residence halls.[82] HEPS chair Eleanor Gliven (class of 1948) said that the committee had debated the question for years, but didn't want to force the issue. Henriksen had been a member of HEPS during her time at NJC, so if these conversations had been taking place for years, then perhaps it was a topic of conversation when she was there. Gliven said, "We need to have a few Negro girls living on campus, so those considering coming to NJC will not hesitate to live on campus. Actual contacts in houses will do a good deal towards breaking down prejudice."[83] Gliven's comment highlights the issue of isolation that black students sometimes faced in predominantly white spaces. On the one hand, administrators could use the fear of isolation as a tactic to discourage black students seeking admission, which is perhaps why Baxter turned down the offer to live on campus. On the other hand, isolation could have also been a real cause of anxiety for black students who may have dreaded being the "only one," or one of a handful.

Despite some pushback from the administration, Gliven and HEPS had student support for their campaign. Emma Andrews and Evelyn Sermons, both of the class of 1949, were the first black women to live on campus. They commuted their first year, but moved onto campus during their sophomore year. Both Andrews and Sermons had state scholarships that covered the cost of tuition, but they did not have the money for room and board. Emma Andrews worked as a waitress in the dining hall to cover some of her educational expenses. HEPS initiated a fundraiser, and the proceeds went toward covering Andrews's room and board. According to Sermons, HEPS solicited a chapter, likely the New Jersey chapter of the National Association of Colored Women's Clubs, who contributed to the fundraiser.[84] The two students also received financial support from the New Brunswick Urban League to stay in dormitories.[85]

Debates about allowing black students to live on campus were embedded within broader questions and ideas about race on campus. Irene Prager (class of 1944) penned a letter that appeared in the *Caellian* questioning why more black women were not admitted. In 1945, the early pages of the *Red Book* contained a message about life at NJC: "It is a social experience in living with others in comradeship, tolerance and cooperation. It is a spiritual experience . . . in working ardently with others toward a goal."[86] This was the first time that language like this appeared in the *Red Book* and probably reflected larger changes in the postwar United States. Young people, and young women in particular, were tasked with the responsibility of building a more tolerant world, both locally and globally.[87]

FIGURE 4.5 *Quair* (1947). Evelyn Sermons and Emma Warren were the first two African American women to live on the campus of NJC. In addition to this notable first, Sermons was also a member of the glee club. She is pictured here in the second row from the front, on the right.

Courtesy of Special Collections and University Archives, Rutgers University.

The first year that Andrews and Sermons lived on campus, they roomed together. However, they lived in separate dormitories their junior and senior years. Sermons lived on the Douglass campus, and Andrews lived on Gibbons. Sermons recalled that "living on campus was 'a very enriching experience.'"[88] According to Sermons, there was one incident of discrimination that she learned about years later; supposedly, she said, "One girl who was in my house [admitted] years later that she got in because someone else was supposed to reside in that home and when her parents found out that there were black women, she couldn't do that. . . . But those things weren't revealed at that time."[89] In fact, Andrews and Sermons seemed to thrive on campus. In their senior year, both served as house chairwomen in their respective dormitories.

In addition to their leadership positions in the dormitories, Andrews and Sermons participated in on-campus extracurricular activities and received various honors. Sermons sung in the choir (see Figure 4.5). Andrews was elected to the Curie Science Club, while Sermons won a Chi Omega Prize for her original sociology research project. Both remembered their time at NJC fondly. Andrews remembered traditions such as the Dean's Tea, the Sacred Path, and attending chapel.[90] Dean Corwin had a tradition of inviting students to her home to meet with chapel speakers, and Sermons was invited to have a meal at her home when African American activist and lawyer Sadie Pace Alexander spoke at chapel.[91] Their involvement extended outside of the institution as well. As members of the Young Adult Chapter of the Urban League, they engaged in volunteer community work.

Friendships with classmates were an important marker of the college experience, but for many, so was socializing with the opposite sex. The *Red Book* laid out the rules for NJC students regarding male guests, or "gentlemen callers." The 1948 edition of the manual, which would have been distributed during the students' junior year, states that women could entertain male guests in the living rooms only at specific times and days in the afternoons and evenings. However, "Gentlemen callers are not to be in the living rooms during the morning hours or during meal hours."[92] Students could entertain gentlemen callers in community spaces like the Cabin, the Lodge, Agora, and Calumet at the discretion of other campus groups. Only male relatives could enter a woman's room, and that was restricted to Sundays between two and six o'clock p.m.[93]

The concern over heterosexual interaction was no doubt heightened by the racial integration of campus dormitories. This is suggested by the conversations that occurred at other women's colleges. For example, when Bryn Mawr began discussing housing policy in 1930, M. Carey Thomas, its former president turned trustee, was apprehensive about allowing black women to room because she believed it would draw black men to the campus. In a letter to Virginia Gildersleeves, dean of Barnard College, she wrote that when four black women were allowed to live on Bryn Mawr's campus during summer school, "whenever entertainments are given by the summer school a solid block of negro men from the neighborhood of Bryn Mawr appears in the audience."[94] There is no written evidence that NJC administrators had similar concerns but the high regulation of women's movements and interaction with men *and* the nationwide hypersensitivity about interracial sex suggest that this was a major concern across the nation and at NJC.

Neither Andrews nor Sermons left anything in the historical record about entertaining gentlemen callers in their residence halls, but Sermons's oral history offers a glimpse into how she and black women at NJC found venues to engage with black men at Rutgers. Print material from the period, which covered news of campus social events for the general white population, echoes the dearth of coed spaces for black students, on either campus, to socialize and hang out. In the postwar period, white students from NJC and Rutgers socialized together at a place called the "Spa," located between George Street and Throop Avenue near downtown. There "everyone gathers, stag, gang or dated; with cokes and juke-box."[95] Black students, by contrast, gathered at the New Brunswick Urban League, which played a big role in facilitating black student socializing. On certain Friday evenings, the organization would host a social at their office to bring together the handful of black students from Rutgers and NJC. It is not clear what year the Urban League began hosting these socials but Sermons noted that the league "realized that there would be a big void for those of us who were African American in terms of social life. So, they welcomed us."[96] In a discussion of her social life at NJC, Emma Andrews recalled, "Yes, we did attend a party or two" with black students at Rutgers and families in New Brunswick. Andrews could not recall who coordinated these gatherings, but based on the details from Sermons's oral history, it is probable that the Urban League facilitated these social interactions.

When asked about the impact of their becoming the first African American students to live on campus, Sermons responded like Baxter did when asked to reflect on being the first African American woman at NJC; she downplayed the moment. Sermons said that she and Andrews "had both been in integrated environments . . . just about all our lives, so we pretty much knew what to do and how to do it. And didn't really feel that this was some great opportunity to prove ourselves or something like that. In a sense, I guess, we just kept on doing what we had been doing."[97]

Though Andrews and Sermon attach little significance to what they had done—at least publicly—NJC did realize how important the integration of the dorms was to its transformation and expansion. In 1949, both received the Heritage Award from the Associate Alumnae, which applauded them for their "soundness of judgment . . . spirit of self-giving, and [their] qualities of leadership."[98] The women received a silver Heritage pin as well as a citation at the 1949 awards ceremony. An excerpt of the citation read:

> Only once in the history of this College will it be our privilege, with this special tribute, to honor the unique contribution you have made to group living at N.J.C. With quiet understanding, rare good judgment, and fine spirit you entered into the dormitory life of this campus, intelligently aware of the importance of your success in the undertaking to those who would follow you. . . . By making the pioneer years of inter-racial living on her campus highly successful ones, you assuredly have made a contribution to her tradition of democratic spirit. You have added to our heritage and have raised our eyes to a future of greater understanding and good will.[99]

The experiences of Andrews and Sermons are instructive for two reasons. First, like African Americans and students of color before them, they were able to assimilate into the campus culture because, like the black women who preceded them, they presented a nonproblematic version of blackness. They did well in their coursework, interacted with peers through social activities, and served their communities. This not only made them ideal NJC students, but ideal students to integrate the dormitories. Histories of the civil rights movement show how the young people chosen to represent the movement embodied the politics of respectability, and because of this, added legitimacy to the movement.[100] Second, selecting Andrews and Sermons as the first recipients of the Heritage Award allowed NJC to congratulate itself for its social progress and move forward with a progressive agenda. It also, for the first time, placed black women squarely within the legacy of the college. They would not just attend but would shape the trajectory of the institution.

As Chapter 3, "The Rutgers Race Man" illustrates, black men at Rutgers were more forthcoming in archival documents and oral reflections than Douglass's African American firsts regarding humiliating instances of racism and discrimination. In 2018, Emma Andrews, the oldest living African American alumna of NJC, did not remember encountering any overt racism as a student, but added that if she did experience any outward racism, she would have probably just let it go, because she felt that there "would have been nothing [she] could do about it."[101] Black men at Rutgers took a different approach. Accounts from Edward Lawson Sr., Clinton Hoggard, and others frankly state that "racism was present" at Rutgers during the first half of the twentieth century.[102] These men left a trail of protest records at the University as evidence of their discontent with racial injustice. This might be explained by their longer history with the university—the first black male entered college in 1888—or it could be that black men's involvement with social clubs and sports activities presented them with broader experiences from which to discern racism. It could also be that some of the women graduates maintained a close relationship with the college and did not wish to appear critical. For example, Constance Andrews worked as a research assistant in the Rutgers Department of Economics between 1946 and 1947, Evelyn Sermons served on the Rutgers Board of Trustees, and, between the mid-1970s and 1980s, Emma Andrews served on the Douglass Alumnae Board of Directors and as president of the Class of 1949.[103] Whatever the reason, black men at Rutgers more confidently made clear their expectations of equal treatment to college administrators.

Historian Rachel Devlin's work on the civil rights movement and the young black women and girls who were school desegregation firsts offers insight into this gendered difference. African American parents, teachers, and community leaders often taught black girls that appearing "socially open" and nice "was a vital component of their femininity."[104] Lucile Bluford, the twenty-eight-year-old journalist who attempted to desegregate the University of Missouri School of Journalism between 1939 and 1942 and was later editor-in-chief of the *Kansas City Call*, chose to not include incidents of violence or verbal harassment in her reports on school desegregation during the 1930s–1950s. Devlin writes, "Bluford made an editorial choice to communicate positive exchanges, it would appear, not because she failed to understand the breadth and depth of racism. Rather, in her reporting she modeled and embodied the attitude and behavior required of any black applicant and desegregation first. Any such pioneer would have to go looking for 'civic decency,' to inspire and accept 'cordial' toleration as the best that could be expected."[105] Like the young women in Devlin's study, the African American women who attended Douglass in the 1930s and 1940s likely received similar instruction about crafting a public image that would "radiate friendliness, sincerity, and openness."[106] Like Bluford, they might have believed that highlighting negative interactions with their white peers, instructors, and administrators would have impeded progress toward equality.

Black women at NJC had experiences that were different from their counterparts at Rutgers. They did not enter a school that had the kind of illustrious history that Rutgers had. Compared to Rutgers which was founded in 1766, Douglass was in its infancy when the first black students arrived, and Mabel Smith Douglass and college trustees had to fight for the existence of the women's college in the first place. Though the founding of the college arrived just before the Nineteenth Amendment granted white women and women of color who escaped Jim Crow terror the right to vote, NJC's stability and longevity as an institution was not a given. It seems likely then that race issues, even in the minds of women who experienced prejudice in the first decade or so of the college, might have taken a backseat to issues of gender. If African American and other nonwhite women dealt with instances of discrimination, they were left unspoken as they sought to assimilate into the newly instituted women's college. A number of black women's experiences at NJC propelled them to more overt race work after college, but while enrolled they kept their eyes on the prize of future opportunities.

And those opportunities bore an abundance of fruit. NJC not only launched the careers of its African American and international students, benefiting not only the women but those they served and interacted with, but as many of these women praised NJC for the start it gave them, NJC/Douglass's reputation as a progressive institution grew. For example, Julia Baxter researched and coauthored the brief that was critical to the win for *Brown v. Board of Education*. She was inducted into the Rutgers Hall of Distinguished Alumni, and Douglass Alumni created a fellowship in her name to support black graduates of Douglass.[107] Maideh Mazda earned a master's in political science from the University of California-Berkeley. She worked as a language instructor at the Naval Intelligence School in Washington, DC, and also at Wayne State University in Detroit. In addition, she published a cookbook in 1960, titled *In a Persian Kitchen: Favorite Recipes from the Near East*.[108] Sermons earned master's degrees in education and library service from Rutgers. She was also a founding trustee of Raritan Valley Community College. She "believed that NJC gave her the opportunity to realize that as a woman, and even as a minority woman, as they say 'you can do anything that you want to do.'"[109]

The Andrews sisters also credited NJC with profoundly shaping their successes. Emma Andrews said, "Douglass was beneficial in preparing me for my career. The caliber of the academic program was excellent and the many opportunities to assume leadership roles were constantly being demonstrated."[110] Constance Andrews worked at Wright Aeronautics Corporation in Paterson right after graduation, and later joined the Rutgers Economics Department. After taking time to get married and have two children, she returned to work at Bell Laboratories as a technical assistant. While at Bell Labs, she was the sole woman on a research team that performed two balloon-launch experiments in 1973 and 1974. Attached to the balloon was a minicomputer Andrews designed and for which she wrote the operating system. The minicomputer controlled the equipment, collected data from the experiment, and sent the results of the experiment back to earth. The balloon measured nitric oxide and water vapor in earth's atmosphere. "The results of the experiment [were] expected to aid environmentalists in determining the future of our atmosphere."[111] Constance Andrews saw her time at NJC and her ability to find role models there as critical to shaping her self-esteem and self-confidence as a woman. She said, "I never once had the feeling that I couldn't make it because I am a woman," even as she progressed in her career in a male-dominated field.[112]

Despite their positive views of the institution, Emma Andrews, now Emma Warren, also realized that being a black woman at NJC had its limitations. Nearly seventy years after graduating from NJC, she admitted that one thing that NJC could not provide were the kinds of professional contacts with other African Americans that her friends who attended historically black colleges and universities (HBCUs) had. She later pledged Delta Sigma Theta and was a charter member of the Central Jersey chapter of the sorority.[113] Anna Carolyn Rice also pledged a sorority after graduating from NJC. She became a member of Alpha Kappa Alpha Sorority.[114]

Epilogue

In her message to the graduates of the class of 2018, Dean Jacquelyn Litt, the tenth dean of Douglass College,[115] welcomed the baccalaureates into the Douglass alumnae family with the words "You are now a special part of this incredible Douglass History." Litt reminded the graduates that "the Douglass mission today is to inspire Douglass women to learn, lead, and live with conviction, creativity and critical insight." She thanked them for contributing to the Douglass community and told them that "my wish is that you continue to make an indelible mark on the world."[116] No doubt, the first graduates, our time travelers, heard a similar message; but by 2018 the context had changed dramatically.

They might not have recognized Douglass. Certainly, the mission had changed. One hundred years earlier, Mabel Smith Douglass and the New Jersey Federation of Women's Clubs lobbied for Douglass on the grounds that it would create opportunities for women in the fields of "librarian, secretarial, nursing, domestic science, art, physical training, and social and civic betterment," and would suit women to become "better citizens, better home makers, better clubwomen." By contrast, Litt told the 2018 graduates to "make an indelible mark on the world. Whether through conducting research, treating patients, instructing students, creating social change, caring for kin, or running your own business."[117] Though dubbed the Negro National Anthem a year after Douglass's founding, our white Anglo-Saxon time travelers would probably have been perplexed to find themselves standing and singing "Lift Every Voice and Sing" right before they heard from Douglass alum Imbolo Mbue (2001) and senior speaker Talyah Basit. Among her other achievements, Basit, a student of Muslim faith, was the director of administration for the Rutgers Global Coalition; Mbue, a native of Cameroon, wrote the award-winning *New York Times* bestselling novel *Behold the Dreamers.* "Lift Every Voice and Sing" was written in 1900 by James Weldon Johnson to recount the history of the African American triumph over slavery and resistance to racism. Indeed, Douglass had transformed and so had its student population.

The women whose brief histories are recounted here played a critical role in that transformation. Without complaint or special patronage, they inserted themselves into NJC/Douglass culture and changed the definition and image of Douglass. In doing so they helped changed it from one that was exclusionary and often racist to one that prepared its students for the multicultural world of the twenty-first century.

5

Race as Reality and Illusion

The Baxter Cousins, NJC, and Rutgers University

SHAUN ARMSTEAD AND JERRAD P. PACATTE

New Jersey local Archibald "Archie" Dunlop graduated from Rutgers University in 1933, the first in his family to attain a college degree. During his four years at the institution, he enjoyed notable success as a football offensive lineman and was celebrated for his ability to "[run] like a streak and with plenty of power."[1] Off the gridiron, Archie Dunlop was a member of the Lambda Chi Alpha fraternity and was admitted to Cap and Skull, a senior honor society. While attending Rutgers, he lived on campus and never shared a dorm room with a black student. Dunlop's experience at Rutgers was unlike students discussed in previous chapters of this text because he identified as a white male student.

Archie Dunlop's self-identification was a source of discomfort for his classmates. His senior yearbook photo refers to Rutgers as his "Alma Mammy," referencing a term referring to enslaved black women who cared for white children and performed other domestic duties within the plantation household (Figure 5.1).[2] Indeed, one documenter of Rutgers history, historian and onetime executive dean, Richard P. McCormick, believed Dunlop might have been concealing his racial identity, writing in his notes that Dunlop "passed for white at Rutgers" (Figure 5.2).[3]

McCormick's suspicion is a compelling one. An undated photo depicting a younger Archie with dark, wavy hair suggests that Dunlop was not only white (Figure 5.3). His alumni file includes a picture of Archie Dunlop as a younger child or teen. In this image, Dunlop is depicted with longer, wavy hair, and his complexion appears darker. His appearance is even more ambiguous in his senior portrait, taken in 1933. There he has shorter hair and fairer skin,

Football (1, 2, 3, 4); Baseball (1, 2, 3, 4); Cap and Skull; Student Council; Junior Prom Committee.

ARCHIE WILLIAM DUNLOP

Irvington   Lambda Chi Alpha   Liberal Arts

CAP and SKULL

Bleech Dunlop came to Rutgers almost broken-hearted because he couldn't go to Beaver, too. The Bell Telephone Co. has offered him a job because they claim that if it were not for his calls from New Brunswick to Jenkintown, Pa., the company would never have weathered the depression. In spite of this, Arch is a true Rutgers son and the old Alma "Mammy" is proud of his record in athletic and campus activities. Such a list of activities in college bespeak of a willingness to do things on the field of life. So here is a wish of luck to go with it, Arch.

FIGURE 5.1 Archie Dunlop's 1933 *Scarlet Letter* senior photo. The caption accompanying his yearbook photo refers to him as "Bleech" and to Rutgers as his "Alma Mammy."

Courtesy of Special Collections, Rutgers University.

cementing his appearance as the white, now college-educated man he purported to be (see Figures 5.1 and 5.4).

We may never know for certain whether or not Archie Dunlop was a person of color. Unfortunately, as an only child who had no children of his own, we cannot determine Dunlop's race by examining other family members. Aside from census records, precious little information exists on Dunlop's parents, a mother from Scotland and a father from Canada. Material on other relatives has not been found. But whether or not Dunlop was white or of mixed-race ancestry is

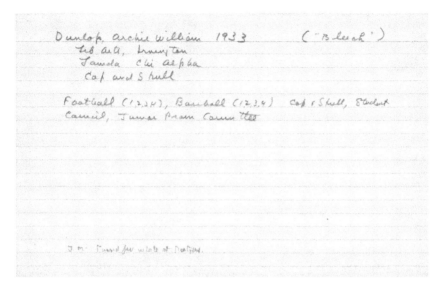

FIGURE 5.2 McCormick's note asserting his belief that Dunlop was passing at Rutgers. Courtesy of Special Collections, Rutgers University.

largely beside the point. Rather, the confusion his appearance evoked encourages us to consider how race and racism have operated historically in the United States and at Rutgers University. The confusion also demonstrates how race exists in the realm of reality and illusion at the same time.

Bound up in American understandings of race and racism are myths of their simplicity. Race is supposedly easy to spot because it is thought to be revealed through complexion and phenotype, which themselves are thought to be markers of the civility, morality, and intelligence of an individual or a group of people.[4] Yet historians have demonstrated that race has never been so clear-cut. From enslaved people masquerading as white to escape slavery to black women passing as white to become Catholic nuns, to the reidentification of the Irish and eastern Europeans as white, race as a category of identity has been anything but stable in U.S. history.[5]

African Americans have been active participants in destabilizing race in America, and nothing demonstrates this more convincingly than the experiences of light-skinned black people, some of whom have passed as white. On the one hand, the way young men like Vermont Allen and Archie Dunlop of Rutgers University and young women like Veronica Henriksen of the New Jersey College for Women (NJC) navigated the racial terrain of their schools demonstrates the fluidity of race as a category of identity.[6] On the other hand, the experiences of light-skinned Julia Baxter Bates and her cousin Malcolm

FIGURE 5.3 Undated photo of Archie Dunlop. Worn in a longer style here, his hair appears wavy. Coupled with his darker complexion, Archie appears here to be a person of color, if not an African American youth.

Courtesy of Special Collections, Rutgers University.

FIGURE 5.4 *Scarlet Letter* (1933). Archie Dunlop (first row, far left), with his Lambda Chi Alpha fraternity brothers. Dunlop's darker complexion in this photograph starkly contrasts with the others depicted.

Courtesy of Special Collections, Rutgers University.

Baxter go beyond this to demonstrate how important racial categories were to Rutgers administrators, and how experiences with color affect African Americans differently.

This essay's focus is on these last two alums. In 1934, Rutgers University and New Jersey College for Women accepted two cousins from a prominent African American family in New Jersey, Malcolm and Julia Baxter. They both came from a family known for its racial and educational activism in Newark in the late nineteenth and early twentieth centuries. The grandfather, James Leroy, was the first black principal in Newark. He used his authority to advocate for integration of the city's schools. And his children furthered his activism. His sons, Drs. J. Leroy and Louis Baxter, as well as his daughter, Grace Baxter Fenderson, founded and presided over NAACP chapters in Newark and Morris County.[7]

Though they both came from this African American activist family, these cousins' relationship to blackness diverged strikingly, demonstrating how unstable race is, how it can be both real and illusory. While Julia's experience at NJC cemented her black identity, the opposite was the case with Malcolm, who eventually slipped into whiteness. In fact, two of his grandchildren did not learn of their African American heritage until they were adults. Just as Archie Dunlop's example teaches us the complications of race, so too do the experiences of Malcolm and Julia Baxter, two Rutgers alums whose stories unfold here.

Becoming a Race Woman: Julia Baxter Bates

Julia Baxter Bates was twenty-one years old when she graduated. Like most undergraduates of NJC, Julia's college years were marked by personal growth and maturity. However, her experience was distinguished by the way she came to understand herself as a black woman. Over the course of four years her knowledge of what it meant to be black in America increased exponentially, something the New Jersey College for Women could take credit for. The school that was to become Douglass College imprinted blackness upon her. She embraced that identity, and working for her race defined her life's work.

Julia Baxter: Racial Ambiguity

Julia Baxter's acceptance to NJC as a young white woman may remain the most notable instance of mistaken identity, but it was certainly not the first time she was misidentified. 1930 census records show that teenaged Julia, her sister, and parents were notated as white. The misidentification was never rectified (Figure 5.5). Admittedly, skin tone most likely contributed significantly to the mistake.[8] A photo of the extended Baxter family in 1940 in Newark shows the entire family to be light-skinned (Figure 5.6).

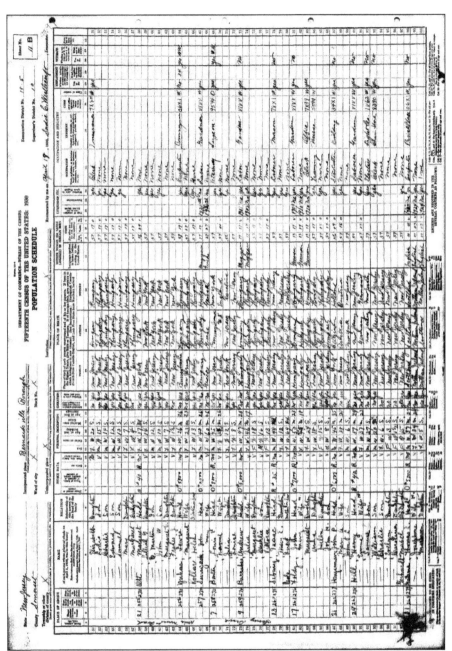

FIGURE 5.5 1930 U.S. Census recording the Bernardsville Baxter family as white.

FIGURE 5.6 The descendants of James M. Baxter gathered at the groundbreaking ceremony for the James M. Baxter Terrace Public Housing Project in Newark, New Jersey, on March 26, 1940. The first low-income, public housing unit built in the city of Newark by the Newark Public Housing Authority, the naming of Baxter Terrace honored the educational activism of Julia and Malcolm Baxter's grandfather.

From Kathleen O'Brien, "Black History Month: Newark Project Honors Influential City Educator James Baxter," *NJ.com*, February 2010, https://www.nj.com/news/index .ssf/2010/02/newark_urban_renewal_project_b.htm

As noted earlier, race is thought to be marked by more than color. The same census that identified the Baxters as white also reported that the Baxter home had the highest monetary value in their neighborhood. As a veterinarian educated at the University of Pennsylvania, Louis Baxter was probably among the most well educated in his neighborhood. No doubt his color, *along with* his economic and educational status, strengthened the appearance of the family as a middle-class white one. His interaction with census takers probably further reinforced their perception of him as a white man.

This point is important. Historian Allyson Hobbs maintains that passing in the United States, meaning those who lived permanently or temporarily as white people, involved more than being light-skinned. In fact, many who believed that race reflected innate behavior often professed their expertise in being able to determine the inner racial nature of others, regardless of their appearance.[9] To be sure, such claims smack of irrationality today. Still, these beliefs reveal that skin tone was not the sole source for constructing ideas about race.

It is likely that the Baxter's racial ambiguity and their middle-class status influenced Julia's fond recollections of her childhood. In one interview, she expressed possessing "only warm memories" of Bernardsville, her hometown, despite being one of only two black families there. She never mentioned a black classmate, nor did she reference the other family by name.[10] It does not appear that her family was especially close to the other African American family in Bernardsville. And this connection may not have been necessary for the Baxters. According to Julia Baxter, her father was a "well-accepted" member of the white community. And, in her case, Baxter felt that being black was inconsequential, stating that in Bernardsville "it didn't matter."[11] While race may not have mattered to a young Julia, it did to her father. He repeatedly reminded his daughter that she was black.

Julia Baxter: Mistaken Identity

So did the New Jersey College for Women. Thinking that she was a young white woman, administrators sent Julia Baxter an acceptance letter, only to try to revoke it after discovering she was black when she arrived on campus for an interview. As Baxter recalled, "There was certainly an attempt to discourage me from coming." In fact, administrators suggested that she enroll at "a negro college."[12] Baxter's father, who had driven her from their home in Bernardsville, asked her to step out of the room so that he could speak to college administrators alone.[13] We may never know what Dr. Baxter said during this private conversation; however, it is important to note that the Baxter family's multigenerational history of breaking down racial barriers to education presumably cemented a firm resolve in Dr. Louis Baxter to see to it that his daughter not be denied an education due to her race.[14] The family's racial activism, financial status, and notoriety further illustrates how markers of class and prestige have historically operated hand-in-hand with color as a means of determining access. Julia Baxter's socioeconomic standing, her family's racial activism, *and* her light skin enabled her to attend NJC during the devastating years of the Great Depression. She might not have attended the institution if her family had been poor or lacked a dedication to racial activism.

For their part, NJC administrators would only go so far in breaking the color line. Departing from their usual insistence that students stay on campus in order to promote community, administrators prohibited Julia Baxter from living on campus.[15] To attend school, Baxter lived with her father's sister, Grace, in Newark, from where she commuted by train to New Brunswick. By barring her from on-campus living, NJC limited Baxter's participation in student life. Indeed, though the caption accompanying her graduating photo-graph mentions her interests in French and teaching, the 1934–1938 NJC year-books, *The Quair*, show no record of her participation in these or any other student clubs (Figure 5.7). That she played soccer her first year is also not recorded.[16] Perhaps commuting from Newark made it too difficult for her to appear in organization photos, or perhaps the omission was deliberate, an attempt to hide the fact that Baxter had broken the color line. Whatever the reasons, the fact that NJC practiced racial segregation in its on-campus hous-ing procedures underscores an important point: by restricting on-campus housing accommodations to white female students only, NJC's actions further illustrate their firm commitment to separating black and white students via de facto measures—a resolve jeopardized by a racially ambiguous student like Julia Baxter Bates.

As noted in Chapter 4, other examples illustrating racial intolerance toward Julia Baxter are few, in part because she did not reveal much. The recounting she provides of her college experience was generally positive. Further, she made sure to disclose that NJC invited her to stay on campus her senior year, an offer she declined because, she explained, she had grown accustomed to taking the train to campus. Given the inconvenience traveling to school weekly must have posed for Julia in terms of time and expense, the reason she provided compels interrogation. Historian Darlene Clark Hine's culture of dissemblance theory offers insight that complicates Julia's own remembrances. Developed to understand how African American women his-torically contended with the trauma and risk of sexual violence, Hine argues that black women publicly portrayed an "openness" that concealed their private "selves from their oppressors."[17] Other scholars have used the cul-ture of dissemblance theory to explain black women's reluctance to disclose the racial injustice they have endured.[18] In other words, rather than give a blow-by-blow description of the sexual, economic, or political exploitation they experienced, thus exposing themselves to critics who could be cruel and vengeful, black women learned to persevere while hiding their true feelings from the public.

Given what we know about the culture of dissemblance, Julia Baxter's recollection of her years at NJC deserves reconsideration. Are we to believe that being banned from the dormitories because of her color did not affect her at all? Also, NJC was not devoid of racism. The year before she enrolled, students performed a play with a "Sambo" character, portrayed by a woman in blackface (Figures 5.8 and 5.9).[19] And while Julia Baxter did not publicly share accounts of intolerant students, she did mention one issue with a faculty member who assigned her a B+ for failing to "recite Chaucer with a southern accent," a performance which would have in effect reinforced the

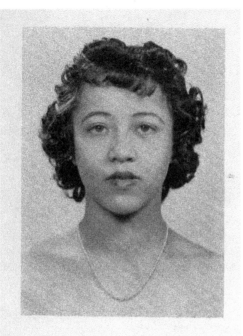

JULIA E. BAXTER

7 Seney Drive, Bernardsville

ENGLISH

Judy is a silver-tongued orator, and when she gets started she can keep on indefinitely. Perhaps she has developed that art from her interest in dramatic speaking, which, she tells us, is one of her hobbies. A good scholar, especially in French, she still has time for tennis and archery; and besides, she pays considerable attention to dog-breeding, dress-designing and cooking. Of paramount interest to her, however, is a teaching career; and, if we know Judy at all, she'll attain that ambition and still have time for the extras.

FIGURE 5.7 *Quair* (1938). Julia Baxter Bates's yearbook photograph and bio describes Baxter as gifted in public speaking as well as an academically rigorous student interested in pursuing a teaching career.

FIGURE 5.8 Stage performance of *Purely Platonic*, depicting a scene with the Sambo character.

Courtesy of Special Collections, Rutgers University.

cultural and intellectual backwardness of African Americans in the white mind.[20] Together, these incidents complicate Baxter's public accounts of her time at NJC. Given that the records of her recollections are in interviews and a speech she presented in honor of her induction into the Rutgers Hall of Distinguished Alumni in 1996, she may have elected not to be critical of the university and let bygones be bygones.

Julia Baxter: Being Black

But Julia Baxter's silence does not preclude an analysis of the impact racism had on her. Lacking unmediated access to Baxter's memories of being the first black student at NJC does not make it impossible to imagine the hardships she may have faced there. In her work on black women in late-nineteenth-century Philadelphia, historian Kali Gross links crimes black women committed to previously experienced trauma. "Reading the violence back into their lives" enables Gross to understand the ordeals of her historical subjects.[21] Similarly, considering Julia's experiences and actions after graduating allows us to understand how hard it was to be at NJC. In short, Julia Baxter Bates's life as a civil rights worker suggests that being the first African American female student at the New Jersey College for Women may not have been as enjoyable or uncomplicated as she claimed.

Purely Platonic

Presented by the Class of 1934

Book by
GWENDOLYN CONDON

Music by
MARJORIE BRINER, DOROTHY CAVE
MILDRED CLARKE

Dances by
DOROTHY PLUMER

Entire production under the supervision of
ALICE NORRIS

Cast of Characters

Fran	RUTH BACHMAN
Ann	ETHEL KIRKPATRICK
Peter	WINIFRED MacCUBBIN
Johnny	MARION WARD
Inez	BERTHA JOSEPHSON
Rene	BERTHA DAY
Aunt Hannah	ELIZABETH BOAN
Isabel	KATHERINE PICKEL
Dog	ELIZABETH MOSER
Gyp	ELEANOR LEHLBACH
Sambo	DAISY KINSTRIX
Willy	EVELYN deRUNDEAU
Dot	MARY GARDNER
Dick	JANE BENDER
Mary	RUTH HUNT

Ensemble

MARY LOUISE BAUER, AUDREY BINZ, ADELINE BROWN, DOROTHY DUNN, MARION EVARTS, DORIS
FRANKLIN, MARY GARDNER, EDITH GODDARD, JANICE HAHN, RUTH HUNT, SUE JENKINS, RUTH
KESSLER, KAY KOEHLER, ARNITA KOZUSKO, CONSTANCE LODGE, HELEN LOUBET, MARIA MARUCCI,
DOROTHY MEYER, MARIE MOUNT, CLAIRE MUSTERMANN, SYLVIA NADLER, CATHERINE O'BRIEN,
LOIS OLSEN, JOHANNA OLSTA, HARRIETT OVERTON, MARY ALMA PARKER, DOT PLUMER, DORIS
ROBINSON, EDNA SMITH, ROSEMARY SMITH, MILDRED SOUTH, SALLY STEVENS, MILDRED STEWART,
CAROLINE THAELER, MARY ELEANOR WATTS.

[274]

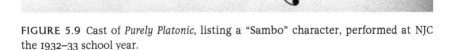

FIGURE 5.9 Cast of *Purely Platonic*, listing a "Sambo" character, performed at NJC
the 1932–33 school year.

The discrimination experienced at NJC continued after graduation. With hopes of becoming a teacher, perhaps out of admiration for her grandfather or aunt, Julia Baxter graduated with an English degree in 1938.[22] She attempted to acquire her license to teach in New Jersey but was denied because she was black. Baxter was not even able to find teaching work in Bernardsville, her hometown.[23] Perhaps necessity compelled her to move back into her parents' home after graduation.

This move is noteworthy because she was living there during the next census period in 1940. As previously mentioned, the family was mistaken for white in 1930, a misidentification that remained uncorrected. In the next census the mistake was repeated. This time, however, the family's race was corrected to "neg" for Negro, as the image illustrates (Figure 5.10). The circumstances leading to the adjustment remain unknown. Perhaps a family member corrected the census taker. This possibility is compelling given the legacy of racial activism in the Baxter family during the late nineteenth century and throughout the twentieth century.[24] Or maybe the person(s) compiling population data for Baxter's neighborhood found out on their own. Whatever the reason for the correction, what is important is that in the decade that it took for the Baxters' official racial designation to change from white to black, Julia Baxter had undergone a transformation of her own. For her, race was no longer a distant concept, and racist rejection was not something that happened to other people elsewhere. In fact, race and racism was something that NJC helped Julia Baxter understand intimately. And dealing with it became part of her life's work.

This new connection to blackness further developed when Julia Baxter migrated south to New Orleans. After efforts to find employment in New Jersey proved hopeless, even with a master's degree in English and comparative literature from Columbia University, she found work at Dillard University, a historically black institution located in the "Crescent City." During her time at Dillard, Baxter saw more visible and strident evidence of racial injustice that she said "demeaned blacks and whites alike and eroded human dignity."[25] When sanctioned for trying to organize an NAACP chapter at the university, she returned to the Northeast to work at NAACP headquarters in New York. While in New York, she worked with civil rights magnates Thurgood Marshall, Walter White, and Roy Wilkens. For over twenty years she served as national director of research and information and coauthored the winning brief in *Brown v. Board of Education of Topeka*, the case that declared segregated schools unconstitutional.

Julia Baxter Bates's authorship of the Brown case deserves consideration for what it suggests about her years at NJC. The Brown case overturned the 1896 *Plessy v. Ferguson* decision that held that facilities for blacks and whites could be separate so long as they were equal, thus upholding Jim Crow

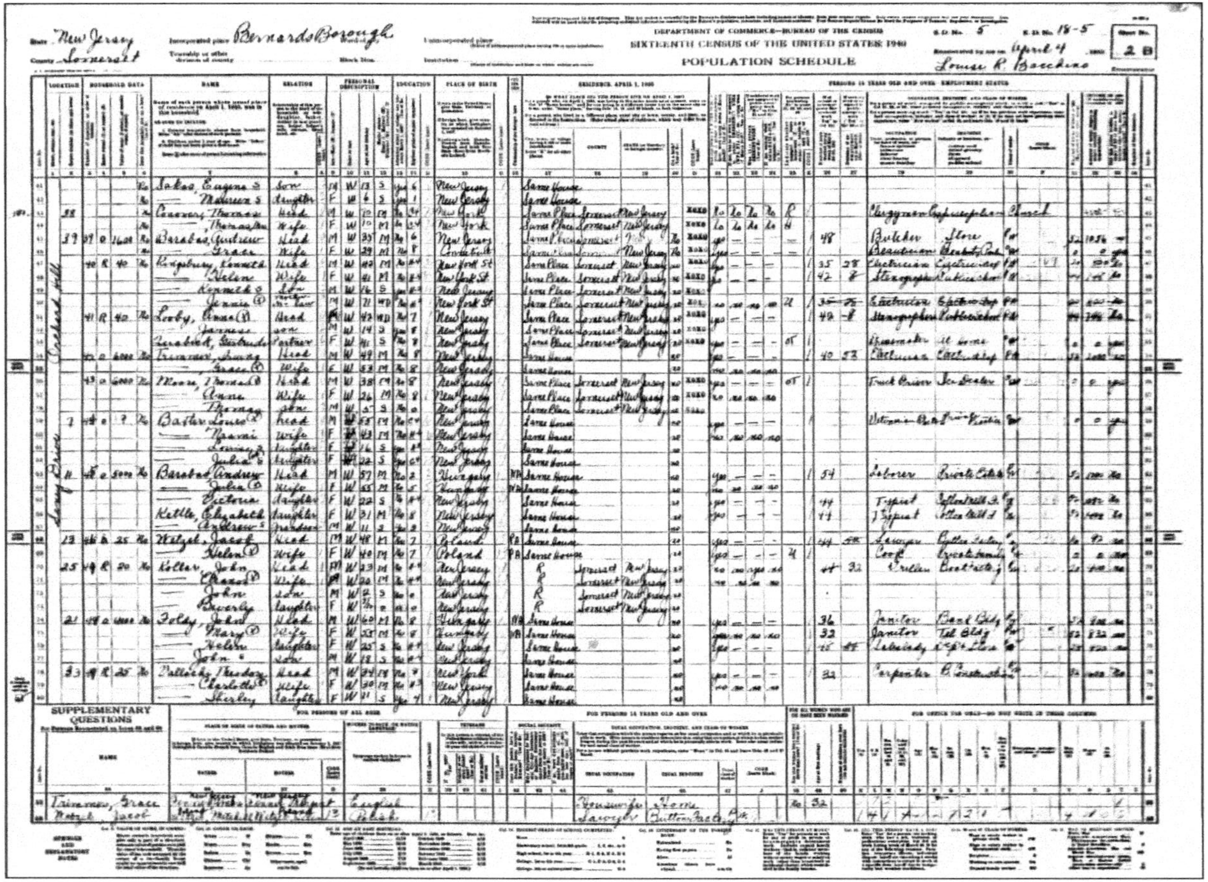

FIGURE 5.10 1940 U.S. Census that lists the family initially as white.

facilities, including, most importantly, segregated schools. The research of psychologists Kenneth and Mamie Clark helped overturn Jim Crow education. The husband and wife team proved that separate schools were inherently unequal because separate schools damaged the self-esteem of black children who, because they were separated from white children, came to view whites as superior. The case was decided in 1954, sixteen years after Julia Baxter Bates graduated from the school that tried to get her to withdraw and go to a black college, forced her to live apart from her classmates, and omitted her photograph from the college clubs. Since we know that Baxter Bates's work on the case included collecting massive amounts of information about segregated schools and the detrimental psychosocial effects of school segregation on black youth, we should understand this work as a byproduct of her experience at NJC. Whether she was conscious of the relationship or not, history should connect the dots. We know that Julia Baxter Bates considered her work on *Brown* her greatest accomplishment. No doubt her connection to it was deeply personal.[26]

Julia Baxter Bates's efforts for racial justice did not stop with this legislative victory. From 1965 until 1973, Baxter Bates worked at the Columbia University School of Social Work Demonstration Center as a researcher. There she contributed to experimental "urban programs in the areas of job training, legal services, housing, health, education, and drug abuse."[27] Following her tenure at Columbia, Bates served as the director of adult education and director of special education for the New Ark School in Newark, a private, alternative education facility, until 1981.[28] Describing her professional aims, Bates wrote her goal was "to work in areas most likely to assure the amelioration of conditions which tend to perpetuate social and cultural privation."[29] To be sure, her activism also extended past her career. When addressing the audience at the Rutgers Hall of Distinguished Alumni Awards in 1996, she called attention to the enduring presence of racism. As she drew to a close, Bates cited the need to "rescue human values" from "any vestige of bigotry."[30]

In many ways, Julia Baxter Bates's life demonstrates that racial identities can change over time. While being black did not seem to matter as a child, it bore significant consequences for her future.[31] Before attending NJC, Baxter's relationship to race was a voluntary assumption. As such, her blackness did not hinder her from developing friends or enjoying a comfortable childhood in an upper-middle-class family in a white town. Indeed, the 1930 census and her admission to NJC underscore that blackness for her was not often imposed upon her body. But her encounter with racial intolerance at the women's college heralded a shift. The events in Baxter's life after her graduation show that race became more central in her life, both as imposed upon her person as well as an identity assumed. In this way, over the course of her lifetime, Julia Baxter Bates became a "Race Woman."

Becoming White: Malcolm Baxter

While Julia's black identity cemented, it faded away for her cousin Malcolm Baxter. Malcolm Baxter's story further demonstrates that there is nothing definitive about race, that similar circumstances impact people dissimilarly.

Unlike his cousin, Malcolm Baxter's racial identity did not follow a clear linear progression. Baxter was born on May 28, 1915. He was raised in Newark, New Jersey, by his father, a dentist, and his mother, a nurse.[32] Baxter lost his mother, Kate Douglass Baxter, to tuberculosis when he was seven.[33] Though his father Leroy Baxter remarried, life was never the same for father and son. Malcolm Baxter's descendants describe Leroy as having "lost his will to live" after the death of his first wife.[34] Malcolm Baxter eventually moved in with his aunt Grace Baxter Fenderson in Newark, a woman whom his daughter, Francine Baxter Shea, remembered "cared for him like a mother."[35]

Based on familial recollections of Malcolm Baxter's childhood, both Baxter's father and his aunt Grace Baxter Fenderson played a pivotal role in the development of his racial consciousness. Socialized in a family of renowned activists and educators, and having grown up in an "enlightened environment" surrounded by men and women who proudly embraced their racial identity, these experiences likely influenced Baxter to live his early life as a young black man.[36] By the time he enrolled at Rutgers University in the fall of 1934, however, Malcolm Baxter's race became contested.

Similar to his cousin Julia Baxter, whose experiences at NJC revealed the institution's systemic racism, Malcolm Baxter's experiences with the politics of race at Rutgers University were equally as complicated. Indeed, Francine Baxter Shea explains that Rutgers did not permit her father to stay on campus. Admittedly, there is evidence that black male students lived in Rutgers dorms during Baxter's attendance. As preceding chapters have shown, however, their presence was not always accepted or welcome.[37] Unwelcome in campus housing, both Malcolm and Julia commuted back and forth from their Aunt Grace's home on Elm Street in Newark to New Brunswick during their four years of study at the New Brunswick campuses.

Francine's recollections suggest that Rutgers designated Malcolm Baxter as black, but this racial casting was not a lasting one. Alumni documentation highlights how Baxter's race mystified university administrators. In two separate instances the institution misidentified his race. The first occurrence happened in the early years after Baxter's graduation. When noting his race on an Alumni data form, it is clear that "white" was designated, then erased to check "negro" instead. This document was most likely created between the late 1930s and early 1940s since Malcolm Baxter is noted as unmarried and without children, both of which change by 1946 (Figure 5.11). For Baxter, his racial ambiguity would continue after graduating from

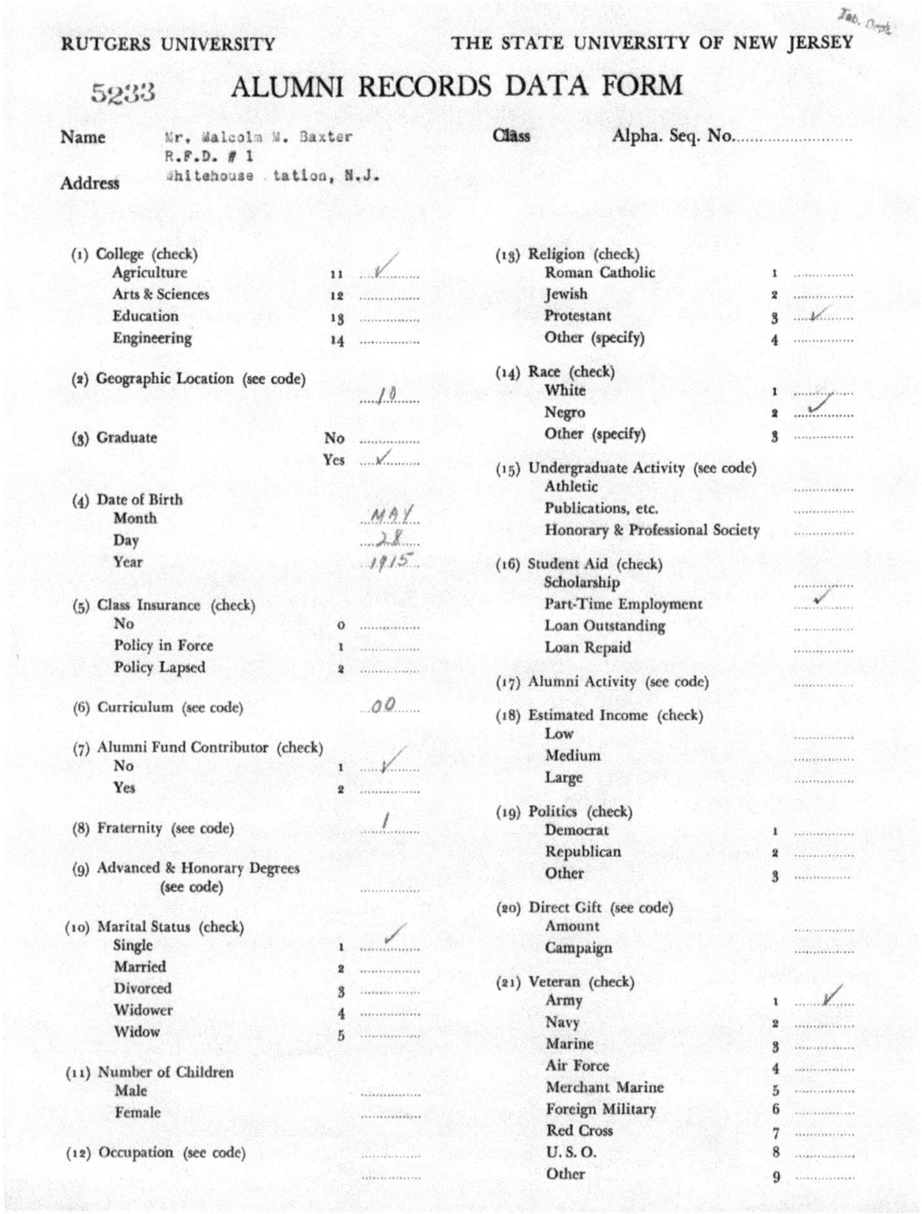

RUTGERS UNIVERSITY THE STATE UNIVERSITY OF NEW JERSEY

5233 ALUMNI RECORDS DATA FORM

Name Mr. Malcolm M. Baxter
R.F.D. # 1
Address Whitehouse Station, N.J.

Class Alpha. Seq. No.

(1) College (check)
Agriculture 11 ✓
Arts & Sciences 12
Education 13
Engineering 14

(2) Geographic Location (see code) 10

(3) Graduate No
Yes ✓

(4) Date of Birth
Month MAY
Day 28
Year 1915

(5) Class Insurance (check)
No 0
Policy in Force 1
Policy Lapsed 2

(6) Curriculum (see code) 00

(7) Alumni Fund Contributor (check)
No 1 ✓
Yes 2

(8) Fraternity (see code) 1

(9) Advanced & Honorary Degrees (see code)

(10) Marital Status (check)
Single 1 ✓
Married 2
Divorced 3
Widower 4
Widow 5

(11) Number of Children
Male
Female

(12) Occupation (see code)

(13) Religion (check)
Roman Catholic 1
Jewish 2
Protestant 3 ✓
Other (specify) 4

(14) Race (check)
White 1 ✓
Negro 2 ✓
Other (specify) 3

(15) Undergraduate Activity (see code)
Athletic
Publications, etc.
Honorary & Professional Society

(16) Student Aid (check)
Scholarship
Part-Time Employment ✓
Loan Outstanding
Loan Repaid

(17) Alumni Activity (see code)

(18) Estimated Income (check)
Low
Medium
Large

(19) Politics (check)
Democrat 1
Republican 2
Other 3

(20) Direct Gift (see code)
Amount
Campaign

(21) Veteran (check)
Army 1 ✓
Navy 2
Marine 3
Air Force 4
Merchant Marine 5
Foreign Military 6
Red Cross 7
U. S. O. 8
Other 9

FIGURE 5.11 Baxter's alumni data form. The document indicates that he was originally listed as white before the correction to "negro" was made.

Courtesy of Special Collections, Rutgers University.

FIGURE 5.12 *Scarlet Letter* (1938). Malcolm Baxter's senior portrait.
Courtesy of Francine Baxter Shea.

Rutgers in 1938, a contested relationship with race magnified by his service
in the Second World War.

Malcolm Baxter's second misidentification by Rutgers University occurred
later in the twentieth century. Rutgers University historian Richard P. Mc-
Cormick failed to include Baxter in his list of African American students at Rutgers before the Second World War. Indeed, discovering Malcolm Baxter for the
purposes of this chapter was fortuitous. His photographs in *Scarlet Letter* year-
books did not confirm he was an African American. Rather his home address,
15 Elm Street—matching the one on file for Julia Baxter when she attended NJC—
confirmed Malcolm's racial identity. Present-day interpretations of Malcolm
Baxter's race could not rely solely on his appearance in photographs. His home
address aside, Baxter appeared nonblack in his senior picture (Figure 5.12).

Malcolm Baxter: Being Black

After graduating from Rutgers, Malcolm Baxter started a food distribution business with his brother Douglas Baxter. Together, the two traveled to Flemington, New Jersey, to purchase milk, eggs, and other dairy products; they then hauled the foodstuffs back to Newark and distributed them to local "Mom and Pop" grocery stores and markets.[38] The Baxter brothers' joint entrepreneurship was short-lived, however, as the attack on Pearl Harbor in December 1941 brought the United States into the Second World War. Drafted in early 1942, Malcolm Baxter served in the United States Army as a staff sergeant in the 269th U.S. Army Battalion.

Racial identification became an issue for Malcolm Baxter when he enlisted in the army. After arriving for military duty, Baxter boarded a train, likely bound for Camp Sutton, a segregated army training camp in North Carolina.[39] According to family history, Baxter was given the option to either enter the white or "colored" sections of the train. His light complexion, green eyes, and Caucasian facial features, as well as his educated demeanor, seemingly extended him the ability to embody the racial classification of his choosing.[40] That Baxter could identify himself as either white or black demonstrates the instability of race, especially as it relates to its alleged biological reality. But the moment also epitomized the lifelong struggle Malcolm Baxter confronted with race. Reared in the home of race activists and uninvited to live on Rutgers University's campus, Baxter's life experiences leading up to this moment likely cemented his decision to enter the passenger car designated for African Americans. For Malcolm Baxter and the thousands of other African American soldiers who served their country during World War II, the fight to end fascism and Nazism abroad coincided with their mission to end racism on the home front, a campaign most famously advocated by the *Pittsburgh Courier* in 1942 and known as the "Double V" campaign.[41]

What is clear from this encounter is that Malcolm Baxter's identity as a black man was voluntary rather than imposed. That he chose not to pass as white suggests he understood the stakes of denying his racial identity. Historian Allyson Hobbs helps us understand Malcolm's choice. She explains that passing was hard for many. Indeed, she calls it "a chosen exile," that required people to sever ties with family and friends.[42] At this moment of decision Malcolm Baxter may have weighed the emotional costs of transforming himself into a white man. By assigning himself to a racially segregated black army unit in the early 1940s Baxter opted for inclusion over exile.

Malcolm Baxter: Becoming White

But over time Malcolm Baxter chose exile. It remains difficult to pinpoint precisely when the erasure or marginalization of blackness began. It was a process that seems to have begun when he married a white Frenchwoman, someone he met while in the military. When the couple moved to Bridgewater, New Jersey, Baxter struggled to provide for their three children. Had they stayed in France, life for the interracial couple might have been easier, but in New Jersey it was hard to make ends meet.[43] It's difficult to say what part race played in his inability to find work; his daughter Francine Shea recalls her father pretended not to be educated in order to find a job. "You know how some people kinda fudge the fact they went on to college and graduated," remarked Francine with ironic laughter, "here's a man who graduated from college who had to fudge that he didn't go to college."[44] His efforts to provide for his family were humbling. Baxter's only surviving son, LeRoy Baxter, remembers his father's belief that he had failed to live up to his family's legacy.[45]

Added to the financial and psychological challenges of fulfilling familial obligations was the overt racism Malcolm Baxter believed he experienced. When Baxter, his wife, and young kids traveled home after visiting family in Newark during the holidays, they were, according to his daughter, routinely stopped by the police. When he and his wife decided that she would drive during these trips, they no longer experienced traffic stops. Though Malcolm was very light-skinned, his daughter attributed these stops to racial profiling. Certainly interracial relationships were frowned upon in the 1950s and while we do not know for sure the precise reasons why Baxter had trouble finding work or why he was stopped by the police, we can surmise that these phenomena had something to do with Malcolm's move toward whiteness.

Baxter's son, LeRoy Baxter, provides additional insight. He maintains that in Bridgewater, instances of antiblackness and misidentification were few. He remembers that Bridgewater in the sixties was very liberal and accepting of his family. "There was no doubt that people knew" his father was black, says LeRoy, but it mattered little. Calling his teenage years "a charmed existence" for the lack of racial hatred, he remembers the "young, up-striving, young people caught up in the Kennedy period" as "genuine" in their acceptance. LeRoy's memories are striking in their positive portrayal of a biracial family openly taking part in social life. He admits that his family life was dissimilar to many, expressing that "I can't fully say that I can feel the pain of what I'm sure other kids in my situation felt."[46] Yet he also discloses that Bridgewater was a white township and that his high school, Bridgewater-Raritan High School, had no black students. LeRoy continued to share that black folks usually resided in neighboring Somerville, which he remembers as a "more . . . racist town than Bridgewater."[47]

LeRoy Baxter's memories suggest that it was easier for his father to let go of a black identity in Bridgewater than it was to embrace it. This was facilitated by the family's appearance: they looked white. While LeRoy mentions that everyone knew his father was African American, he acknowledges that his father appeared "very, very light, you know, very . . . more Hispanic."[48] And LeRoy shares that he, his brother, and his sister "definitely don't look . . . we don't have . . . we just fit in with just everybody," hinting that they did not phenotypically appear to be black. Clearly then, the color of Malcolm Baxter's family, its whiteness, insulated them from racial antagonism.

Malcolm Baxter: Compromising Race

Whether or not Malcolm Baxter's blackness was acknowledged by his neighbors, his relationship to blackness eventually changed. As his children grew up, married, and started families of their own, "compromises were made," says his daughter, and the family slipped into whiteness.[49] While the family Baxter was born into connected him with blackness, the one he created with his wife connected him to whiteness.

The marriage of Baxter's son, Malcolm Baxter II, to Diana Frankenfield, a white woman of Bridgewater, in 1970, ushered the family further into whiteness.[50] Malcolm II's son, Malcolm "Duke" Baxter III, recalls his surprise when he discovered his and his two other siblings' African American heritage. Noting that he was well into adulthood when he found out, Duke recalls that "[his] family never really knew we come from a colored background."[51] Duke's older sister, Renee, explains that their father, Malcolm II, was, like their grandfather, very light-skinned, which was a source of anxiety throughout his lifetime as well. Her father, she said, struggled with identifying as a black man while others perceived him as white. Indeed, his appearance made people comfortable expressing racial humor in his presence, something he found offensive. Despite his discomfort, the decision to marry Diana seems to have been a fateful one, for after that the family made a conscious decision to hide their black ancestry.

The decision was clearly a compromise. Malcolm Baxter's daughter, Francine, remembers that the family's expansion allowed "new individuals . . . into our home life."[52] But it also seems to have been devastating, even catastrophic. Francine notes that "my father's background was basically eviscerated."[53] Bearing out historian Allyson Hobbs's claim that blacks who passed committed themselves to a life of exile, Francine continues:

> By that I mean there were very strict instructions not to discuss any family background, my mother or my father. Information about my father was not allowed to be shared and um I think it caused my father a lot of anguish for that reason but uh the you know the compromise was that the grandchildren could come and um you know so everyone had to you know . . . kinda play it out a little bit, play it out totally, and . . . I feel sorry for my father that way you know . . . it was huge a compromise, a tremendous compromise my father made uh uh . . . for to see his grandchildren. Um to this day I kinda regret it. I think we all regret it.[54]

Her brother LeRoy Baxter's recollections differ. He insists that his nephews and nieces must have known about their father and grandfather's racial identity. "I think," LeRoy explains, "my nephews and nieces may have closed their eyes to the obvious." LeRoy might be right since his niece, Renee, did indeed remember that her father, Malcolm Baxter's son, expressed frustration over being black in a white skin.[55] At first glance these experiences and understandings conflict. Yet perhaps these accounts are harmonious. The evidence of blackness, which LeRoy Baxter sees as plain, may have been hidden in plain sight. Rather than actively endeavoring to pass as white, perhaps race as a topic was just evaded. That it could be is evidence that race, itself, is illusory.

Malcolm Baxter: A "Hardworking Man"

Aside from Malcolm Baxter's decision to enter the African American train car during his wartime service or the recollections of his surviving family, not much exists about Baxter's personal views about race. Many of the alums mentioned in this volume made their views as racial activists evident. Even his cousin Julia Baxter Bates has left behind records describing her views on race and proof of her actions to dismantle racism. Not so for Malcolm Baxter. In a questionnaire he answered and returned to Rutgers University in 1972, his racial identity is never asked and he made no mention of it. No conspicuous reference to race is evident in the document. He notes that his political affiliations are none, identifying himself as an "independent." And when disclosing his organization memberships, he mentions associations such as Boys Town, Indian Foundation, and the Salvation Army. Since a number of Baxters worked with the NAACP, it is significant that Malcolm Baxter does not refer to this group. Responding to the final question inquiring about any additional information he would like the institution to know, Baxter declared in a bold flourish that he was a "hardworking man."[56]

Malcolm Baxter's proud assertion of his manhood recalls similar proclamations made by African American men during the climax of the civil rights movement. And this connection may have been intentional. Or perhaps his explicit claim to masculinity stemmed from earlier experiences attending Rutgers. Perhaps Baxter's utterance reveals that race had become an increasingly diminished factor in his life, a consequence of the compromises he made. As a result, accessing masculinity may have been his effort to salvage an identity that was whole. Most likely both of these possibilities were true.

Race Matters

Julia Baxter Bates and Malcolm Baxter were cousins who in 1938 graduated from NJC and Rutgers University, respectively. Both were commuter students. Both came from African American families that were solidly middle to upper middle class. Both came from an extended family that was highly respected in New Jersey for its committed work on African American civil rights, and both had light to almost white skin.

As similar as were their backgrounds, their relationship to blackness diverged starkly, something this chapter has chronicled but cannot be conclusive about. We will probably never know why Julia Baxter identified as black and continued her family's legacy of civil rights work while Malcolm Baxter slipped into whiteness. No doubt, gender was significant because men and women do not experience day-to-day living the same way. Related to gender is the way marriage impacts men and women. Julia Baxter married a black man while Malcolm married a white woman. Children also impact identity decisions. Julia had no children, but Malcom had three. Additionally, men and women do not experience the world of work the same way. Both Julia and Malcolm Baxter were discriminated against in the workplace, but the racism Julia found pushed her toward blackness, while for Malcolm it seemed an impetus in the other direction. Malcolm's mother also died early, but how her death impacted his identity decisions may never be known. In short, there are any number of reasons for the difference we see in Julia's and Malcolm's self-identification.

The Baxter cousins' experiences show that race is real and illusory at the same time. The discrimination the cousins experienced was real. Julia Baxter Bates would not have been the first African American to graduate from the New Jersey College for Women had she not been mistaken as white. Nor would she have had that distinction if her father had backed down and sent her to a "negro college," as NJC administrators insisted. Discrimination kept Julia Baxter's picture from appearing with her club members in the college yearbook. They both attended college when a climate of racism pervaded the campuses, and both Julia and Malcolm Baxter commuted to campus because racism kept them out of the dorms. In this way racism was/is real and race had/has real consequences.

But it was/is illusory as well. This is one way to explain the mistaken identity that both Julia and Malcolm experienced, Julia at NJC and Malcolm at Rutgers. Despite Malcolm Baxter's African American heritage he was repeatedly mistaken as white, so much so that historians of African Americans at Rutgers did not list him as an African American alum. Here was a black man who was hidden in plain sight, proof that race is not something immediately apparent, or an indication of morality, civility, education, or economic well-being. Here was/is proof that race is, after all, a social construction, albeit one that is very real.

Epilogue

The Forerunner Generation

DEBORAH GRAY WHITE

> Someone once said that the best punishment for Hitler would be to paint him black and send him to the United States. This was no joke. To struggle up as a black boy in America; to meet jeers and blows; to meet insult with silence and discrimination with a smile; to sit with fellow students who hated you and work and play for the honor of a college that disowned you—all this was America for Paul Robeson.
>
> —W.E.B. Du Bois, "The Real Reason behind Robeson's Persecution"

Two thousand nineteen marked the one-hundredth anniversary of Paul Robeson's graduation from Rutgers University. Celebrations took place, and a few, like the groundbreaking for the Paul Robeson Memorial Plaza on the College Avenue campus, brought residents from the New Brunswick black community to campus to celebrate with faculty, staff and administrators. The tributes are more than appropriate, for as we have noted in this volume, as class valedictorian; member of Phi Beta Kappa and Cap and Skull; and star football, basketball, track, and baseball player, Robeson was the quintessential Rutgers Man. A Race Man as well, Robeson advocated for workers, for anticolonialism abroad, and against racism and lynching at home. During the McCarthy era, he was blacklisted and lost his lucrative theatrical and singing career because he refused to retract his statements against American apartheid.

As alluded to by W.E.B. Du Bois, however, Rutgers did not always honor or revere Robeson.[1] Indeed, when he first took the Rutgers football field his teammates attacked him, spectators and opponents shouted racial epithets, and at least one team forced him to the bench because they would not play against a black man. Barred by race from having too much social contact with fellow students, Robeson could not live on campus or participate fully in campus life.[2]

Still, he persevered in all areas of his life and his legacy has emerged on the right side of history. In 1998, the editors of *Freedomways*, a journal of African American political and cultural thought, published "Paul Robeson: The Great Forerunner." In it they highlight all of the tributes organized to celebrate the centennial anniversary of his birth. They noted that although Robeson is "being recognized in most books today as one of the great world figures of the 20th century," when he died on January 23, 1976, "there was a virtual blackout of favorable stories about him."[3] Similarly, in his introduction to the book, Paul Robeson Jr. addressed the silence and negativity and his regret that "not only had a web of lies and falsifications been institutionalized, but his entire record of achievement had been all but eradicated in the United States."[4]

Actually, Robeson's son missed the turnabout that had happened at Rutgers a few years before Robeson died. In 1970, President Mason Gross protested the National Football Foundation's snub of Robeson.[5] Both he and the head football coach, John Bateman, sent letters protesting the foundation's failure to admit Robeson into their Hall of Fame that honored great college athletes.[6] Even before that, student pressure on both the Newark and New Brunswick campuses pushed administrators to honor Robeson. Consequently, in 1968 Newark named its new campus center, and in 1972 New Brunswick named its African American cultural center, after Robeson.[7] At the Newark dedication, then president Edward J. Bloustein called Robeson a man who "transcended his time, his race, and his own person to join that select group of souls who speak for all humanity." He proclaimed Robeson a man who "through his worldwide acclaim brought esteem to our nation and our university." With the words "today, after a period of neglect by this university of which I am ashamed, we return to Paul Robeson some small portion of that great honor he brought us,"[8] Bloustein all but apologized for Rutgers's treatment of Robeson.

No doubt, this centennial of Robeson's graduation will continue that apology, but it should and can do what we have tried to do here: recover, acknowledge, and celebrate *all* of the forerunners of desegregation at Rutgers. Robeson has the most august history as a Rutgers Race Man, but like those we have covered here, there were other Race Men and Women. They plowed through Jim Crow America by not admitting that they were unworthy or inferior. If they were daunted by their exceptionalism or exclusion, they did not and could not show it. Rather they competed fiercely, completed their degrees, and many went on to leadership positions in the race and nation.

While we celebrate them we should not lose sight of the complexity or the painfulness of their story. Robeson's struggle was a very public one, but for all of these forerunners the struggle was lonely. If we have not written about their pain it is because theirs was a situation that did not allow for transparency. However, there are slivers, ever-so-tiny glimpses, of the difficult choices they had to make, the first being to attend Rutgers. We should not forget that these pioneers chose to forego attendance at an historically black college or university (HBCU) where they would have been in the majority and escaped the racial anxieties they endured. Instead, they chose Rutgers, which in the early part of the century practiced informal Jim Crow segregation and incubated a white supremacist ideology that it spread throughout the nation and abroad. While these forerunners give us a lot more to explore, for now it is important to remember that they *could not* fail. They had to get their foot in the door. Their success made it possible for African American baby boomers, or the desegregation generation, to push that door wide open.

The next and final volume of *Scarlet and Black* will explore Rutgers and African Americans from World War II to the present with particular emphasis on the desegregation and diversification of Rutgers. It will illuminate and differentiate the student organizing at Rutgers Camden, Newark, and New Brunswick, as well as explore the class and gendered dimensions of student organizing on the Douglass and Livingston campuses. This necessarily forces us to focus on the development of African American studies, Puerto Rican studies, the Educational Opportunity Program, and antiapartheid organizing. It also concentrates our lens on certain key events like the Conklin Hall protest, the Bell Curve incident involving President Lawrence, and the Imus Affair. As we have done here and with Volume 1 we will look at the intellectual climate fostered by professors and administrators as a way of exploring campus-wide discussions about race and how faculty and administrators helped or hindered the Rutgers process of diversity. And, as we did in the first two volumes, we will look at the transformation of Rutgers in the context of the nation and communities around it. This is important because the diversification of Rutgers occurred in the context of the Black Freedom Struggle, a signal event that was an impetus for the democratization of education nationwide.

Like W.E.B. Du Bois, Paul Robeson did not live to see history or justice bend in his favor, and only a very few of the forerunners of desegregation survived to see Rutgers become the diverse institution we take pride in today. Though largely invisible, the forerunners' legacy lives on Rutgers campuses. It has been the honor of the Scarlet and Black Project to make this legacy visible not only to pay homage to these forgotten trailblazers but to allow them to demonstrate the many lessons that history can teach.

ACKNOWLEDGMENTS

This book was a community effort and while it might be obvious we feel it important to acknowledge this fact, for not every university undertaking the inquiry into its relation to African American slavery and discrimination, and the legacy of racism at their institution, has willingly given as much support as has the Rutgers academic community. Therefore we thank everyone connected with this project and apologize in advance if we do not mention everyone.

We continue to thank former Chancellor Richard Edwards who conceived, initiated and helped fund the three volume project, and Vice President for Academic Affairs Karen Stubaus for their continued support. Christopher Molloy, the current Chancellor of Rutgers University – New Brunswick, and Executive Vice Chancellor of Administration and Planning at Rutgers, New Brunswick, Felicia McGinty, have been unwavering in their commitment, as has Jacquelyn Litt, the Dean of Douglass Residential College; Peter March, the Executive Dean of the School of Arts and Sciences; and Michele Stephens, the Dean of Humanities at Rutgers, New Brunswick.

The work undertaken by our researchers was made possible by committed librarians and faculty. We extend special thanks to University Archivist Erika Gorder for guiding our graduate and undergraduate researchers through the maze of documents in the Special Collections and University Archives. John Coakley, the emeritus L. Russell Feakes Memorial Professor of Church History, once again helped us with the connections between the New Brunswick Theological Seminary and Rutgers University. Also we thank Professor Mary Hawkesworth, and librarians Fernanda Perrone, and Kayo Denda, for extending a copy of the book *The Douglass Century: Transformation of the Women's College at Rutgers University* before it was published. This was a tremendous help to our researchers of Douglass College.

We are especially grateful to the staff of the History Department for calmly wading through the Rutgers bureaucratic labyrinth to ensure that our researchers were compensated and otherwise cared for. Tiffany Berg, Quiyana

Butler, and Matthew Leonaggeo are surely among the most unflappable people at Rutgers.

Finally, we are appreciative of the commitment of Rutgers University Press to the dissemination of this raced history of Rutgers and African Americans. We thank Director Micah Kleit and Executive Editor Peter Mickulas for working with us and backing this project.

NOTES

INTRODUCTION

1. W.E.B. Du Bois, *The Souls of Black Folk* (Chicago: A. C. McClurg and Company, 1903), 1.
2. Ibid., 2.
3. Data on African American attendance at Rutgers is difficult to attain, in part because of spotty record-keeping, but also because, as evidence suggests, some passed as white. Researchers for this collection identified twenty-five black men who graduated by 1943 and found information on seven black women who graduated as well1949. For other estimates see Kayo Denda, Mary Hawkesworth, and Fernanda Perrone, *The Douglass Century: Transformation of the Women's College at Rutgers University* (New Brunswick, NJ: Rutgers University Press, 2018), 144.
4. Thomas Frusciano and Benjamin Justice, "History & Politics," in *Rutgers: A 250th Anniversary Portrait*, ed. Nita Congress (London: Third Millennium Publishing, 2015), 47.
5. Stefan M. Bradley, *Upending the Ivory Tower: Civil Rights, Black Power and the Ivy League* (New York: New York University Press, 2018), 25–26.
6. Craig Steven Wilder, *Ebony and Ivy: Race, Slavery, and the Troubled History of America's Universities* (New York: Bloomsbury Press, 2013), 263–264.
7. See Marisa J. Fuentes and Deborah Gray White, eds., *Scarlet and Black: Slavery and Dispossession in Rutgers History* (New Brunswick, NJ: Rutgers University Press, 2016).
8. See David Oshinsky, *Worse than Slavery: Parchman Farm and the Ordeal of Jim Crow Justice* (New York: Free Press, 1996); Douglas A. Blackmon, *Slavery by Another Name: The Re-Enslavement of Black Americans from the Civil War to World War II* (New York: Anchor Books, 2008).
9. Thomas J. Sugrue, *Sweet Land of Liberty: The Forgotten Struggle for Civil Rights in the North* (New York: Random House, 2008), xv.
10. Graham Russell Gao Hodges, *Black New Jersey: 1664 to the Present Day* (New Brunswick, NJ: Rutgers University Press, 2018), 142–143.
11. Ibid., 136–138.
12. Ibid., 132–134; Hodges throughout the entire book details New Jersey's history of inequality.
13. See Matthew J. Countryman, *Up South: Civil Rights and Black Power in Philadelphia* (Philadelphia: University of Pennsylvania Press, 2006); Malaika Adero, ed., *Up South: Stories, Studies, and Letters of This Century's Black Migrations* (New York: New Press,

1993); Brian Purnell, Jeanne Theoharis, and Komozi Woodard, eds., *The Strange Career of the Jim Crow North: Segregation and Struggle outside the South* (New York: New York University Press, 2019).

14. Hodges, *Black New Jersey*, 110.

15. David Litsokin, Dorothea Berkhout, and James W. Hughes, *New Brunswick, New Jersey: The Decline and Revitalization of Urban America* (New Brunswick, NJ: Rutgers University Press, 2016), 54.

CHAPTER 1: All the World's a Classroom

1. See Marisa J. Fuentes and Deborah Gray White, eds., *Scarlet and Black: Slavery and Dispossession in Rutgers History* (New Brunswick, NJ: Rutgers University Press, 2016).

2. For more on race and American imperialism following the Civil War, see Paul A. Kramer, *The Blood of Government: Race, Empire, the United States, and the Philippines* (Chapel Hill: University of North Carolina Press, 2006); Eric T. Love, *Race over Empire: Racism and U.S. Imperialism, 1865–1900* (Chapel Hill: University of North Carolina Press, 2004); Gary Gerstle, *American Crucible: Race and Nation in the Twentieth Century* (Princeton, NJ: Princeton University Press, 2001); Gail Bederman, *Manliness and Civilization: A Cultural History of Gender and Race in the United States, 1880–1917* (Chicago: University of Chicago Press, 1995), 170–217.

3. John W. Coakley, *New Brunswick Theological Seminary: An Illustrated History, 1784–2014* (Grand Rapids, MI: Eerdmans, 2014).

4. Eric Foner, *Reconstruction: America's Unfinished Revolution, 1863–1877* (New York: HarperCollins, 1989), 91.

5. Ibid.

6. John Howard Raven, *Biographical Record: New Brunswick Theological Seminary, 1784–1934* (New York, NY: Printed by Columbia University, 1934), 143.

7. Evie Ruth (Hill) Grady, likely a relative of Walden, "Islay Walden Biography," Unpublished typescript, Walden Papers, Special Collections and University Archives, Rutgers University, *RCA Photos & Resources*, http://rcaarchives.omeka.net/items/show/27.

8. Ibid., 1–2.

9. Islay Walden, *Walden's Miscellaneous Poems* (Washington, DC: Author, 1873), 80–83.

10. Grady, "Islay Walden Biography," 1–2.

11. Coakley, *New Brunswick Theological Seminary*, 43–44.

12. Ibid. Grady, "Islay Walden Biography," 1–2.

13. Board of Superintendents Minutes, vol. 3 (April 17, 1877), New Brunswick Theological Seminary Archives, New Brunswick, New Jersey; Board of Superintendents Minutes, vol. 3 (May 10, 1877), New Brunswick Theological Seminary Archives, New Brunswick, New Jersey.

14. See Craig Steven Wilder, *Ebony and Ivy: Race, Slavery, and the Troubled History of America's Universities* (New York: Bloomsbury Press, 2013).

15. Board of Superintendents Minutes, vol. 3 (May 10, 1877), New Brunswick Theological Seminary Archives, New Brunswick, New Jersey.

16. "College Gossip," *The College Courant*, December 10, 1870, 358, (New Haven, CT: Yale University), Special Collections and University Archives, Rutgers University.

17. Bayard, "That Ex-Slave at Rutgers," *The Targum*, January 1871, 3 (New Brunswick, NJ: Rutgers University), Special Collections and University Archives, Rutgers University.

18. Ibid.

19. Ibid.

20. For more on black criminality, see Kali N. Gross, *Colored Amazons: Crime, Violence, and Black Women in the City of Brotherly Love, 1880–1910* (Durham, NC: Duke University Press, 2006); Cheryl D. Hicks, *Talk With You Like a Woman: African American Women, Justice, and Reform in New York 1890–1935* (Chapel Hill: The University of North Carolina Press, 2010); Khalil Gibran Muhammad, *The Condemnation of Blackness: Race, Crime, and the Making of Modern Urban America* (Cambridge, MA: Harvard University Press, 2010).

21. Muhammad, *The Condemnation of Blackness*, 19–34.

22. For more on social control of black life see Shaun Armstead, Brenann Sutter, Pamela Walker, and Caitlin Wiesner, "'And I Poor Slave Yet': The Precarity of Black Life in New Brunswick, 1766–1833" in *Scarlet and Black: Slavery and Dispossession in Rutgers History,* ed. Deborah Gray White and Marisa J. Fuentes (New Brunswick: Rutgers University Press, 2016): 91-122; Beatrice Adams, Tracey Johnson, Daniel Manuel, and Meagan Wierda, "From the Classroom to the American Colonization Society: Making Race at Rutgers," in *Scarlet and Black,* 123–149.

23. Inventory to the Records of the Philoclean Society of Rutgers College, 1825–1927, Box 5, Folder 1. Special Collections and University Archives, Rutgers University.

24. C. Vann Woodward, *Reunion and Reaction: The Compromise of 1877 and the End of Reconstruction* (Oxford: Oxford University Press, 1951), 8.

25. William H. S. Demarest, *A History of Rutgers College: 1766–1924* (New Brunswick, NJ: Rutgers College, 1924), 419; "Atherton: Our Candidate for Congress," *The Targum*, September 1876, 5–6.

26. "Atherton: Our Candidate for Congress."

27. Islay Walden, Letter to William Demarest, September 21, 1878, *RCA Photos & Resources*, Special Collections and University Archives, Rutgers University.

28. The authors assume that Walden was not able to preach at local churches because of his institutional affiliation with the Dutch Reformed Church (which, according to seminary scholar Dr. John Coakley, did not have its own African American churches). The African Methodist Church leadership in New Brunswick hosted "circuit" preachers who stayed anywhere from one to three years. The church did not have a permanent pastor until the 1930s. The authors venture that if the A.M.E. Church was consistently hiring preachers, Walden would have been able to preach there from time to time, but since he did not we can assume that it is because he was not A.M.E. The double-bind for Walden is, Dr. John Coakley asserts, "he as a 'colored' person is tied, at that moment, for purposes of his education in ministry, to a denomination that both 'has no colored churches' and apparently would not welcome him to its pulpits." Email communication from Dr. John Coakley to Tracey Johnson.

29. Islay Walden, Letter to William Demarest, September 21, 1878, *RCA Photos & Resources*, Special Collections and University Archives, Rutgers University.

30. The earliest literary societies at Queen's College were the Athenian, Polemical, and Calleopean Societies. Owing to the financial instability of and low enrollment at the

college between its founding and the early nineteenth century, however, they did not survive.

31. Nicholas L. Syrett, *The Company He Keeps: A History of White College Fraternities* (Chapel Hill: University of North Carolina Press, 2009), 9.

32. RG 48/A2/01, Box 4, Folder 1 (May 18th, 1827; November 2nd, 1827), Inventory to the Records of the Philoclean Society of Rutgers College, 1825-1927 by Vincent S. Larkin (December, 1993) Special Collections and University Archives, Rutgers University.

33. For more on the election of Andrew Jackson and the Indian Removal Act (1830), see Nicholas Guyatt, *Bind Us Apart: How Enlightened Americans Invented Racial Segregation* (New York: Basic Books, 2016); Daniel Walker Howe, *What Hath God Wrought: The Transformation of America, 1815–1848* (New York: Oxford University Press, 2010); Anthony F. C. Wallace, *The Long, Bitter Trail: Andrew Jackson and the Indians* (New York: Hill and Wang, 1993).

34. RG 48/A2/01, Box 4, Folder 1 [February 6th, 1829; September 18th, 1829; October 9th, 1829; May 6th, 1831], Inventory to the Records of the Philoclean Society of Rutgers College, 1825-1927 By Vincent S. Larkin (December, 1993) Special Collections and University Archives, Rutgers University.

35. RG 48/A2/01, Box 4, Folder 2 [February 6th, 1835], Inventory to the Records of the Philoclean Society of Rutgers College, 1825-1927 By Vincent S. Larkin (December, 1993) Special Collections and University Archives, Rutgers University.

36. See RG 48/A2/01, Box 5, Folder 1 [October 26th, 1855], Inventory to the Records of the Philoclean Society of Rutgers College, 1825-1927 By Vincent S. Larkin (December, 1993) Special Collections and University Archives, Rutgers University. For more on the history of the Fugitive Slave Law, see R.J.M. Blackett, *The Captive's Quest for Freedom: Fugitive Slaves, the 1850 Fugitive Slave Law, and the Politics of Slavery* (New York: Cambridge University Press, 2018); Angela F. Murphy, *The Jerry Rescue: The Fugitive Slave Law, Northern Rights, and the American Sectional Crisis* (New York: Oxford University Press, 2016); Eric Foner, *Gateway to Freedom: The Hidden History of America's Fugitive Slaves* (New York: W. W. Norton & Company, 2015); Ousmane K. Power-Greene, *Against Wind and Tide: The African American Struggle against the Colonization Movement* (New York: New York University Press, 2014), 95–129.

37. For more on the relationship between Rutgers and the American Colonization Society see Beatrice Adams, Tracey Johnson, Daniel Manuel, and Meagan Wierda, "From the Classroom to the American Colonization Society: Making Race at Rutgers," in *Scarlet and Black: Slavery and Dispossession in Rutgers History*, eds. Marisa J. Fuentes and Deborah Gray White (New Brunswick, NJ: Rutgers University Press, 2016), 123–149. See also Wilder, *Ebony & Ivy*.

38. Beatrice Adams, Tracey Johnson, Daniel Manuel, and Meagan Wierda, "From the Classroom to the American Colonization Society: Making Race at Rutgers," in *Scarlet and Black: Slavery and Dispossession in Rutgers History*, eds. Marisa J. Fuentes and Deborah Gray White (New Brunswick, NJ: Rutgers University Press, 2016), 123–149.

39. Philip Milledoler, *Address, Delivered to the Graduates of Rutgers College: At Commencement Held in the Reformed Dutch Church, New Brunswick, NJ, July 20, 1831* (New York: Rutgers Press, 1831). For more about the ACS, see Ousmane K. Power-Greene, *Against Wind and Tide: The African American Struggle against the Colonization Movement* (New York: New York University Press, 2014); Beverly Tomek, *Colonization and Its Discontents: Emancipation, Emigration, and Antislavery in Antebellum Pennsylvania* (New York: New York University Press, 2011); Eric Burin, *Slavery and the Peculiar*

Solution: A History of the American Colonization Society (Gainesville: University Press of Florida, 2005).

40. "Ultraism," *Rutgers Literary Miscellany* I, no. II (Nov., 1842), 167.

41. Manisha Sinha explores the tensions between slavery's defenders and detractors during the antebellum period in *The Slave's Cause: A History of Abolition* (New Haven, CT: Yale University Press, 2016). For more on amalgamation and anxieties over sex and race in the antebellum North, see Leslie M. Harris, *In the Shadow of Slavery: African Americans in New York City, 1626–1863* (Chicago: University of Chicago Press, 2003), 247–263; Patrick Rael, *Black Identity and Black Protest in the Antebellum North* (Chapel Hill: University of North Carolina Press, 2002), 169–170, 216–217. On the related question of anti-abolitionist riots, see David Grimsted, *American Mobbing, 1828–1861: Toward Civil War* (New York: Oxford University Press, 1998), 3–33; Carl E. Prince, "The Great 'Riot Year': Jacksonian Democracy and Patterns of Violence in 1834," *Journal of the Early Republic* 5, no. I (Spring 1985): 1–19; John Runcie, "'Hunting the Nigs' in Philadelphia: The Race Riot of August 1834," *Pennsylvania History* 39, no. 2 (April 1972): 187–218; Linda K. Kerber, "Abolitionists and Amalgamators: The New York City Race Riots of 1834," *New York History* 48, no. I (January 1967): 28–39. On the Senate "gag rule," see Daniel Wirls, "'The Only Mode of Avoiding Everlasting Debate': The Overlooked Senate Gag Rule for Antislavery Petitions," *Journal of the Early Republic* 27, no. I (Spring 2007): 115–138.

42. Joseph Yannielli explores accusations of insanity levied against abolitionists during the nineteenth century in "George Thompson among the Africans: Empathy, Authority, and Insanity in the Age of Abolition," *Journal of American History* 96, no. 4 (2010): 979–1000. See also John Stauffer, *The Black Hearts of Men: Radical Abolitionists and the Transformation of Race* (Cambridge, MA: Harvard University Press, 2001), 43–44.

43. "Ultraism," *Rutgers Literary Miscellany* I, no. II (November 1842): 167–168; "Prudence," *Rutgers Literary Miscellany* I, no. 6 (June 1842): 91–94.

44. "Old Fogyism," *Rutgers College Quarterly* I, no. 3 (October 1858): 112–115.

45. Blackett, *The Captive's Quest for Freedom*; Murphy, *The Jerry Rescue*; Foner, *Gateway to Freedom*. For more on "Bleeding Kansas" and John Brown, see Kristen Epps, *Slavery on the Periphery: The Kansas-Missouri Border in the Antebellum and Civil War Eras* (Athens: University of Georgia Press, 2016); Nicole Etcheson, *Bleeding Kansas: Contested Liberty in the Civil War Era* (Lawrence: University Press of Kansas, 2004); Stephen B. Oates, *To Purge This Land with Blood: A Biography of John Brown* (Amherst: University of Massachusetts Press, 1970). Regarding the Dred Scott decision, see Sinha, *The Slave's Cause*, 567–574; Kelly M. Kennington, *In the Shadow of Dred Scott: St. Louis Freedom Suits and the Legal Culture of Slavery in the Antebellum Period* (Athens: University of Georgia Press, 2016), 170–174; Paul Finkelman, *Dred Scott v. Sandford: A Brief History with Documents* (Boston: Bedford Books, 1997).

46. William Lloyd Garrison, "The American Union," *The Liberator*, January 10, 1845.

47. William Lloyd Garrison, "Remarks of Mr. Garrison," *The Liberator*, March 12, 1858.

48. "Our Enlightened Age," *Rutgers College Quarterly* 2, no. 4 (April 1860): 160.

49. "A Trip to the Bahamas (concluded.)," *Rutgers College Quarterly* 2, no. 4 (April 1860): 173–174.

50. Ibid.

51. Ibid., 174–175.

52. Ibid., 177.

53. For a very abridged list of works dealing with the history of racial science, see Britt Russert, *Fugitive Science: Empiricism and Freedom in Early African American Culture* (New York: New York University Press, 2017); Ann Fabian, *The Skull Collectors: Race, Science, and America's Unburied Dead* (Chicago: University of Chicago Press, 2010); Colin Kidd, *The Forging of Races: Race and Scripture in the Protestant Atlantic World, 1600–2000* (Cambridge: Cambridge University Press, 2006); Bruce Dain, *A Hideous Monster of the Mind: American Race Theory in the Early Republic* (Cambridge, MA: Harvard University Press, 2002); Mia Bay, *The White Image in the Black Mind: African-American Ideas about White People, 1830–1925* (New York: Oxford University Press, 2000).

54. "A Trip to the Bahamas," 177.

55. "Library Inventory," RG 48/A2/01, Box 13, Folder 4, Special Collections and University Archives, Rutgers University Archives.

56. "Meeting minutes of the Natural History Society," RG 48/B1, Box 1, Folder 3 [March 3rd, 1858 and March 17th, 1858], Special Collections and University Archives, Rutgers University.

57. Timothy J. Williams, *Intellectual Manhood: University, Self, and Society in the Antebellum South* (Chapel Hill: University of North Carolina Press, 2015), 63–64.

58. Theodore Sanford Doolittle, "The College as a Religious Thermometer" [Editorial], *Christian at Work*, February 23, 1888, Box 2, Folder 1, Coll. R-MC 002, Theodore Sanford Doolittle Papers, Special Collections and University Archives, Rutgers University.

59. Ibid.

60. Theodore Sanford Doolittle, "Is the World Growing Better," *Christian at Work*, May 11, 1876, Box 1, Folder 2, T. S. Doolittle Papers.

61. Doolittle, "The College as a Religious Thermometer."

62. Theodore Sanford Doolittle, "The Relation of the Bible to Science" [Editorial], *Christian at Work*, March 15, 1888, Box 2, Folder 1, T. S. Doolittle Papers.

63. Theodore Sanford Doolittle, "The Sunday School: Practical Religion" [Column], *Christian at Work*, August 21, 1879, Box 3, Folder 1, T. S. Doolittle Papers.

64. Theodore Sandford Doolittle, "Fourth of July Reflections" [Editorial], *Christian at Work*, July 3, 1879, Box 1, Folder 2, T. S. Doolittle Papers.

65. Theodore Sandford Doolittle, "The Nation's Birthday," *Christian at Work*, July 5, 1877, Box 1, Folder 1, T. S. Doolittle Papers.

66. Theodore Sanford Doolittle, "Thomas Carlyle: His Character and Work" [Editorial], *Christian at Work*, February 10, 1881, Box 1, Folder 2, T. S. Doolittle Papers.

67. Theodore Sanford Doolittle, A *Sermon Delivered in the First Reformed Dutch Church* (Schenectady, New York: 1866), 15, Box 2, Folder 4, T. S. Doolittle Papers.

68. Ibid., 19.

69. Ibid.

70. Ibid.

71. For data on black population increase between 1850 and 1900 in the entire country, see Claudette E. Bennett, Barbara Martin, and Kymberley DeBarros, *We the Americans: Blacks* (Washington, DC: U.S. Department of Commerce, Economics and Statistics Administration, Bureau of the Census, 1993), 2, https://www.census.gov/prod/cen1990/wepeople/we-1.pdf. For a discussion about the growth of the black population in New Jersey, see Giles Wright, *Afro-Americans in New Jersey: A Short History* (Trenton: New Jersey Historical Commission, 1989), 45–46.

72. While Doolittle is not listed as the author of this article, its location in the archive suggests that he wrote the entry. It appears as a separate document along with his other editorials. See Article, *Christian at Work*, July 12, 1888, Box 2, Folder 1, T. S. Doolittle Papers.

73. Ibid.

74. See Leon Litwack, *Been in the Storm So Long: The Aftermath of Slavery* (New York: Vintage Books, 1980), 462–465; Graham Russell Hodges, *Root and Branch: African Americans in New York and East Jersey, 1613–1863*.(Chapel Hill, NC: University of North Carolina Press).

75. Article, *Christian at Work*, July 12, 1888, Box 2, Folder 1, T. S. Doolittle Papers.

76. Theodore Sanford Doolittle, "Morality Divorced from Religion" [Editorial], *Christian at Work*, November 13, 1890, Box 2, Folder 1, T. S. Doolittle Papers.

77. "A Mystery of New York Law," *Daily Alta California*, August 9, 1879, the California Digital Newspaper Collection, University of California-Riverside, https://cdnc.ucr.edu/cgi-bin/cdnc?a=d&d=DAC18790809.2.28. See also Courtney Thompson, "The Curious Case of Chastine Cox: Murder, Race, Medicine and the Media in the Gilded Age," *Social History of Medicine* (February 2018): 1–21.

78. John Muller, *Frederick Douglass in Washington, D.C.: The Lion of Anacostia* (Charleston, SC: The History Press, 2012).

79. Doolittle, "Morality Divorced from Religion," [Editorial], *Christian at Work*, November 13, 1890, Box 2, Folder 1, T.S. Doolittle Papers.

80. Doolittle was not alone in equating black liturgical styles with uncivilized behavior. See Litwack, *Been in the Storm So Long*, 458–459.

81. Doolittle, "Morality Divorced from Religion," 623.

82. Ibid.

83. Theodore Sanford Doolittle, "Thou Shalt Not Bear False Witness" [Editorial], *Christian at Work*, March 29, 1888, Box 2, Folder 1, T. S. Doolittle Papers.

84. Derek Chang, *Citizens of a Christian Nation: Evangelical Missions and the Problems of Race in the Nineteenth Century* (Philadelphia: University of Pennsylvania Press, 2011), 4.

85. Theodore Sanford Doolittle, "What to Be Thankful For" [Editorial], *Christian at Work*, November 24, 1887, Box 2, Folder 1, T. S. Doolittle Papers.

86. Theodore Sanford Doolittle, "Charles Darwin on Missions" [Editorial], *Christian at Work*, February 7, 1889, Box 2, Folder 2, T. S. Doolittle Papers.

87. Ibid; for Doolittle's use of Stanley, see Doolittle, "The Relation of the Bible to Science."

88. Doolittle, "Charles Darwin on Missions."

89. Muhammad, *The Condemnation of Blackness*, 15–34.

90. Theodore Sanford Doolittle, "The Immigrant Question" [Editorial], *Christian at Work*, August 15, 1887, Box 2, Folder 1, T. S. Doolittle Papers.

91. Ibid.

92. Ibid.

93. Doolittle, "Charles Darwin on Missions."

94. Theodore Sanford Doolittle, "College Students and Church Life" [Editorial], *Christian at Work*, August 15, 1889, Box 2, Folder 2, T. S. Doolittle Papers.

95. Theodore Sanford Doolittle, "A Corean Exile," *Christian at Work*, January 17, 1889, Box 2, Folder 2, T. S. Doolittle Papers.

96. William R. Hutchison, *Errand to the World: American Protestant Thought and Foreign Missions* (Chicago: University of Chicago Press, 1987), 4–5.

97. Wilder, *Ebony & Ivy*, 246–247.

98. John Howard Raven, *Catalogue of the Officers and Alumni of Rutgers College, 1766–1916* (Trenton, NJ: State Gazette Publishing, 1916), 66–309, https://archive.org/details /catalogueofofficoorutgrich. The alumni between 1910 and 1916 show little connection to foreign missions.

99. Ibid., 79, 83, 86; Gerald De Jong, "Mission to Borneo," *The Historical Society of the Reformed Church in America Occasional Papers* 1 (1987): 1–83.

100. Regarding foreign missions of the Reformed Church in America, see Gerald F. De Jong, *The Reformed Church in China: 1842–1951* (Grand Rapids, MI: Eerdmans, 1992); Eugene P. Heideman, *From Mission to Church: The Reformed Church in America Mission to India* (Grand Rapids, MI: Eerdmans, 2001); Gordon M. Laman, *Pioneers to Partners: The Reformed Church in American and Christian Mission with the Japanese* (Grand Rapids, MI: Eerdmans, 2013).

101. Raven, *Catalogue of the Officers and Alumni of Rutgers College*, 106, 107, 109; untitled item in "Scudder, Samuel D., 1847," Rutgers University Biographical Files: Alumni (Classes of 1774–1922), Special Collections and University Archives, Rutgers University Lirbraries; untitled item in "Scudder, Joseph, 1848," Rutgers University Biographical Files: Alumni (Classes of 1774–1922), Special Collections and University Archives, Rutgers University. Their father John Scudder, however, did not study at Rutgers College. Untitled item in "Ray, Charles, 1849," Rutgers University Biographical Files: Alumni (Classes of 1774–1922), Special Collections and University Archives, Rutgers University.

102. Like American Christian missions in general, India and China were the most common destinations among missionaries of Rutgers alumni. In particular, the Scudder and Talmage families had strong ties with India and China, respectively. Regarding Hawai'i, see Alvin Ostrom (class of 1856) and Frank Seymour Scudder (class of 1885). Regarding Japan, see, for instance, James Hamilton Ballagh (class of 1857), Henry Stout (class of 1865), and Eugene Samuel Booth (class of 1876). Regarding Arabia, see Henry Rufus Lankford Worrall (class of 1884) and Frederick Jacob Barny (class of 1894). Regarding British East Africa, see Elwood Linnell Davis (class of 1902) and Theodore Romeyn Westervelt (class of 1909). Their biographical files are available in the Rutgers Special Collections and University Archives. Regarding the seminary, see Coakley, *New Brunswick Theological Seminary*, 44–49.

103. However, through the case of Hawai'i, Joy Schulz emphasizes that the citizenship of white missionary children was ambiguous. Joy Schulz, *Hawaiian by Birth: Missionary Children, Bicultural Identity, and U.S. Colonialism in the Pacific* (Lincoln: University of Nebraska Press, 2017), chap. 5.

104. John Higham, *Strangers in the Land: Patterns of American Nativism, 1860–1925* (New Brunswick, NJ: Rutgers University Press, 1955); Erika Lee, *At America's Gates: Chinese Immigration during the Exclusion Era, 1882–1943* (Chapel Hill: University of North Carolina Press, 2003); Mae M. Ngai, *Impossible Subjects: Illegal Aliens and the Making of Modern America* (Princeton, NJ: Princeton University Press, 2004); Hidetaka Hirota, *Expelling the Poor: Atlantic Seaboard States and the Nineteenth-Century Origins of American Immigration Policy* (Oxford: Oxford University Press, 2017).

105. Recent research juxtaposes US foreign missions with immigration, which are often separated in previous scholarship. See for example, Andrew Urban, "Yun Ch'i-Ho's

Alienation by Way of Inclusion: A Korean International Student and Christian Reform in the 'New' South, 1888–1893," *Journal of Asian American Studies* 17, no. 3 (2014): 305–336.

106. Raven, *Catalogue of the Officers and Alumni of Rutgers College*, 145.

107. Ibid., 336; "Catalogue of the Officers and Students of Rutgers College, at New Brunswick, N.J., 1895–96," n.d., 112, *Rutgers College Catalogue*, Rutgers Special Collections and University Archives.

108. "Catalogue of the Officers and Students of Rutgers College, New Brunswick, N.J., 1876–77," n.d., 42, *Rutgers College Catalogue*, Rutgers Special Collections and University Archives; "Catalogue of the Officers and Students of Rutgers College, at New Brunswick, N.J., 1895–96," 110; "Catalogue of Rutgers College at New Brunswick, N.J., 1899–1900," n.d., 103, *Rutgers College Catalogue*, Rutgers Special Collections and University Archives.

109. John Howard Raven, *Biographical Record: Theological Seminary New Brunswick, 1784–1911* (New Brunswick, NJ, 1912), 229, https://archive.org/details/biographical recoooonewb; Raven, *Catalogue of the Officers and Alumni of Rutgers College* 316. The fact that the same person, Raven, compiled the alumni catalogues of both schools also indicates the affinity between the two.

110. Raven, *Catalogue of the Officers and Alumni of Rutgers College*, 186, 204. In addition to Chamberlain and Scudder, the alumni catalogue tells us that Philip Wilson Pitcher (Van Doren winner of 1885, class of 1882) became the missionary of the Reformed Church in America to China, and Frank Stelle Booth (1900 Van Vechten and 1902 Van Doren winner, class of 1903) was born in Tokyo, Japan, as a missionary son. Their biographical files are available at Rutgers Special Collections and University Archives.

111. "Catalogue of the Officers and Students of Rutgers College, at New Brunswick, N.J., 1895–96," 110.

112. Henry Johnstone Scudder, "Methods of City Missionary Work" (Rutgers College, 1896), Van Doren Prize for Essay on Missions, Rutgers Special Collections and University Archives.

113. These titles of available essays at Rutgers Special Collections may be useful for future researchers. Van Doren Prize: Frederick Joseph Collier, "The Missionary Enterprises the Safeguard of the Church" (c.1878); Isaac William Gowen, "Christian Missions" (c.1879), Edwin Francis See, "Christian Missions" (c.1880); Afel H. Huzinga, "Christian Missions" (c.1881); Daniel Wesley Skellenger, "The Missionary Spirit" (c.1882), George Zarriskie Collier, "Christian Missions" (c.1883); William Paterson Bruce, "Christian Missions" (c.1884); Philip Wilson Pitcher, "The Introduction of Missions in the Fiji Islands" (c.1885); William Isaac Chamberlain, "The Historical Argument for Christian Missions" (c.1886); Thurston Walker Challen, "The Spirit of Missions" (c.1887); Oscar McMurtrie Voorhees, "Foreign Missions" (c.1888); Maurice Joseph Thompson, "Foreign Missions. An Appeal for Immediate Action" (1889); Warren Redcliffe Schenck, "The Speedy Triumph of Missions" (1890); James Westfall Thompson, "The Greatest Thing in the World" (1891); James Westfall Thompson, "The Greatest Thing in the World" (1892); Henry Chales Cussler, "Missions in China" (1893); Herman Charles Weber, "Progress of Home Missions during the Last Twenty Five Years" (1895); Henry Johnstone Scudder, "Methods of City Missionary Work" (1896); Howard Rutsen Furbeck, "Present Methods of Institutions, Maintaining and Conducting Missions" (1899); Henry John Vyverberg, "Past and Present Mission Work among the Freedmen

in the South" (1900); Arthur Perlee Brokaw, "Missions in India during the Reign of Victoria" (1901); Frank Stelle Booth, "The History of Missions in the Hawaiian Islands" (1902); Henry John Vyverberg, "A Conspectus of Missions Maintained at the Present Time throughout the World by Denominations in the United States" (1903); Henry John Vyverberg, "The Missionaries in China during the Boxer Rebellion" (1904); J. Harvey Murphy, "The Work of the Society for the Propagation of the Gospel in the American Colonies of Great Britain" (1906); Royal Arthur Stout, "Self-Support of the Christian Church in Foreign Lands" (1907); Andrew Hansen, "Bearing of Foreign Missions on International Relations" (1909); Royal Arthur Stout, "Protestant Missions in Persia" (1910); Seymour Parker Gilbert Jr., "William Carey: His Life, Work and Results" (1911); George Edward Hagemann, "Industrial Education in Foreign Missions" (1912); Levi Simmons Ernst, "Protestant Missions among Mohammedans" (1913); Levi Simmons Ernst, "The Unoccupied Mission Fields of the World" (1914). Van Vechten Prize: John Mitchell Allen, "Foreign Missions of the Reformed (Dutch) Church in America" (1885); Asa Wynkoop, "Foreign Mission Analysis" (1886); Giles Herbert Sharpley, "Africa as a Mission Field" (1887); Oscar McMurtrie Voorhees, "Foreign Missions: Their Recent Progress and Our Attendant Responsibility" (1888); Harold Diossy Force, "Foreign Missions; Their Growth and Results" (1889); James Harvey Keeling, "Christian Missions in India" (1889); Warren Redcliffe Schenck, "Two Phases of Missions" (1890); Charles Edward Corwin, "Modern Missions, a Revival of the Apostolic Spirit" (1891); Charles Edward Corwin, "The Unseen Power Working for Missions" (1892); Ellis Robert Woodruff, "The Prospects of Christianity among the Mohammedans" (1893); John Henry Thompson, "The Theory of Education in Foreign Missions" (1894); Herman Carl Weber, "Industrial Missions and the Self-Supporting Theory" (1895); James Macdonald Martin, "The Service Rendered to the World" (1896); William Reese Hart, "The Americans. Their Church; History; and the Missionary Work Done among Them" (1897); Charles Frederick Benjamin Jr., "The Present State of Mission Work in Africa" (1898); Henry John Vyverberg, "Civilization and Missions" (1899); Frank Stelle Booth, "Education as a Missionary Agency in India" (1900); Henry John Vyverberg, "The Secular Results of Foreign Missions" (1901); Frederic Elmer Foertner, "Protestant Missions in Alaska" (1902); Simon Blocker, "The Change Wrought in Japan by Christianity" (1903); Simon Blocker, "Modern Missionary Methods Compared with Mediaeval and Apostolic" (1904); Simon Blocker, "Missions in the Philippines since the American Occupation" (1905); J. Harvey Murphy, "Moravian Missions in the Eighteenth and Twentieth Centuries" (1906); Samuel Arthur Devan, "Moravian Missions in the Eighteenth and Twentieth Centuries" (1906); Andrew Hansen, "A History of Medical Missions" (1907); Andrew Hansen, "The Elements of Foreign Missions in the Development of Japan" (1908); William Abel Rogniat Russum, "Foreign Missions and the Awakening of China" (1909); Seymour Parker Gilbert Jr., "The Influence of Christian Missions in Turkey" (1910); Seymour Parker Gilbert Jr., "The Great Missionary Councils" (1911); George Edward Hagemann, "Missionary Work in the Philippines" (1912); David Bevier Van Dyck, "Korean Christianity" (1913); George Henry Whisler, "The Present and Future of Islam" (1914). Despite such varieties of subjects, essays on missionaries to American Indians and people in Latin America are absent.

114.	There is a growing body of scholarship on Christian foreign missions along with U.S. empire—for instance, Ian R. Tyrrell, *Reforming the World: The Creation of America's Moral Empire* (Princeton, NJ: Princeton University Press, 2010); Emily Conroy-Krutz, *Christian Imperialism: Converting the World in the Early American Republic* (Ithaca, NY: Cornell University Press, 2015); Barbara Reeves-Ellington, Kathryn Kish Sklar, and

Connie Anne Shemo, eds., *Competing Kingdoms: Women, Mission, Nation, and the American Protestant Empire, 1812–1960* (Durham, NC: Duke University Press, 2010).

115. Daniel T. Rodgers, "American Exceptionalism Revisited," *Raritan* 24, no. 3 (2004): 23; Nikhil Pal Singh, *Black Is a Country: Race and the Unfinished Struggle for Democracy* (Cambridge, MA: Harvard University Press, 2004), 17–18.

116. Thomas Bender, *A Nation Among Nations: America's Place in World History* (New York: Hill and Wang, 2006), chap. 4; Paul A. Kramer, "Power and Connection: Imperial Histories of the United States in the World," *The American Historical Review* 116, no. 5 (2011): 1348–1391.

117. The Anti-Imperialist League, whose membership was dominated by white Protestant professional men, idealized the Founding Fathers, who we know today as slave owners. Kristin L. Hoganson, *Fighting for American Manhood: How Gender Politics Provoked the Spanish-American and Philippine-American Wars* (New Haven, CT: Yale University Press, 1998), 156.

118. On U.S. Christian missions in the Philippines, see Kenton Clymer, *Protestant Missionaries in the Philippines, 1898–1916: An Inquiry into the American Colonial Mentality* (Urbana: University of Illinois Press, 1986).

119. George Edward Hagemann, "Missionary Work in the Philippines" (Rutgers College, 1912), Van Vechten Prize Essay on Christian Missions, Special Collections and University Archives, Rutgers University. These essays are handwritten and the page numbers are unavailable.

120. Paul A. Kramer, *The Blood of Government: Race, Empire, the United States, and the Philippines* (Chapel Hill: University of North Carolina Press, 2006), chap. 2.

121. Simon Blocker, "Missions in the Philippines since the American Occupation" (Rutgers College, 1905), Van Vechten Prize Essay on Christian Missions, Rutgers Special Collections and University Archives.

122. Ibid.

123. On Alaskan history in relation to U.S. empire, see Robert Campbell, *In Darkest Alaska: Travel and Empire along the Inside Passage* (Philadelphia: University of Pennsylvania Press, 2008); Anthony Urvina and Sally Urvina, *More Than God Demands: Politics and Influence of Christian Missions in Northwest Alaska, 1897–1918* (Fairbanks: University of Alaska Press, 2016).

124. Frederic Elmer Foertner, "Protestant Missions in Alaska" (Rutgers College, 1902), Van Vechten Prize Essay on Christian Missions, Rutgers Special Collections and University Archives.

125. While climatic determinism can be traced back to Aristotle, scholars have paid attention to several modern moments in which such scientific knowledge became authoritative, including the Enlightenment and the rise of anthropology, tropical medicine, and climatology. See David N. Livingstone, "Race, Space and Moral Climatology: Notes toward a Genealogy," *Journal of Historical Geography* 28, no. 2 (2002): 159–180; Mike Hulme, "Reducing the Future to Climate: A Story of Climate Determinism and Reductionism," *Osiris* 26, no. 1 (2011): 245–266.

126. Foertner, "Protestant Missions in Alaska."

127. Frank Stelle Booth, "The History of Missions in the Hawaiian Islands" (Rutgers College, 1902), Van Doren Prize for Essay on Missions, Rutgers Special Collections and University Archives.

128. Booth, "The History of Missions in the Hawaiian Islands."

129. Schulz, *Hawaiian by Birth*; Sally Engle Merry, *Colonizing Hawai'i: The Cultural Power of Law* (Princeton, NJ: Princeton University Press, 2000); Jennifer Fish Kashay, "Agents of Imperialism: Missionaries and Merchants in Early-Nineteenth-Century Hawaii," *The New England Quarterly* 80, no. 2 (2007): 280–298. Thomas Lafon Gulick (class of 1865) had a missionary father, Peter Johnson Gulick, and attended foreign missions in Spain and British East Africa. His brother John Thomas Gulick is well known for his evolution theory and missionary service in Hawai'i. "Material or General Catalogue of Rutgers University," in "Gulick, Thomas L., 1865," Rutgers University Biographical Files: Alumni (Classes of 1774–1922), Rutgers Special Collections and University Archives. Raven, *Catalogue of the Officers and Alumni of Rutgers College*, 142.

130. Natalie J. Ring, *The Problem South: Region, Empire, and the New Liberal State, 1880–1930* (Athens: University of Georgia Press, 2012).

131. Henry John Vyverberg, "Past and Present Mission Work among the Freedmen in the South" (Rutgers College, 1900), Van Doren Prize for Essay on Missions, Rutgers Special Collections and University Archives.

132. Untitled item in "Vyverberg, Henry J., 1901," Rutgers University Biographical Files: Alumni (Classes of 1774–1922), Rutgers Special Collections and University Archives.

133. Vyverberg, "Past and Present Mission Work among the Freedmen in the South." While mentioning their paternalism and racial prejudice, Joe M. Richardson asserts that the American Missionary Association, one of the major Christian missionary organizations for freedmen in the South, supported black suffrage. Joe Martin Richardson, *Christian Reconstruction: The American Missionary Association and Southern Blacks, 1861–1890* (Athens: University of Georgia Press, 1986).

134. Vyverberg, "Past and Present Mission Work among the Freedmen in the South."

135. Ibid.

136. On the reciprocal process of modernization between metropole and colony, see Alfred W. McCoy and Francisco A. Scarano, eds., *Colonial Crucible: Empire in the Making of the Modern American State* (Madison: University of Wisconsin Press, 2009); Ann Laura Stoler and Frederick Cooper, "Between Metropole and Colony: Rethinking a Research Agenda," in *Tensions of Empire: Colonial Cultures in a Bourgeois World*, ed. Frederick Cooper and Ann Laura Stoler (Berkeley: University of California Press, 1997), 1–56.

137. One of the Christian rescue embodiments was the removal of Native American children from their families to boarding schools. Scholars have discussed the implementation of this assimilation policy, its catastrophic impacts on indigenous communities, and their contestations. See David Wallace Adams, *Education for Extinction: American Indians and the Boarding School Experience, 1875–1928* (Lawrence: University Press of Kansas, 1995); Brenda J. Child, *Boarding School Seasons: American Indian Families, 1900–1940* (Lincoln: University of Nebraska Press, 1998); Ward Churchill, *Kill the Indian, Save the Man: The Genocidal Impact of American Indian Residential Schools* (San Francisco: City Lights, 2004).

CHAPTER 2: In the Shadow of Old Queens

1. Thomas J. Frusciano, "From 'Seminary of Learning' to Public Research University: A Historical Sketch of Rutgers," https://www.libraries.rutgers.edu/scua/rutgers-historical-sketch, Special Collections and University Archives, Rutgers University.

2. Shaun Armstead, Brenann Sutter, Pamela Walker, and Caitlin Wiesner, "'And I Poor Slave Yet': The Precarity of Black Life in New Brunswick, 1766–1835," in *Scarlet and Black: Slavery and Dispossession in Rutgers History*, ed. Marisa J. Fuentes and Deborah Gray White (New Brunswick, NJ: Rutgers University Press, 2016), 98.

3. David Listokin, Dorothea Berkhout, and James W. Hughes, *New Brunswick, New Jersey: The Decline and Revitalization of Urban America* (New Brunswick, NJ: Rutgers University Press, 2016), 54.

4. State of New Jersey, "New Jersey State Population Trends, 1790–2000," New Jersey State Data Center, http://www.state.nj.us/labor/lpa/census/2kpub/njsdcp3.pdf.

5. Ibid.

6. Armstead, Sutter, Walker, and Wiesner, "And I Poor Slave Yet," 91.

7. See Bureau of the Census, Department of Commerce, *Tenth United States Federal Census* (1880): Middlesex County, New Brunswick, New Jersey; Bureau of the Census, Department of Commerce, *Eleventh United States Federal Census* (1890): Middlesex County, New Brunswick, New Jersey; Bureau of the Census, Department of Commerce, *Twelfth United States Federal Census* (1900): Middlesex County, New Brunswick, New Jersey; Bureau of the Census, Department of Commerce, *Thirteenth United States Federal Census* (1910): Middlesex County, New Brunswick, New Jersey; Bureau of the Census, Department of Commerce, *Fourteenth United States Federal Census* (1920): Middlesex County, New Brunswick, New Jersey, all available via Ancestry.com.

8. Darlene Clark Hine, "Black Migration to the Urban Midwest: The Gender Dimension," in *The Great Migration in Historical Perspective: New Dimensions of Race, Class and Gender*, ed. Joe Trotter (Bloomington: Indiana University Press, 1991), 127.

9. James P. Hackett, *The New Jersey Citizen* (New Brunswick, NJ: Rutgers University Press, 1957), 23.

10. New Jersey Section of the 1850 Census, Bureau of the Census, Department of Commerce, *Seventh Census of the United States* (1850), 136 and 139, https://www2.census.gov/library/publications/decennial/1850/1850a/1850a-23.pdf?#. Accessed 9/18/18.

11. L. A. Greene, "A History of Afro-Americans in New Jersey," *Journal of the Rutgers University Libraries* 56, no. 1 (1994): 33.

12. Listokin, Berkhout, and Hughes, *New Brunswick, New Jersey*, 57.

13. "The Colored Voters," *New Brunswick Daily Times*, July 30, 1872.

14. Marion Manola (Thompson) Wright, *The Education of Negroes in New Jersey* (American Education: Its Men, Ideas, and Institutions II) (New York: Bureau of Publications, Teachers College, Columbia University, 1941), 114–115.

15. *New Brunswick Directory 1855*, 30, Rutgers Special Collections and University Archives.

16. Ibid.

17. Ibid.

18. Ibid.

19. Public school education in New Jersey during this time period was a three-tiered system of primary, grammar, and high school, where primary provided a basic foundation, while grammar and high school provided more advanced study. See Donald Raichle, "Stephen Congar and the Establishment of the Newark Public School System," *The Journal of the Rutgers University Libraries* 38, no. 2 (1976): 66–67.

20. The French Street Building remained in use until it was demolished in 1899. See *The City of New Brunswick; Its History, Its Homes & Its Industries* (The Times Publishing Company, 1908), 60; *New Brunswick Directory 1893*, 1893, Rutgers Special Collections and University Archives.

21. S. E. Weir Jr., *Map of the City of New Brunswick*, 200 to an inch (W. C. Dripps, 1877).

22. Wright, *The Education of Negroes in New Jersey*, 161–162.

23. Ibid.

24. Armstead, Sutter, Walker, and Wiesner, "And I Poor Slave Yet," 99.

25. "Cream Ridge in Changing Color," *New Brunswick Times*, March 11, 1911, 3.

26. Charles D. Deshler, "The Vanished Things of My Time, Part II" (New Brunswick Historical Club, January 15, 1903), 19–20, Rutgers Special Collections and University Archives.

27. *New Brunswick Directory 1865–66*, Rutgers Special Collections and University Archives.

28. *New Brunswick Directory 1872–73*, Rutgers Special Collections and University Archives; *New Brunswick Directory 1883–84*, Rutgers Special Collections and University Archives.

29. Brian P. Luskey, "Special Marts: Intelligence Offices, Labor Commodification, and Emancipation in Nineteenth-Century America," *The Journal of the Civil War Era* 3, no. 3 (2013): 360–361, https://doi.org/10.1353/cwe.2013.0046; *New Brunswick Directory: 1883–84*, Rutgers Special Collections and University Archives.

30. John P. Wall and Harold E. Pickersgill, *History of Middlesex County, New Jersey, 1664–1920*, vol. 1 (Lewis Historical Publishing Company, 1921), 287.

31. Vivian Neal Stewart, "The Black Community," in *The Tercentennial Lectures, New Brunswick, New Jersey*, ed. Ruth Marcus Platt (New Brunswick, NJ: The City of New Brunswick, 1982), 78. Created in May 1915 by naval architect, engineer, and Tammany Hall affiliate Lewis Nixon, the Nixon Nitration Plant produced some 2,000 million pounds of smokeless powder for the United States and its allies during World War I. The Nixon Plant experienced frequent labor strikes during the war years, and in March 1924, a massive explosion felt as far away as Staten Island claimed the lives of some twenty persons; see "Fertilizer Plant Blows Up," *New York Times*, March 2, 1924; "Nixon, New Jersey, Nitration Works Disaster," in Disasters and Tragic Events, *An Encyclopedia of Catastrophes in American History*, ed. Kelley Newton-Matza (Santa Barbara, CA: ABC-CLIO, 2014), 271–273.

32. Bureau of the Census, Department of Commerce, *Fourteenth United States Federal Census* (1920): "Rodgers C. Birt, Sr.," New Jersey, Middlesex County, https://www.ancestry.com/interactive/6061/4384841_00987/71319882?backurl=https://www.ancestry.com/family-tree/person/tree/104885793/person/190042330789/facts#?imageId=4384841_00986.

33. Joe William Trotter Jr., "The Great Migration," *OAH Magazine* 17, no. 1 (2002): 31.

34. According to the 1930 U.S. Federal Census, Pelton Swann (see also Suan) lived at 27 Lorane Street in New Brunswick's 6th Ward. Born circa 1888 in Maryland, Swann's occupation is listed as "laborer for roads state," suggesting that he likely still worked as a driver for Johnson & Johnson or in some other capacity as a driver. See Bureau of the Census, Department of Commerce, *Fifteenth Census of the United States* (1930): "Pelton Swann," Middlesex County, New Brunswick, New Jersey; Stewart, "The Black Community," 78.

35. Armstead, Sutter, Walker, and Wiesner, "And I Poor Slave Yet," 110.

36. "WANTED: TWO COLORED GIRLS," *New Brunswick Daily Home News*, April 5, 1887.

37. For more on African American women's devalued domestic labor after emancipation, see Leslie Harris, *In the Shadow of Slavery: African Americans in New York, 1626–1863* (Chicago: University of Chicago Press, 2003); Erica Armstrong Dunbar, *A Fragile Freedom: African American Women and Emancipation in the Antebellum City* (New Haven, CT: Yale University Press, 2008); Seth Rockman, *Scraping By: Wage Labor, Slavery, and Survival in Early Baltimore* (Baltimore: Johns Hopkins University Press, 2009); Enobong Hannah Branch, *Opportunity Denied: Limiting Black Women to Devalued Work* (New Brunswick, NJ: Rutgers University Press, 2011).

38. "WANTED: TWO COLORED GIRLS," *New Brunswick Daily Home News*, April 5, 1887; "WANTED: COLORED WAITER," *New Brunswick Daily Home News*, June 14, 1887; "WANTED: A WOMAN COLORED PREFERED," *New Brunswick Daily Home News*, March 24, 1887; "WANTED: A LAUNDRESS TO ASSIST IN KITCHEN," *New Brunswick Daily Home News*, July 11, 1887.

39. "CRIMINALS IN COURT: IGNORANT ITALIANS AND A MORE IGNORANT NEGRESS," *New Brunswick Daily Home News*, August 17, 1887. The juxtaposition of Italian immigrants and an African American woman in the title of this article reveals the fluidity of racial categorization in the late-nineteenth- and early-twentieth-century United States. At that time, immigrants from Southern and Eastern Europe (including Italians) were not considered white. Like African Americans, these groups were racialized as inherently ignorant and criminal. Italians and other European immigrants would gradually be accepted as white by the 1930s and lose their association with rampant criminality. For more on the changing ideas of race and criminality in the early-twentieth-century United States, see Khalil Gibran Muhammad, *The Condemnation of Blackness: Race, Crime and the Making of Modern Urban America* (Cambridge, MA: Harvard University Press, 2011).

40. Ibid.

41. "Robbery in Rutgers Dormitory," *New York Times*, April 15, 1894.

42. Ibid.

43. Kali Gross, *Colored Amazons: Crime, Violence, and Black Women in the City of Brotherly Love* (Durham, NC: Duke University Press, 2006).

44. Isabel Wilkerson, *The Warmth of Other Suns: The Epic Story of America's Great Migration* (New York: Random House, 2010).

45. Litsokin, Berkhout, and Hughes, *New Brunswick, New Jersey*, 56–59.

46. "Help Wanted," *New Brunswick Daily Home News*, April 11, 1916.

47. "The Irresponsible Character," *New Brunswick Daily Home News*, December 18, 1893.

48. Ibid.

49. "Southern Colored Help Furnished," *New Brunswick Daily Home News*, May 19, 1903.

50. Litsokin, Berkhout, and Hughes, *New Brunswick, New Jersey*, 53.

51. Branch, *Opportunity Denied*, 59.

52. "SITUATION WANTED: MALE, YOUNG MAN (colored)" *New Brunswick Daily Home News*, March 9, 1904.

53. Litsokin, Berkhout, and Hughes, *New Brunswick, New Jersey*, 45–46.

54. "WANTED Chambermaid or Waitress, White or Colored," *New Brunswick Daily Home News*, February 2, 1903; "WANTED: White Girl for General Housework," *New*

Brunswick Daily Home News, February 4, 1903; "WANTED: Girl for General Housework, German or Hungarian Prefered," *New Brunswick Daily Home News*, February 23, 1903; "WANTED Competent Waitress or chambermaid, colored preferred," *New Brunswick Daily Home News*, March 24, 1903, "WANTED, in small family cook and laundress, must be white," *New Brunswick Daily Home News*, April 11, 1903; "WANTED competent cook, white," *New Brunswick Daily Home News*, May 1, 1903; "WANTED Good cook, white or colored," *New Brunswick Daily Home News*, June 29, 1903; "WANTED Girl for general housework, white or colored," *New Brunswick Daily Home News*, July 1, 1903; "WANTED young white girl as waitress," *New Brunswick Daily Home News*, September 14, 1903.

55. Kathy Peiss, *Cheap Amusements: Working Women and Leisure in Turn-of-the-Century New York* (Philadelphia: Temple University Press, 1986).

56. "How Girls Make Money," *New Brunswick Daily Home News*, January 14, 1903.

57. Ibid.

58. "Maid and Mistress Freed in Plot," *Baltimore Afro-American*, October 29, 1927, 2.

59. Litsokin, Berkhout, and Hughes, *New Brunswick, New Jersey*, 58–59.

60. "Southern Colored Help Furnished," *New Brunswick Daily Home News*, May 5, 1911.

61. Litsokin, Berkhout, and Hughes, *New Brunswick, New Jersey*, 52.

62. "WANTED At Wells General Hospital Colored Maids," *New Brunswick Daily Home News*, April 1, 1911; "WANTED A white woman to work by day," *New Brunswick Daily Home News*, May 19, 1911; "WANTED small girl colored preferred," *New Brunswick Daily Home News*, July 10, 1911; "WANTED a young girl to help with light housework white preferred," *New Brunswick Daily Home News*, August 18, 1911; "WANTED an experienced girl white or colored," *New Brunswick Daily Home News*, September 13, 1911; "WANTED Strong capable colored woman," *New Brunswick Daily Home News*, October 17, 1911; "WANTED white woman as laundress," *New Brunswick Daily Home News*, November 2, 1911; "WANTED White woman to do laundry," *New Brunswick Daily Home News*, November 21, 1911.

63. Branch, *Opportunity Denied*, 56–57. For more on immigrant women's transition from domestic service to factory employment in the early twentieth century, see Alice Kessler Harris, *Out to Work: A History of Wage Earning Women* (New York: Oxford University Press, 1982); Peiss, *Cheap Amusements*; Premilla Nadasen, *Household Workers Unit: The Untold Story of African American Women Who Built a Movement* (Boston: Beacon Press, 2015).

64. "WANTED: Colored woman desiring face bleach," *New Brunswick Daily Home News*, December 12, 1908.

65. Tiffany Gill, *Beauty Shop Politics: African American Women's Activism in the Beauty Industry* (Urbana: University of Illinois Press, 2010), 18.

66. "WANTED Colored girl for general housework," *New Brunswick Daily Home News*, October 31, 1913; "WANTED at Wells Hospital competent colored maid," *New Brunswick Daily Home News*, April 11, 1911.

67. Jacqueline Jones, *Labor of Love, Labor of Sorrow: Black Women, Work, and the Family from Slavery to the Present*, rev. ed. (New York: Basic Books, 2010), 142.

68. "Colored Women to Do Track Work on Pennsy Railroad," *New Brunswick Daily Home News*, August 27, 1918.

69. Jones, *Labor of Love, Labor of Sorrow*, 144.

70. Ibid., 145.

71. "Situation Wanted," *New Brunswick Daily Home News*, January 21, 1918.

72. " WANTED woman to wash on Monday, preferred white," *New Brunswick Daily Home News*, January 3, 1918; "WANTED two colored girls at once," *New Brunswick Daily Home News*, January 5, 1918; "WANTED Maid for housework, white or colored," *New Brunswick Daily Home News*, January 12, 1918; "WANTED White woman as cook and laundress," *New Brunswick Daily Home News*, October 4, 1918; WANTED COLORED GIRL FOR LAUNDRY WORK, *New Brunswick Daily Home News*, October 24, 1918; "FEMALE Help wanted (two) white or colored," *New Brunswick Daily Home News*, October 30, 1918.

73. Cynthia M. Blair, *I've Got to Make My Livin': Black Women's Sex Work in Turn-of-the-Century Chicago* (Chicago: University of Chicago Press, 2010), 3.

74. "Thirty-Two Caught in Raid on Bellmore Hotel: Police Found Flourishing Business Going On and Soon Had All the Cells at the Lock-Up Filled with Prisoners—Several Women in the Party," *New Brunswick Times*, September 19, 1920, 1, 5.

75. Ruth Rosen, *The Lost Sisterhood: Prostitution in America, 1900–1918* (Baltimore: Johns Hopkins University Press, 1982), 4.

76. "Thirty-Two Caught in Raid on Bellmore Hotel," 1, 5.

77. "Arrests Made to Promote Public Health," *New Brunswick Daily Home News*, September 16, 1918, 4.

78. "WANTED Competent laundress, white or colored," *New Brunswick Daily Home News*, January 30, 1919; WANTED White girl for general housework," *New Brunswick Daily Home News*, February 1, 1919; "WANTED White girl to work in lunchroom," *New Brunswick Daily Home News*, March 13, 1919; "WANTED A white woman part of every day," *New Brunswick Daily Home News*, April 15, 1919; "WANTED White woman for cleaning," *New Brunswick Daily Home News*, August 14, 1919; "WANTED a competent waitress or chambermaid (white)," *New Brunswick Daily Home News*, September 4, 1919; "WANTED White waitress," *New Brunswick Daily Home News*, October 30, 1919; "WANTED Clean white girl to assist in housework," *New Brunswick Daily Home News*, March 30, 1920; "WANTED A good cook (white)," *New Brunswick Daily Home News*, May 29, 1920; "WANTED White girl for housework," *New Brunswick Daily Home News*, September 27, 1920; "WANTED a competent cook (white), *New Brunswick Daily Home News*, October 2, 1920; "WANTED white girl for general housework," *New Brunswick Daily Home News*, December 16, 1920; "WANTED White cook," *New Brunswick Daily Home News*, April 16, 1921; "WANTED Middleaged colored woman," *New Brunswick Daily Home News*, May 10, 1921; "WANTED White girl for general housework," *New Brunswick Daily Home News*, June 4, 1921; "WANTED competent white cook," *New Brunswick Daily Home News*, December 23, 1921; "GIRL (white) wanted," *New Brunswick Daily Home News*, January 5, 1922; "MAID (white) wanted," *New Brunswick Daily Home News*, March 8, 1922; "COLORED GIRL wanted to do laundry," *New Brunswick Daily Home News*, June 10, 1922; "WHITE girl wanted," *New Brunswick Daily Home News*, September 1, 1922; "WHITE girl wanted," *New Brunswick Daily Home News*, December 5, 1922; "WANTED Neat white laundress," *New Brunswick Daily Home News*, March 1, 1923;"WHITE girl for general housework," *New Brunswick Daily Home News*, January 4, 1924; "YOUNG girl wanted (white)," *New Brunswick Daily Home News*, March 14, 1924; "WHITE woman wanted," *New Brunswick Daily Home News*, August 30, 1924; "WHITE girl as cook," *New Brunswick Daily Home News*, October 30, 1924; "GENERAL houseworker, white or colored," *New Brunswick Daily Home News*, March 6, 1925; "WHITE

girl as cook," *New Brunswick Daily Home News*, May 6, 1925; "REFINED colored girl to wait tables," *New Brunswick Daily Home News*, December 9, 1925; "WHITE woman to wash dishes," *New Brunswick Daily Home News*, January 13, 1926; "WHITE woman as plain cook," *New Brunswick Daily Home News*, August 13, 1926; "GIRL for general housework, white," *New Brunswick Daily Home News*, October 1, 1926; "WANTED Two white girls," *New Brunswick Daily Home News*, March 10, 1927; "WANTED white girl for general housework," *New Brunswick Daily Home News*, July 1, 1927; "WHITE maid wanted," *New Brunswick Daily Home News*, November 22, 1927; "WHITE girl wanted for general housework," *New Brunswick Daily Home News*, February 23, 1928; "WHITE girl for general housework," *New Brunswick Daily Home News*, April 26, 1928; "WANTED experienced white girl," *New Brunswick Daily Home News*, August 17, 1928; "WHITE maid for general housework," *New Brunswick Daily Home News*, December 5, 1928; "TWO white girls," *New Brunswick Daily Home News*, May 1, 1929; "WHITE girl, general housework and cooking," *New Brunswick Daily Home News*, September 5, 1929; "CONFIDENT white girl for general housework," *New Brunswick Daily Home News*, January 3, 1930; "WANTED colored woman," *New Brunswick Daily Home News*, July 5, 1930; "EXPERIENCED shirt ironer wanted, white or colored," *New Brunswick Daily Home News*, December 4, 1930; "COLORED girl or woman, live in," *New Brunswick Daily Home News*, May 1, 1931; "WHITE girl wanted for general housework," *New Brunswick Daily Home News*, September 2, 1931; "MAID white or colored, live in," *New Brunswick Daily Home News*, October 17, 1931; "EXPERIENCED young white woman," *New Brunswick Daily Home News*, January 4, 1931; "WHITE girl, housework," *New Brunswick Daily Home News*, May 8, 1932; "WHITE girl assist," *New Brunswick Daily Home News*, June 3, 1932.

79. Litsokin, Berkhout, and Hughes, *New Brunswick, New Jersey*, 53.

80. Ibid.

81. Mae Ngai, *Impossible Subjects: Illegal Aliens and the Making of Modern America* (Princeton, NJ: Princeton University Press, 2014), 3.

82. "PRESSERS wanted, colored girls," *New Brunswick Daily Home News*, September 22, 1926.

83. "COLORED girls wanted as pressers," *New Brunswick Daily Home News*, February 23, 1928.

84. "WANTED Reliable man as janitor," *New Brunswick Daily Home News*, September 27, 1920.

85. "WANTED At Women's College," *New Brunswick Daily Home News*, December 7, 1920.

86. "WANTED woman to clean at fraternity house," *New Brunswick Daily Home News*, March 13, 1919.

87. "WANTED Cook for fraternity house," *New Brunswick Daily Home News*, October 2, 1920; "WANTED Reliable cook for college fraternity," *New Brunswick Daily Home News*, October 2, 1920; "WANTED waitresses for college dining hall," *New Brunswick Daily Home News*, September 22, 1926.

88. "WANTED Strong white woman," *New Brunswick Daily Home News*, March 27, 1923.

89. "WANTED Competent white girl," *New Brunswick Daily Home News*, August 21, 1924.

90. "COLORED girl desires position," *New Brunswick Daily Home News*, March 2, 1928; "WANTED by reliable colored girl," *New Brunswick Daily Home News*, February 1, 1926; "EXPERIENCED cook, colored," *New Brunswick Daily Home News*, February 4, 1924.

91. "EXPERIENCED Cook, colored," *New Brunswick Daily Home News*, February 4, 1924; "COLORED girl desires position as chambermaid," *New Brunswick Daily Home News*, March 2, 1928; "COLORED woman desires laundry work," *New Brunswick Daily Home News*, April 8, 1927.

92. For more on specializing domestic labor as a strategy for black women's resistance, see Tera Hunter, *To 'Joy My Freedom: Southern Black Women's Lives and Labors after the Civil War* (Cambridge, MA: Harvard University Press, 1997); Leslie Schwalm, *A Hard Fight for We: Women's Transition from Slavery to Freedom in South Carolina* (Urbana: University of Illinois Press, 1997); Thavolia Glymph, *Out of the House of Bondage: The Transformation of the Plantation Household* (New York: Cambridge University Press, 2003).

93. "COLORED girl wishes housework," *New Brunswick Daily Home News*, December 19, 1930.

94. "COLORED woman wishes part-time work," *New Brunswick Daily Home News*, February 21, 1932; "COLORED woman wants part time or day's work," *New Brunswick Daily Home News*, May 1, 1931; "WOMAN colored desires position," *New Brunswick Daily Home News*, August 4, 1928.

95. "COLORED woman wishes fine dry washes at home," *New Brunswick Daily Home News*, September 22, 1929; "COLORED woman desires washing or ironing at home," *New Brunswick Daily Home News*, November 22, 1927; "WOMAN colored will do bundle washing," *New Brunswick Daily Home News*, February 11, 1924.

96. Jones, *Labor of Love, Labor of Sorrow*, 143.

97. "WOMAN, colored wanted housework," *New Brunswick Daily Home News*, January 2, 1930.

98. Martin Summers, *Manliness and Its Discontents: The Black Middle Class and the Transformation of Masculinity, 1900–1930* (Chapel Hill: University of North Carolina Press, 2004), 26.

99. "Samaritans in Session," *Daily Times*, June 4, 1885, 3.

100. Mildred L. Rice Jordan, *Reclaiming African American Students: Legacies, Lessons, and Prescriptions: The Bordentown School Model* (Bloomington, IN: iUniverse, 2017), 82–83.

101. *A Place Out of Time: The Bordentown School*, directed by Dave Davidson (2010; United States: Hudson West Productions, 2009), DVD.

102. Ibid.

103. "Steal Smothered: Middlesex to Keep Its Territory—Highland Park Borough Bill Lost—Legislature Adjourns," *Daily Times*, March 26, 1898; "Board of Education," *Daily Times*, November 3, 1898; "Died of Paralysis: Rev. Walter A. S. Rice Passes Away after Short Illness," *Daily Times*, January 5, 1899, 1.

104. "Where Help May Be Obtained," *Daily Times*, November 11, 1898, 7.

105. *A Place Out of Time: The Bordentown School*, directed by Dave Davidson.

106. Thomas Jesse Jones, ed., *Negro Education: A Study of the Private and Higher Schools for Colored People in the United States*, 2 vols. (U.S. Department of the Interior, Bureau of Education, Bulletin 1916, No. 38) (Washington, DC: Government Printing Office, 1917), 695. Unfortunately, exigent records only suggest the name of one possible part-time instructor, Ira L. Vanderveer, a black engineering student in the class of 1924. Rutgers University, *Annual Catalogue, 1920–1921* (New Brunswick, NJ: Rutgers University Press), 264.

107. "Rice School Accomplishing a Big Work: Little School on Comstock Street Is a Great Power for Good—Will Have Donation Day There Wednesday, May 28," *New Brunswick Daily Home News*, May 22, 1913, 8.

108. "Think Boy, Alarmed, Ran Away: Fire Reported to Have Been Started by Upsetting of Oil Stove," *New Brunswick Daily Home News*, October 3, 1925, 1.

109. "Xmas for Colored Industrial Home," *New Brunswick Daily Home News*, December 19, 1918, 3.

110. "Colored School's Annual Report: Annual Meeting of the Trustees of the Rice Industrial and Literary Institute," *Daily Times*, July 14, 1906, 4.

111. Ibid., 4; "Notice of Sale of Lands for Unpaid Taxes of 1908," *New Brunswick Daily Home News*, September 11, 1909, 8; "Notice of Sale of Lands for Unpaid Taxes 1916," *New Brunswick Daily Home News*, October 20, 1917, 10.

112. "Rice Institute Commencement Thursday Night," *New Brunswick Daily Home News*, June 25, 1912, 2.

113. "Industrial School Closes: Pleasing Exercises Held in Mt. Zion A. M. E. Church," *Daily Times*, June 22, 1900, 2; "Industrial School Concert," *Daily Times*, October 9, 1897.

114. Jones, *Negro Education*, 6, 695.

115. "Personals," *The Crisis* 21, no. 5 (March 1921): 227; "Pig Roast and Picnic in Aid of Rice School," *Daily Home News*, August 29, 1921, 12.

116. "Announcement: The Rice Memorial School," *Baltimore Afro-American*, January 26, 1929, 4.

117. "Class Letters and Personal Items," *Rutgers Alumni Monthly* 1, no. 3 (December 1921): 78.

118. "Think Boy, Alarmed, Ran Away," 1.

119. "Rice School Wins Debate with Team from High School," *Sunday Times*, February 26, 1922, 10.

120. Ibid.

121. Bernard Bush, "Ku Klux Klan," in *Encyclopedia of New Jersey*, ed. Maxine N. Lurie and Marc Mappen (New Brunswick, NJ: Rutgers University Press, 2004), 446.

122. "Press Finds Klan Is Quiet in Jersey: Activities Are Reported Only from Hoboken, Paterson and Bayonne: ACTS OF CHARITY NOTED: Survey of State Shows Lack of Interest in Many Towns—Silent in Trenton," *New York Times*, February 16, 1923, 8.

123. "Leaders Are Chased By 'Ku Klux': Local Youths Have Fright of Their Lives Near Milltown Last Night—Police Believe Meeting of 'Klan' Was Hoaxed," *New Brunswick Daily Home News*, September 10, 1921, 1, 2; "Where Was the Brass Band?," *New Brunswick Daily Home News*, March 30, 1923, 15.

124. "The Greatest of the Photoplays Now at the Opera House," *New Brunswick Times*, March 7, 1916, 3.

125. "Masquerades Had No Trouble Keeping Warm," *New Brunswick Times*, May 13, 1911, 1.

126. "Press Finds Klan Is Quiet in Jersey," 8.

127. Lindsay Denison, "The Klan Holds a 'Klavern,'" *New York World*, May 3, 1923, reprinted in *Deadline Artists: Scandals, Tragedies and Triumphs: More of America's Greatest Newspaper Columns*, ed. John P. Avlon, Jesse Angelo, and Errol Louis (New York: The Overlook Press, 2012), 40; "12,000 of Klan out at Jersey Meeting: Hold Heavily Guarded Initiation on a Lonely Farm Near New Brunswick: 500 Automobiles Parked: Some from as Far as Florida and Georgia—Guards Posted, Hostile Visitors

Threatened," *New York Times*, May 3, 1923, 1, 5; "Klan to Hold More Jersey Klaverns: Gathering at Hobbs's Farm First of a Series—Many Small Meetings," *New York Times*, May 4, 1923, 6.

128. Denison, "The Klan Holds A 'Klavern,'" 40, 41.

129. Ibid., 42.

130. Ibid., 43.

131. "12,000 of Klan out at Jersey Meeting," 1, 5.

132. "10,000 Klansmen Gather in Great Klan Ceremony: New Brunswick Is Scene of One of the Greatest Ku Klux Demonstrations: Gigantic Cross Is Burned as Almost One Thousand Candidates Are Initiated," *The Fiery Cross* (Indiana ed.), May 11, 1923, 8.

133. "Ku Klux Cross Near J. & J. Plant; South River Also: Police Promptly Extinguish Flames—Klan Emblems Draped: Few People Saw South River Cross," *New Brunswick Daily Home News*, August 10, 1923, 1; "Ku Klux Cross On Comstock St.: Second For City: Bonfire of Wooden Structure, Nine Feet High, Attracts Small Notice: First Cross Was Burned August 10," *New Brunswick Daily Home News*, August 24, 1923, 1.

134. "Klan Cross, Thirty Feet High, Burns: Erected on Easton Avenue Last Night Opposite Buccleuch Park: Other Crosses Found on Fire," *New Brunswick Daily Home News*, June 29, 1924, 1.

135. "Immense Crowd Is Attracted by Cross: Proof That Klan Is Active at New Brunswick Is Impressed on Citizens," *The Fiery Cross* (New Jersey ed.), February 8, 1924, 1.

136. "110 Girls Want to Enter College for Women Here in October," *New Brunswick Daily Home News*, May 7, 1915.

137. "Charter Granted to Local Klan: Rutgers Klan Title of Local Chapter of the Ku Klux Klan: State Charter Issued March 17," *New Brunswick Daily Home News*, March 7, 1926, 1.

138. "Nearly 500 at Big Klan Meeting," *New Brunswick Daily Home News*, May 23, 1926, 1.

139. "New Jersey: Rutgers Klan No. 44," *Kourier* 9, no. 10 (September 1933): 39.

140. Kathleen M. Blee, *Women of the Klan: Racism and Gender in the 1920s* (Berkeley: University of California Press, 1991), 175.

141. For more information about the founding, organization, and history of the first African Methodist Episcopal Church, see Richard S. Newman, *Freedom's Prophet: Bishop Richard Allen, the AME Church, and the Black Founding Fathers* (New York: New York University Press, 2009); Jualynne E. Dodson, *Engendering Church: Women Power and the AME Church* (Lanham, MD: Rowman and Littlefield, 2002).

142. Unknown author, Pamphlet Celebrating the 150th Anniversary of the Mt. Zion AME Church, for Mt. Zion, 1977, unprocessed, Alice Jennings Archibald History Room, Mt. Zion AME Church, New Brunswick, NJ. Division Street runs perpendicular to Somerset Street, which becomes Route 27.

143. Secondary sources to date and those in Mt. Zion's Archibald Library do not definitively state that the church was the first black church, but it is widely accepted as fact, as it is often listed first in histories of black religious organizations in New Brunswick. For more, see H. Solomon Hill, "The Negro in New Brunswick, New Jersey, as Revealed by a Study of One Hundred Families" (PhD diss., Drew University, 1942), Alice Jennings Archibald History Library, Mt. Zion AME Church, New Brunswick, NJ.

144. Armstead, Sutter, Walker, and Wiesner, "And I Poor Slave Yet," 112–121.

145. While no scholar has suggested a direct relationship between the African Association of New Brunswick and Mt. Zion A.M.E. Church, I hypothesize that there is
actually a direct connection between the disbanding of the African Association and
the founding of the church. More research should be conducted to examine if there
exists overlapping membership, but skepticism of white leaders would indeed have
been a theme gleaned from the association. Section two of the 1827 charter alludes
to this idea: "None shall be eligible as Trustees except free men, descendants of Africans and above the age of twenty-one years." Proposed Amendments to the Charter
of Incorporation of the African Methodist Episcopal, Mount Zion Church of New
Brunswick, New Jersey, April 15, 1868, Alice Jennings Archibald Historical Library,
Mt. Zion A.M.E. Church, New Brunswick, New Jersey.

146. Dodson, *Engendering Church*; Cheryl Townsend Gilkes, "Exploring the Religious
Connection," in *Women and Religion in the African Diaspora*, ed. R. Marie Griffith and
Barbara Dianne Savage (Baltimore: Johns Hopkins University Press, 2006) 179-198;
Evelyn Brooks Higginbotham, *Righteous Discontent: The Women's Movement in the
Black Baptist Church, 1880–1920* (Cambridge, MA: Harvard University Press, 1993).

147. Eddie S. Glaude, *Exodus!: Religion, Race, and Nation in Early Nineteenth-Century Black
America* (Chicago: University of Chicago Press, 2000), 88.

148. "The Jersey Convention," *Christian Recorder*, May 15, 1870.

149. For more information about colored conventions of the nineteenth century, see
Leslie M. Alexander, *African or American?: Black Identity and Political Activism in New
York City, 1784–1861* (Urbana: University of Illinois Press, 2008); John Ernest, *A
Nation within a Nation: Organizing African-American Communities before the Civil War*
(Chicago: Ivan R. Dee, 2011); Philip Sheldon Foner and George Elizur Walker, eds.,
Proceedings of the Black State Conventions: 1840–1865, 2 vols. (Philadelphia: Temple
University Press, 1979); Eric Gardner, *Black Print Unbound: The Christian Recorder,
African American Literature, and Periodical Culture* (New York: Oxford University Press,
2015); Steven Hahn, *A Nation under Our Feet: Black Political Struggles in the Rural South
from Slavery to the Great Migration* (Cambridge, MA: Harvard University Press, 2003);
John Stauffer, *The Black Hearts of Men: Radical Abolitionists and the Transformation of
Race* (Cambridge, MA: Harvard University Press, 2002).

150. Letter from Rev. Benjamin Lynch, *Christian Recorder*, September 23, 1965.

151. Ibid.

152. Unknown author, Pamphlet Celebrating the 150th Anniversary of the Mt. Zion AME
Church. Rosters for the members of the church have not yet been located as the
collection is unprocessed.

153. "For the Christian Recorder," *Christian Recorder*, March 7, 1863.

154. Mt. Zion AME Chuch Ledger (1979-1902), 157, 159, 263, unprocessed, Alice Jennings
Archibald History Room, Mt. Zion AME Church, New Brunswick New Jersey.

155. Ultimately, the church would not reach economic stability until the pastoral leadership of Rev. Solomon K. Hill (1938–1949), the first pastor to serve more than a
three-year term. Unknown author, Pamphlet Celebrating the 150th Anniversary of
the Mt. Zion AME Church.

156. See Higginbotham, *Righteous Discontent*; Dodson, *Engendering Church*.

157. Dodson, *Engendering Church*, 86.

158. Ibid., 87.

159. Ibid., 84.

160. This is a term established by historian Glenda Gilmore, who argued that *class* had different meanings for African Americans during the Jim Crow and Progressive era. "Middle Class" as a term for blacks is "too rigid" and therefore suggests the term "better class" for African Americans who saw themselves as ambassadors to the white power structure. Jennings view of herself as a negotiator, rather than a radical, suggests that she too, like her aunt, would align herself with a cohort of better class blacks in New Jersey. Glenda Gilmore, *Gender and Jim Crow: Women and the Politics of White Supremacy in North Carolina, 1896–1920* (Chapel Hill: University of North Carolina Press, 1996).

161. Anderson Funeral Service (New Brunswick New Jersey),"Alice Gertrude Jennings Archibald Funeral Program," December 23, 2002, New Brunswick Men and Women, Folder A, New Brunswick Free Public Library Collection, New Brunswick, NJ.

162. Alice Jennings Archibald, oral interview, March 14, 1997, by G. Kurt Peihler and Eve Snyder, Rutgers Oral History Archives, http://oralhistory.rutgers.edu/images/PDFs/archibald_alice_jennings.pdf.

163. It is likely that Jennings's aunt, Gertrude Pierce, is a relative of Jeremiah Pierce, Mt. Zion A.M.E. pastor from 1868 to 1870. There are Mt. Zion A.M.E. quarterly conference ticket stubs for Joseph Titus and Gertrude Titus for years as early as 1851 and 1853, respectively.

164. Alice Jennings Archibald, oral interview.

165. Ibid.

166. Ibid.

167. Ibid. Jennings also served as class historian, was a member of the National Honor Society, and ran track and played basketball.

168. It is not known if Jennings applied to New Jersey College for Women in 1923 or 1924. NJC would not accept its first known black student until 1934.

169. Alice Jennings Archibald, oral interview.

170. Ibid.

171. Ibid.

172. Alice Jennings Archibald, "Sketch of the Willing Workers Club of Mt. Zion AME Church," 1991, unprocessed, Alice Jennings Archibald History Room, Mt. Zion A.M.E. Church, New Brunswick, NJ.

173. Archibald, "Sketch of the Willing Workers Club of Mt. Zion AME Church"; Alice Jennings Archibald, oral interview; Alice Jennings Archibald to the Editor of the *Daily Home News*, "What the Negro Wants," June 23, 1942, unprocessed, Alice Jennings Archibald History Room, Mt. Zion A.M.E. Church, New Brunswick, NJ.

174. Ibid.

175. Ibid.

176. Katie Brennan, *Civic League of Greater New Brunswick: An Evolution of Success* (Community Development Case Study) (New Brunswick, NJ: Edward J. Bloustein School of Planning and Public Policy, 2010).

177. Alice Jennings Archibald, oral interview; Kayo Denda, Mary Hawkesworth, and Fernanda Perrone, *The Douglass Century: Transformation of the Women's College at Rutgers University* (New Brunswick, NJ: Rutgers University Press, Forthcoming), 139.

178. Alice Jennings Archibald, oral interview.

CHAPTER 3: The Rutgers Race Man

1. "1915 Class History," *Scarlet Letter* (New Brunswick, NJ, 1916), 33, Special Collections and University Archives, Rutgers University.

2. Social Darwinism has a long and global history reaching back to the mid-nineteenth century when race knowledge acquired the legitimacy of "scientific" proof. These epistemologies later served as the foundation to eugenics ideas in the early to mid-twentieth century in the United States, which also extended the veneer of fact to white racial hegemony. These racialized sentiments were interwoven in forging notions of masculinity at Rutgers College. See Johanna Schoen, *Choice and Coercion: Birth Control, Sterilization, and Abortion in Public Health and Welfare* (Chapel Hill: University of North Carolina Press, 2005); Pippa Holloway, *Sexuality, Politics, and Social Control in Virginia, 1920–1945* (Chapel Hill: University of North Carolina Press, 2006).

3. Lemon Ade, "The Fable of the Guy Who Made Good," *Scarlet Letter* (New Brunswick, NJ, 1916), 222, Special Collections and University Archives, Rutgers University.

4. Ibid.

5. *Scarlet Letter* (New Brunswick, NJ, 1916), 34, Special Collections and University Archives, Rutgers University.

6. Gail Bederman, *Manliness and Civilization: A Cultural History of Gender and Race in the United States, 1880-1917,* (Chicago: University of Chicago Press, 1996).

7. John Higham, *Strangers in the Land: Patterns of American Nativism, 1860-1925* (New Brunswick, NJ: Rutgers University Press, 2002), 103.

8. To be sure, scholars have considered constructions of masculinity—discursive and otherwise—through time and space. And many historians have considered gender identities and their relation to nonwhite Others. Yet scholars have not equally interrogated whiteness alongside their intellectual analyses on masculinity. Those specializing in whiteness studies have demonstrated that this category is also a construction. As such, whiteness is as much a historically situated concept and fabrication (with real consequences) as other racial identities. See Nayan Shah, *Stranger Intimacy: Contesting Race, Sexuality and the Law in the North American West* (Berkeley: University of California Press, 2011); Glenda Gilmore, *Gender and Jim Crow: Women and the Politics of White Supremacy in North Carolina, 1896–1920* (Chapel Hill: University of North Carolina Press, 1996); Gail Bederman, *Manliness and Civilization: A Cultural History of Gender and Race in the United States, 1880–1917* (Chicago: University of Chicago Press, 1996); Kristin Hoganson, *Fighting for American Manhood: How Gender Politics Provoked the Spanish-American and Philippine-American Wars* (New Haven, CT: Yale University Press, 1998); Danielle McGuire, *At the Dark End of the Street: Black Women, Rape, and Resistance—A New History of the Civil Rights Movement from Rosa Parks to the Rise of Black Power* (New York: Alfred A. Knopf, 2010); Deborah Gray White, *Lost in the USA: American Identity from the Promise Keepers to the Million Mom March* (Urbana: University of Illinois Press, 2017); Linda Gordon, *The Great Arizona Orphan Abduction* (Cambridge, MA: Harvard University Press, 2001).

9. These nicknames are likely references to the "Mutt and Jeff" comic strip that was popular in the early twentieth century. *Scarlet Letter* (New Brunswick, NJ, 1914), 55, Special Collections and University Archives, Rutgers University.

10. Janaki Challa, "Why Being 'Gypped' Hurts the Roma More Than It Hurts You," *NPR*, December 13, 2013, https://www.npr.org/sections/codeswitch/2013/12/30/242429836/why-being-gypped-hurts-the-roma-more-than-it-hurts-you.

11. W.E.B. Du Bois, *The Talented Tenth* (New York: James Pott and Company, 1903. For more on the notion of the "talented tenth" see Joy James, *Transcending the Talented Tenth: Black Leaders and American Intellectuals* (New York: Routledge, 2014); Zachery R. Williams, *In Search of the Talented Tenth: Howard University Public Intellectuals and the Dilemmas of Race, 1926–1970* (Columbia: University of Missouri Press, 2010); Ella F. Sloan, *W.E.B. Du Bois's "Talented Tenth": A Pioneering Conception of Transformational Leadership* (San Diego: Night Star Press, 2016).

12. Hazel V. Carby, *Race Men* (Cambridge, MA: Harvard University Press, 2000), 4.

13. W.E.B. Du Bois and Augustus Granville Dill, *The College-Bred Negro American: Report of a Social Study Made by Atlanta University under the Patronage of the Trustees of the John F. Slater Fund: With the Proceedings of the 15th Annual Conference for the Study of the Negro Problems, Held at Atlanta University, on Tuesday, May 24th, 1910* (Atlanta, GA: Atlanta University Press, 1910), 52.

14. Martin Summers, *Manliness and Its Discontents: The Black Middle Class and the Transformation of Masculinity, 1900–1930* (Chapel Hill: The University of North Carolina Press, 2004), 7.

15. In 1876 the New Brunswick Theological Seminary admitted two African American men, Islay Walden and John Bergen. However, the seminary was officially a separate institution from Rutgers College at this time.

16. For more on Will see Bayker, Jesse, Christopher Blakley, and Kendra Boyd. "His Name Was Will: Remembering Enslaved Individuals in Rutgers History." In *Scarlet and Black: Slavery and Dispossession in Rutgers History*, edited by Marisa J. Fuentes and Deborah Gray White, 58–81. Rutgers University Press, 2016.

17. Peter Mazzei, "James Dickson Carr: First Black Graduate of Rutgers College," *The Journal of the Rutgers University Libraries* 47, no. 2 (1985): 93; "A Baltimore Boy," *The Afro American*, August 10, 1895. The Preparatory School was founded in 1766 as the Queen's College Grammar School. In 1883, the Rutgers College Grammar School was renamed the Rutgers Preparatory School. In 1964 the building was renamed Alexander Johnston Hall and today it houses Rutgers University administrative offices. D. Clark, "Rutgers College Grammar School Photograph," 1870, photographs from the William Elliot Griffis Collection, Special Collections and University Archives, Rutgers University, https://doi.org/doi:10.7282/T37M08D5.

18. Mazzei, "James Dickson Carr: First Black Graduate of Rutgers College," 93.

19. Henry Kimball Davis, "The Classes 1892," *Rutgers Alumni Quarterly*, October 1920, 57; Rutgers University Biographical Files: Alumni (Classes of 1774–1922), Special Collections and University Archives, Rutgers University.

20. Henry Kimball Davis, "The Classes 1892," 57.

21. Mazzei, "James Dickson Carr: First Black Graduate of Rutgers College," 95–96.

22. "A Credit to His Race," *New York Times*, June 16, 1892.

23. Davis, "The Classes 1892," 57.

24. Ibid., 58.

25. "Class Day Exercises—Kirkpatrick Chapel Crowded with College Students and Visiting Friends," *Daily Times*, June 20, 1892.

26. Mazzei, "James Dickson Carr: First Black Graduate of Rutgers College," 97.

27. "The United Colored Democracy," 1939, Schomburg Center for Research in Black Culture, Manuscripts, Archives and Rare Books Division, The New York Public

Library, New York Public Library Digital Collections, https://digitalcollections.nypl
.org/items/c56824b0-80d2-0133-62be-00505686a51c.

28. Ibid.

29. "Some Sharp Contrast," *Broad Ax*, November 4, 1899.

30. "The United Colored Democracy," 1939.

31. Mazzei, "James Dickson Carr: First Black Graduate of Rutgers College," 97.

32. "James Dickson Carr, a Young Negro Lawyer," *Statesville Record and Landmark*, Octo-
ber 10, 1899; "Brief Telegrams," *McCook Tribune*, October 20, 1899; "Brief Telegrams,"
North Platte Semi-Weekly Tribune, October 17, 1899; "General News," *Chronicle*,
October 18, 1899; "General News," *Goldsboro Weekly Argus*, October 12, 1899; "James
Dickson Carr," *Roanoke Beacon*, October 20, 1899; "Office for a Colored Lawyer," *The
Sun*, October 3, 1899; "Personal," *Morning News*, October 11, 1899; "Personal and Gen-
eral Notes," *Times-Picayune*, October 9, 1899; "Personalities," *Daily Arkansas Gazette*,
October 10, 1899.

33. "Inconsistency," *Davie Record*, October 11, 1899.

34. "James Dickson Carr, a Young Negro Lawyer."

35. Mazzei, "James Dickson Carr: First Black Graduate of Rutgers College," 97.

36. "'92 James Dickson Carr," *Targum*, March 31, 1904, Rutgers University Biographical
Files: Alumni (Classes of 1774–1922), Special Collections and University Archives,
Rutgers University; Davis, "The Classes 1892."

37. "James Dickson Carr, 1892," Rutgers University Biographical Files: Alumni (Classes of
1774–1922), Box 82, Special Collections and University Archives, Rutgers University.

38. Robeson and Carr's relationship appears to have been fairly intimate; when Carr
died in 1920, Robeson served as a pallbearer at his funeral in Harlem. "Sudden
Death Meets James Dickson Carr," *New York Age*, March 16, 1920.

39. Edward Lawson to Irving S. Upson, January 20, 1904, Rutgers Biographical Files:
Alumni (1774–1922), Box 128, Folder Edward Lawson, Special Collections and University Archives, Rutgers University.

40. Michael R. Hill, "Jesse Lawson and the National Sociological Society of 1903," in
Diverse Histories of American Sociology, ed. Anthony J. Blasi (Boston: Brill, 2005), 127.

41. Jesse Lawson to Irving S. Upson, June 1, 1904, Rutgers College Administration
Records, Box Irving S. Upson, Folder Jesse Lawson, Special Collections and University Archives, Rutgers University.

42. For more on the politics of respectability, see the final chapter in Evelyn Brooks Higginbotham, *Righteous Discontent: The Women's Movement in the Black Baptist Church,
1880–1920* (Cambridge, MA: Harvard University Press, 1994).

43. *Scarlet Letter* (New Brunswick, NJ, 1908), 93, 114, Special Collections and University
Archives, Rutgers University; Jesse Lawson to Irving Upson, June 27, 1907, Rutgers
University Biographical Files: Alumni (Classes of 1774–1922, Box 128, Folder May
24, 1904–March 18, 1908, Special Collections and University Archives, Rutgers
University.

44. Jesse Lawson to Irving Upson, April 8, 1906, Rutgers Biographical Files (1774–1922),
Box 128, Folder Jesse Lawson, Special Collections and University Archives, Rutgers
University.

45. "Student Accused of Stealing," *Washington Bee*, November 30, 1907.

46. "The Wicked Waiter," *Daily Times*, November 2, 1893.

47. The *Washington Bee* newspaper (Washington, DC) reprinted the *Evening Star*'s original article and Edward Lawson's letter to the editor that appeared in the same paper. "Student Accused of Stealing," *Washington Bee*, November 30, 1907.

48. Ibid.

49. Rutgers Faculty Minutes, November 22, 1907, Box Faculty Minutes, Folder June 21, 1906–June 8, 1916, Special Collections and University Archives, Rutgers University; Edward Lawson, "Material for History of Class of 1908," Rutgers University Biographical Files Alumni (1774–1922), Box 128, Folder Edward Lawson, Special Collections and University Archives, Rutgers University.

50. Edward Lawson, "Material for History of Class of 1908."

51. Jesse Lawson to Irving Upson, February 19, 1908, Rutgers Biographical Files (1774–1922), Box 128, Folder Jesse Lawson, Special Collections and University Archives, Rutgers University.

52. Edward Lawson to the Administration Committee, April 16, 1909, Rutgers College Administration Records, Box Irving S. Upson, Folder Edward Lawson, Special Collections and University Archives, Rutgers University.

53. Edward Lawson to W.H.S. Demarest, May 16, 1910, Rutgers Biographical Files (1774–1922), Box 128, Folder Edward Lawson, Special Collections and University Archives, Rutgers University.

54. Charles T. Thompson to Edward Lawson, n.d., Rutgers Biographical Files (1774–1922), Box 128, Folder Edward Lawson, Special Collections and University Archives, Rutgers University.

55. Irving S. Upson to Registrar from the Board of Education of the District of Columbia, June 29, 1908, Rutgers Biographical Files (1774–1922), Box 128, Folder Edward Lawson, Special Collections and University Archives, Rutgers University.

56. Edward Lawson Sr. to D. J. Fisher, June 9, 1915, Rutgers Biographical Files (1774–1922), Box 128, Folder Edward Lawson, Special Collections and University Archives, Rutgers University.

57. Ibid.

58. Rutgers College Questionnaire, 1932, Rutgers Biographical Files (1774–1922), Box 128, Folder Edward Lawson, Special Collections and University Archives, Rutgers University.

59. Martin Bauml Duberman, *Paul Robeson* (New York: Ballantine Books, 1989), 4–5.

60. Ibid., 9, 17.

61. "Local Student Gets Scholarship," *Courier-News*, July 16, 1915; Duberman, *Paul Robeson*, 9–12; "Raritan," *The Courier-News*, May 1, 1915.

62. "Somerville Notes," *Courier-News*, April 23, 1915.

63. "Somerville School Won County Meet," *Courier-News*, May 25, 1914.

64. "Local Boys Star in Rutgers - S. T. S. Tilt," *Courier-News*, November 1, 1915.

65. Robert Van Gelder, "Robeson Remembers," *New York Times*, January 16, 1944, cited in Duberman, *Paul Robeson*, n.3, 572.

66. Duberman, *Paul Robeson*, 21.

67. "Paul Leroy Robeson," *Targum*, June 1919, Paul Robeson Collection (R-MC 011), Box 4, Folder 26, Special Collections and University Archives, Rutgers University; "Robeson Is Hero of Rutgers; Newport Reserves Defeated," *Chicago Defender*, December 1, 1917; "Looms Up Again as Hero," *Chicago Defender*, November 2, 1918; "Robeson Twice

Beaten," *Chicago Defender*, May 10, 1919; "Starred in Football Game," *Courier-News*, October 8, 1917.

68. "Paul L. Robeson (Left End)," *Targum*, December 19, 1917, Paul Robeson Collection (R-MC 011), Box 4, Folder 17, Special Collections and University Archives, Rutgers University.

69. Duberman, *Paul Robeson*, 22–23.

70. Mazzei, "James Dickson Carr: First Black Graduate of Rutgers College," 98.

71. Ibid., 93.

72. James D. Carr to William H. Demarest, June 6, 1919, Rutgers University Biographical Files: Alumni (Classes of 1774–1922), Special Collections and University Archives, Rutgers University.

73. Ibid.

74. Ibid.

75. Kenneth W. Mack, *Representing the Race: The Creation of the Civil Rights Lawyer* (Cambridge, MA: Harvard University Press, 2012), 4.

76. William H. Demarest to James D. Carr, June 16, 1919, Rutgers University Biographical Files: Alumni (Classes of 1774–1922), Special Collections and University Archives, Rutgers University.

77. Duberman, *Paul Robeson*, 24.

78. "Elmer French Takes Prize at Rutgers," *Courier-News*, June 2, 1916.

79. "Wins Speaking Prize," *Courier-News*, September 16, 1916; "Robeson Wins Extemporaneous Speaking Contest," *Targum*, 1919, Paul Robeson Collection (R-MC 011), Box 4, Folder 22, Special Collections and University Archives, Rutgers University; "Robeson Wins Contest," *Courier-News*, June 14, 1917; "Robeson A Varsity Debater," *Courier-News*, February 11, 1918; "Robeson in Phi Betta Kappa," *Courier-News*, February 24, 1919.

80. Duberman, *Paul Robeson*, 19.

81. "Sudden Death Meets James Dickson Carr," *New York Age*, March 16, 1920.

82. Mazzei, "James Dickson Carr: First Black Graduate of Rutgers College," 96–97.

83. "Paul Leroy Robeson," *Targum*, June 1919.

84. Francis E. Lyons, "Prophesy of the Class of '19," *Targum*, June 1919, Paul Robeson Collection (R-MC 011), Box 4, Folder 24, Special Collections and University Archives, Rutgers University.

85. Duberman, *Paul Robeson*, 32–33.

86. Ibid., 43–45.

87. Ibid., 55–67.

88. Paul Robeson, "The Culture of the Negro," *Spectator* 152 (1934): 916–917.

89. Duberman, *Paul Robeson*, 211–232. For more on the life and activism of Paul Robeson, see Gerald Horne, *Paul Robeson: The Artist as Revolutionary* (London: Pluto Press, 2016); Jordan Goodman, *Paul Robeson: A Watched Man* (New York: Verso, 2013); Sheila Tully Boyle and Andrew Bunie, *Paul Robeson: The Years of Promise and Achievement* (Amherst: University of Massachusetts Press, 2001); Freedomways, *Paul Robeson: The Great Forerunner* (New York: International Publishers, 1998); Ron Ramdin, *Paul Robeson: The Man and His Mission* (London: Peter Owen Publishers, 1992); Duberman, *Paul Robeson*; Paul Robeson, *Paul Robeson Speaks: Writings, Speeches, and*

Interviews, a Centennial Celebration (New York: Citadel Press, 1978); Marie Seton, *Paul Robeson* (London: Dennis Dobson, 1958); Paul Robeson, *Here I Stand* (Boston: Beacon Press, 1958).

90. Duberman, *Paul Robeson*, 184–191.

91. For more on African Americans and the Communist Party in the United States, see Mark I. Solomon, *The Cry Was Unity: Communists and African Americans, 1917–36* (Jackson: University Press of Mississippi, 1998); Mark Naison, *Communists in Harlem during the Depression, Blacks in the New World* (New York: Grove Press, 1984); Robin D. G. Kelley, *Hammer and Hoe: Alabama Communists during the Great Depression* (Chapel Hill: University of North Carolina Press, 1990); Minkah Makalani, *In the Cause of Freedom: Radical Black Internationalism from Harlem to London, 1917–1939* (Chapel Hill: University of North Carolina Press, 2011); Wilson Record, *The Negro and the Communist Party* (Chapel Hill: University of North Carolina Press, 1951); Harry Haywood, *Black Bolshevik: Autobiography of an Afro-American Communist* (Chicago: Liberator Press, 1978).

92. In the 1930s the Comintern's International Labor Defense (ILD) represented African Americans in key legal battles. This was a major factor in black support of the Communist Party during the depression years. The most notable case the ILD took up was that of the Scottsboro Boys. Nine black teenagers were arrested in 1931 in Scottsboro, Alabama, and falsely accused of raping two white women while riding the rails. After eight of the nine were convicted and sentenced to death, the ILD was the first to offer its assistance. For more on the Scottsboro Boys case, see Dan T. Carter, *Scottsboro: A Tragedy of the American South* (Baton Rouge: Louisiana State University Press, 1969); Wilson Record, *Race and Radicalism: The NAACP and the Communist Party in Conflict* (Ithaca, NY: Cornell University Press, 1964); James E. Goodman, *Stories of Scottsboro* (New York: Vintage Books, 1995); James A. Miller, Susan D. Pennybacker, and Eve Rosenhaft, "Mother Ada Wright and the International Campaign to Free the Scottsboro Boys, 1931–1934," *The American Historical Review* 106, no. 2 (2001): 387–430.

93. John Lewis Gaddis, *The United States and the Origins of the Cold War, 1941–1947* (New York: Columbia University Press, 1972); Stephen J. Whitfield, *The Culture of the Cold War* (Baltimore: Johns Hopkins University Press, 1996); Richard Gid Powers, *Not without Honor: The History of American Anticommunism* (New Haven, CT: Yale University Press, 1998); Ellen Schrecker, *Many Are the Crimes: McCarthyism in America* (Princeton, NJ: Princeton University Press, 1999); David M. Oshinsky, *A Conspiracy So Immense: The World of Joe McCarthy* (Oxford, UK: Oxford University Press, 2005); Melvyn P. Leffler, *For the Soul of Mankind: The United States, the Soviet Union, and the Cold War* (New York: Farrar, Straus and Giroux, 2008); David K. Johnson, *The Lavender Scare: The Cold War Persecution of Gays and Lesbians in the Federal Government* (Chicago: University of Chicago Press, 2009); Landon R. Y. Storrs, *The Second Red Scare and the Unmaking of the New Deal Left* (Princeton, NJ: Princeton University Press, 2013).

94. For more on civil and human rights activism in the Cold War era, see Brenda Gayle Plummer, *Rising Wind: Black Americans and U.S. Foreign Affairs, 1935–1960* (Chapel Hill: University of North Carolina Press, 1996); Penny M. Von Eschen, *Race against Empire: Black Americans and Anticolonialism, 1937–1957* (Ithaca, NY: Cornell University Press, 1997); Mary L. Dudziak, *Cold War Civil Rights: Race and the Image of American Democracy* (Princeton, NJ: Princeton University Press, 2000); Carol Anderson, *Eyes*

off the Prize: The United Nations and the African American Struggle for Human Rights, 1944–1955 (New York: Cambridge University Press, 2003); Thomas Borstelmann, *The Cold War and the Color Line: American Race Relations in the Global Arena* (Cambridge, MA: Harvard University Press, 2003).

95. Robeson, *Here I Stand*, 63.

96. Ibid., 64.

97. "Congress, House, Committee on Un-American Activities, Investigation of the Unauthorized Use of U.S. Passports, 84th Congress, Part 3, June 12, 1956," in *Thirty Years of Treason: Excerpts from Hearings before the House Committee on Un-American Activities, 1938–1968*, ed. Eric Bentley (New York: Viking Press, 1971), 770.

98. Ibid.

99. Ibid.

100. John H. Morrow, interview by Celectine Tutt, Transcript, May 11, 1981, 115–16, The Foreign Affairs Oral History Collection of the Association for Diplomatic Studies and Training, Library of Congress, http://www.loc.gov/item/mfdipbib001604.

101. "Boy, 19, Wins Phi Beta Kappa Key," *The Chicago Defender*, October 18, 1930.

102. Morrow, interview, 115.

103. For example, Morrow's roommate Walter Alexander was the first African American to graduate from Rutgers with a degree in engineering and could not find a job in engineering after World War II. Alexander opted to go to dental school instead. Angela Delli Santi, "The Trailblazer—Walter G. Alexander II," *Rutgers Magazine*, July 9, 2009, http://soe.rutgers.edu/story/trailblazer-walter-g-alexander-ii.

104. "Boy, 19, Wins Phi Beta Kappa Key."

105. Morrow, interview, 115.

106. Ibid., 116.

107. Ibid., 117.

108. Ibid., 120.

109. Ibid., 115–116.

110. Michael Krenn, *Black Diplomacy: African Americans and the State Department, 1945–69* (New York: Routledge, 1999), 109.

111. Morrow, interview, 121.

112. Ibid., 126.

113. Martha Biondi, *The Black Revolution on Campus* (Berkeley: University of California Press, 2014), 3.

114. Morrow, interview, 124.

115. Ibid.

116. "Education," *Jet*, February 6, 1964.

117. "On the Inside of Democracy at Work," *Rutgers Alumni Monthly*, December 1942.

118. Harvard Sitkoff, *A New Deal for Blacks: The Emergence of Civil Rights as a National Issue: The Depression Decade* (New York: Oxford University Press, 2008), 49.

119. Edward Lawson, "Soup's On," *The Crisis* November 1936. .

120. Edward Lawson, "Recreation for Negro Youth," *Opportunity: Journal of Negro Life* 15, no. 7 (1937)" 202-204.

121. Nancy Joan Weiss, *Farewell to the Party of Lincoln* (Princeton, NJ: Princeton University Press, 1983), 137. See also photograph titled "Twenty Afro-American Members of

Franklin Roosevelt's 'Black Cabinet,' Posed, Standing outside of Building," Library of Congress, http://hdl.loc.gov/loc.pnp/cph.3c07174.

122. The formation of the FEPC, like the formation of the Black Cabinet and political shifts associated with the New Deal, are part of the first stage of organizing associated with what historians call the Long Civil Rights Movement, which expanded the temporal and ideological boundaries of the "Classic Civil Rights Movement" to include organizing and activism around civil rights that happened prior to *Brown v. Board of Education* and after the death of Martin Luther King Jr. See Merl Elwyn Reed, *Seedtime for the Modern Civil Rights Movement: The President's Committee on Fair Employment Practice, 1941–1946* (Baton Rouge: Louisiana State University Press, 1991), 4–5.

123. Edward Lawson, *Encyclopedia of Human Rights* (Washington, DC: Taylor & Francis, 1996), ix.

124. Ibid.

125. Ibid., xvi.

126. James Clinton Hoggard, interview by William McKinney, James Clinton Hoggard Papers, Box 1, Folder 1, Schomburg Center for Research in Black Culture, New York.

127. Jay Hoggard, interview by Tracey Johnson, New Brunswick, New Jersey August 9, 2017.

128. James Hoggard, interview by William McKinney.

129. Ibid.

130. Ibid.

131. Ibid.

132. Ibid.

133. For more on Islay Walden see Chapter 1 of this volume, "All the World's A Classroom: The First Black Students Encounter the Racial, Religious, and Intellectual Life of the University."

134. Fraser Metzger to Harold H. Tryon, April 5, 1939, Rutgers Student Files, Box 351, Special Collections and University Archives, Rutgers University.

135. James Clinton Hoggard to Edward McNall Burns, February 18, 1953, James Clinton Hoggard Papers, Box 1, Folder 2, Schomburg Center for Research in Black Culture, New York.

136. Edward McNall Burns to James Clinton Hoggard, February 25, 1953, James Clinton Hoggard Papers, Box 1, Folder 2, Schomburg Center for Research in Black Culture, New York.

137. James Clinton Hoggard, "Report of the Department of Foreign Missions, A.M.E. Zion Church," August 1957, James Clinton Hoggard Papers, Box 7, Folder 7, Schomburg Center for Research in Black Culture, New York.

138. Fraser Metzger, Law School Recommendation Letter, May 21, 1943, Rutgers University Biographical Files Alumni, Harry Hazelwood Jr. Class of 1943, University Special Collections and University Archives, Rutgers University.

139. Ibid.

140. Fraser Metzger, Law School Recommendation Letter, May 21, 1943; Harry Hazelwood Jr. and George Thomas, "Wills—Presumption of Undue Influence: Attorney as Testamentary Beneficiary," *Current Legal Thought* 12, no. 4 (April 1946): 264–267.

141. "Harry Hazelwood Jr.," *The Daytona Beach News Journal*, October 2, 2007.

142. "Harry Hazelwood Jr.—Newark Student Council's 'Man of the Year,'" *Newark Evening News*, May 1957.

143. "Liberalized Admission for Negro Lawyers to Be Urged at U.S. Bar Groups Convention," *Special to The New York Times*, September 5, 1949, 15.

144. "Run-Off Election in Newark Near: Choice of Council of 9 Due on Tuesday—18 Are in Race—Light Vote Is Expected," *New York Times*, June 13, 1954, Special to the *New York Times* edition, 64.

145. "Webb Gets 2 New Aids: Sarcone, Hazelwood Sworn to Staff of Prosecutor," *Newark Evening News*, February 1, 1956.

146. "Not as a Candidate," *Newark Evening News*, January 11, 1958.

147. "Negro Judgeships at Record High," *Ebony Magazine*, July 1962, 83.

148. Ibid., 79.

149. George Hallam, "Hazelwood Credo: Devotion to Duty," *Newark Evening News*, December 12, 1969; "Negro Judgeships at Record High," 83.

150. "Weekly Almanac," *Jet Magazine*, June 18, 1959, 27.

151. Hallam, "Hazelwood Credo: Devotion to Duty," "National Report: Confirm 1st Negro Judge in Newark New Jersey," *Jet*, November 20, 1958, 11.

152. "5 to Receive Brotherhood Awards," *Newark Evening News*, February 2, 1968.

153. Clement Alexander Price, "Blacks and Jews in the City of Opportunity: Newark, New Jersey, 1900–1967," 1994, 3, http://andromeda.rutgers.edu/~natalieb/Price BlacksJews.pdf.

154. "City NAACP Installs Slate: Hazelwood Returns to Presidency; Housing Assistant Heard," *Newark Evening News*, January 1, 1957; "Harry Hazelwood Heads Colored Unit," *Newark Evening News*, December 31, 1947.

155. "Harry Hazelwood Jr.," *The Daytona Beach News Journal*, October 2, 2007.

156. Rick Rojas and Khorri Atkison, "Five Days of Unrest That Shaped, and Haunted, Newark," *New York Times*, July 11, 2017.

CHAPTER 4: Profiles in Courage

1. At its founding in 1918 Douglass was called the New Jersey College for Women. It became Douglass College in 1955. Although this article covers the period when the campus was the New Jersey College for Women, it will use the terms NJC and Douglass College interchangeably.

2. Kayo Deneda, Mary Hawkesworth, and Fernanda Perrone, *The Douglass Century: Transformation of the Women's College at Rutgers University*, (New Brunswick, NJ: Rutgers University Press, 2018), 15–16. Historian Linda Kerber describes the intellectual idea of "Republican Motherhood" during and after the Revolutionary War in her book *Women of the Republic: Intellect & Ideology in Revolutionary America*. "Republican Motherhood" was the image that white women constructed to merge the domestic realm with political participation through the notion that women provided moral guidance for their husbands and sons. This ideal was an avenue for women's limited participation in politics and, later, was the ideal through which women sought to advance female education and gendered Progressive Era reform. Kerber, *Women of the Republic: Intellect & Ideology in Revolutionary America* (Chapel Hill: University of North Carolina Press, 1980), 15-16.

3. Kayo Denda, Mary Hawkesworth, and Fernanda Perrone, *The Douglass Century: Transformation of the Women's College at Rutgers University* (New Brunswick, NJ: Rutgers University Press, 2018), 14–17.

4. The notion of "Anglo-Saxon" narrowly defined whiteness in the early-twentieth-century United States. Italian Americans, Irish Americans, Asian Americans, and Jewish Americans were racialized as ethnic, nonwhite. In this chapter, we employ broadly the terms *ethnic* and *nonwhite* to discuss the early trickle of female students, some of whom were international students, admitted to NJC who were not considered white or Anglo-Saxon. When applicable, we indicate more precisely milestone students—"firsts," such as the first African American student admitted to NJC, etc.

5. Denda, Hawkesworth, and Perrone, *The Douglass Century*, 47; "Handbook of Information for Students/New Jersey College for Women," Special Collections and University Archives (SPCOL/UA), R-PUBS, LD 7071.5.A32, 1921, 5, 9; "Handbook of Information for Students," 1924, 50; "Handbook of Information for Students," 1937.

6. "Handbook of Information for Students," 1921, 15.

7. Ibid., 20.

8. Denda, Hawkesworth, and Perrone, *The Douglass Century*, 48.

9. Previously, students were not allowed to smoke, but the 1930s edition of the *Red Book* mentions a smoking room. Additionally, gentlemen callers were not restricted to just the living rooms. "Handbook of Information for Students," 1930, 24.

10. Denda, Hawkesworth, and Perrone, *The Douglass Century*, 70–71.

11. Rutgers University Athletics, "Why Knights," *ScarletKnights.com*, http://www.scarlet knights.com/sports/2017/6/11/trads.aspx.

12. Prom Number, *The Chanticleer* (November 1924), Special Collections and University Archives, Rutgers University.

13. Inaugural Number, *The Chanticleer* (June 1923), Special Collections and University Archives, Rutgers University; Freshman Number, *The Chanticleer* (September 1925), Special Collections and University Archives, Rutgers University.

14. For more information on the prevalence of the modern girl imagery during the interwar period, see Alys Eve Weinbaum, Lynn Thomas, Pritis Ramamurthy, Uta G. Poiger, Madeline Y. Dong, and Tani Barlow, eds., "The Modern Girl as Heuristic Device: Collaboration, Comparison Multidirectional Citation," in *Modern Girl Around the World: Consumption, Modernity, and Globalization* (Durham, NC: Duke University Press, 2008). Image of "The Snake Charmer" and "An Old Fashioned Necking Party" are found on the very same page of the first edition of the *Chanticleer*.

15. For more information about the history and nature of Jim Crow, see C. Vann Woodward, *The Strange Career of Jim Crow* (New York: Oxford University Press, 1955); Howard Rabinowitz, *Race Relations in the Urban South* (New York: Oxford University Press, 1978); Jennifer Ritterhouse, *Growing Up Jim Crow: How Black and White Southern Children Learn Race* (Chapel Hill: University of North Carolina Press, 2006); Blair Kelley, *Right to Ride: Streetcar Boycotts and African American Citizenship in the Era of Plessy v. Ferguson* (Chapel Hill: University of North Carolina Press, 2010).

16. For readings on blackface minstrelsy, see Yuval Taylor and Jake Austen, *Black Minstrelsy from Slavery to Hip-Hop* (New York: W. W. Norton, 2012); Anne Marie Beams, *Inside the Minstrel Mask: Readings in 19th Century Blackface Minstrelsy* (Hanover, NH: Wesleyan University Press, 1996); Eric Lott, *Love and Theft: Blackface Minstrelsy and the*

American Working Class (Oxford: Oxford University Press, 2013); John Strausbaugh, and Darius James, *Black Like You: Blackface, Whiteface, Insult, and Imitation* (New York: Penguin, 2006); Lawrence Levine, *Highbrow/Lowbrow: The Emergence of Cultural Hierarchy in America* (Cambridge, MA: Harvard University Press, 1990).

17. Tracey Owens Patton, "Jim Crow on Fraternity Row: A Study of the Phenomenon of Blackface in the White Southern Fraternal Order," *Visual Communication Quarterly* 15 (July–September 2008) 150–168.

18. Ibid., 2.

19. "Charter Granted to Local Klan: Rutgers Klan Title of Local Chapter of the Ku Klux Klan: State Charter Issued March 17," *New Brunswick Daily Home News*, March 7, 1926, 1; "12,000 of Klan Out at Jersey Meeting: Hold Heavily Guarded Initiation on a Lonely Farm Near New Brunswick: 500 Automobiles Parked: Some from as Far as Florida and Georgia—Guards Posted, Hostile Visitors Threatened," *New York Times*, May 3, 1923, 1, 5.

20. Lafayette Number, *The Chanticleer* (November 1926), Special Collections and University Archives, Rutgers University.

21. Ibid.

22. Girls' Number: "Fraterni-tea," "Bo and Say," "Nico-teens," *The Chanticleer* (April 1926), Special Collections and University Archives, Rutgers University.

23. "Sophomore Club," *Quair* (1938 Douglass College Yearbook), Special Collections and University Archives, Rutgers University.

24. "NJC Service League," *Quair* (1939 Douglass College Yearbook), Special Collections and University Archives, Rutgers University.

25. "Jumping Jive," *Quair* (1940 Douglass College Yearbook), Special Collections and University Archives, Rutgers University.

26. Julia Feller Feist, quoted in Denda, Hawkesworth and Perrone, *The Douglass Century*, 41.

27. Denda, Hawkesworth, and Perrone, *The Douglass Century*, 19.

28. "Emilia Caballero," Personal History Records," Box: A-D, College Hall, Douglass Residential College.

29. Ibid.

30. Ibid.

31. "Emilia Caballero," *Quair* (1930 Douglass College Yearbook), Special Collections and University Archives, Rutgers University.

32. "Doris Cohn," *Quair* (1930 Douglass College Yearbook), Special Collections and University Archives, Rutgers University.

33. "Eleanor Tilton" and "Phyllis Muriel Tracy," *Quair* (1944 Douglass College Yearbook), Special Collections and University Archives, Rutgers University.

34. "Jean Gordon," *Quair* (1945 Douglass College Yearbook), Special Collections and University Archives, Rutgers University.

35. See, for example, Karen Brodkin, *How Jews Became White Folks and What That Says about Race in America* (New Brunswick, NJ: Rutgers University Press, 1998); Matthew Frye Jacobson, *Whiteness of a Different Color: European Immigrants and the Alchemy of Race* (Cambridge, MA: Harvard University Press, 1998); David Roediger, *Working Toward Whiteness: How America's Immigrants Became White* (New York: Basic Books, 2005).

36. "Angeline Grace Maruca," *Quair* (1945 Douglass College Yearbook), Special Collections and University Archives, Rutgers University.

37. "Barbara Louise Moreno," *Quair* (1946 Douglass College Yearbook), Special Collections and University Archives, Rutgers University.

38. "Catherine Kashiwa," *Quair* (1939 Douglass College Yearbook), Special Collections and University Archives, Rutgers University.

39. "Memo," Folder: Ayala, Sara (1945), AADC Bio Files, Associate Alumnae of Douglass College; "Too Much Cold," *Central New Jersey Home News*, December 18, 1943, 4.

40. "Too Much Cold," 4.

41. "Junior Women Hold Conference Here," *Bernardsville News*, October 25, 1945, 1.

42. "February Profile," Folder: Mazda, Maideh (1947), AADC Bio Files, Associate Alumnae of Douglass College (hereafter AADC).

43. New Jersey College for Women Department of Public Information, "Maideh Mazda," Folder: Mazda, Maideh (1947), AADC.

44. "February Profile," Folder: Mazda, Maideh (1947), AADC.

45. Denda, Hawkesworth, and Perrone, *The Douglass Century*, 79.

46. Linda M. Perkins, "The African American Female Elite: The Early History of African American Women in the Seven Sister Colleges, 1880–1960," *Harvard Educational Review* 67, no. 4 (Winter 1997): 722.

47. Ibid., 726.

48. "NJC Alumnae Are Scattered over Somerset; 31 Girls from County Now Attending College," *Courier-News*, May 14, 1938, 55.

49. Tom Perry, "She Broke Barrier, Kept Ego in Check," *Courier Post*, April 14, 1996, A-10, Folder: Baxter, Julia (1938), AADC.

50. Ibid.

51. Ibid.

52. Ibid.

53. Judith Osborne, "Julia Baxter Bates: A Profile," *Douglass Alumnae Bulletin* (Spring 1989): 5, Folder: Baxter, Julia (1938), AADC. Baxter Bates does not explain this in the article, but in *The Douglass Century*, Hawkesworth et al. describe some of the challenges that NJC faced in the 1930s. The largest challenge was the struggle over the autonomy of the college. The Great Depression also forced the college to reduce its faculty from 131 in 1930/1931 to 107 in 1933/1934. The Depression also caused a drop in enrollment. Corwin's comments might have been a reference to what she saw as her role in remedying these issues. See Denda, Hawkesworth, and Perrone, *The Douglass Century*, 60–64.

54. Denda, Hawkesworth, and Perrone, *The Douglass Century*, 40–41.

55. Ibid., 64.

56. Bates, Julia Baxter, "Rutgers Hall of Distinguished Alumni Awards," Rutgers University, New Brunswick, April 13, 1996, AADC.

57. New Jersey College for Women Department of Public Information, "Baxter, Julia Esteve" Folder: Baxter, Julia Esteve (1938), AADC.

58. Osborne, 5, AADC.

59. Denda, Hawkesworth, and Perrone, *The Douglass Century*, 67.

60. Perry, "She Broke Barrier, Kept Ego in Check," 2, AADC.

61. Quoted in Denda, Hawkesworth, and Perrone, *The Douglass Century*, 83.

62. Ibid., 110; Carol Elmore, "Whatever You Put Your Mind To," *Douglass Alumnae Bulletin* (Winter 1980): 4, Folder: Andrews, Emma (1949), AADC.

63. Bureau of the Census, Department of Commerce, *Fifteenth Census of the United States* (1930): Census Place: *Plainfield, Union, New Jersey*; Roll: *1388*; Page: *11B*; Enumeration District: *0108*; FHL microfilm: *2341123*.

64. U.S. Social Security Applications and Claims Index, 1936–2007 [database online], *Ancestry.com*, 2015. https://search.ancestry.com/cgi-bin/sse.dll?_phsrc=wLe48&_ph start=successSource&usePUBJs=true&indiv=1&dbid=60901&gsfn=Veronica &gsln=Henriksen&msfng=Englehardt&msfns=Henriksen&msmng=Genevieve &msmns=Sweeney&msbdy=1923&msbdm=4&msbdd=23&msbpn__ftp=plainfield ,%20union,%20new%20jersey,%20usa&msbpn=9869&msddy=1998&msddm=12& msddd=17&new=1&rank=1&uidh=amw&redir=false&msT=1&gss=angs-d&pcat=36&f h=0&h=47971019&recoff=&ml_rpos=1

65. Bureau of the Census, Department of Commerce, *Fifteenth Census of the United States* (1930): "History: 1930," https://www.census.gov/history/www/through_the_decades /index_of_questions/1930_1.html.

66. "Recital Here Tuesday by Montclair Chorus," *Courier-News*, December 7, 1940, 3.

67. "Choral Club Plans Recital," *Courier-News*, June 4, 1948, 20.

68. Associate Alumnae of Douglass College, "Oral History Project Interview: Evelyn Field '49," conducted and transcribed by Susan Schwirck, Folder: Evelyn Sermons Field (1949), AADC.

69. Denda, Hawkesworth, and Perrone, *The Douglass Century*, 101.

70. "Veronica Henriksen," *Quair* (1944 Douglass College Yearbook), Special Collections and University Archives, Rutgers University.

71. "Constance Andrews," *Quair* (1945 Douglass College Yearbook), Special Collections and University Archives, Rutgers University.

72. Elmore, "Whatever You Put Your Mind To," 4, AADC.

73. "(Anna) Carolyn Rice," *Quair* (1942 Douglass College Yearbook), Special Collections and University Archives, Rutgers University.

74. Bureau of the Census, Department of Commerce, *Sixteenth Census of the United States* (1940): Census Place: *Plainfield, Union, New Jersey*; Roll: *T627_2387*; Page: *6B*; Enumeration District: *20–67*; National Archives, St. Louis, Missouri, *World War II Draft Cards (Fourth Registration) for the State of New Jersey*: Record Group Title: *Records of the Selective Service System, 1926–1975*; Record Group Number: *147*; Series Number: *M1986*; Bureau of the Census, Department of Commerce, *Fifteenth Census of the United States* (1930): Census Place: *Manhattan, New York, New York*; Roll: *1576*; Page: *10A*; Enumeration District: *1001*; FHL microfilm: *2341311*.

75. Bureau of the Census, Department of Commerce, *Fourteenth Census of the United States* (1920): Census Place: *Princeton, Mercer, New Jersey*; Roll: *T625_1053*; Page: *7A*; Enumeration District: *47*; Bureau of the Census, Department of Commerce, *Fifteenth Census of the United States* (1930): Census Place: *Princeton, Mercer, New Jersey*; Roll: *1362*; Page: *8B*; Enumeration District: *0100*; FHL microfilm: *2341097*; Bureau of the Census, Department of Commerce, *Sixteenth Census of the United States* (1940): Census Place: *Princeton, Mercer, New Jersey*; Roll: *T627_2357*; Page: *9B*; Enumeration District: *11–62*.

76. Cecilia Avon Rahner, "Douglass Convocation in Vorhees Chapel," Douglass College, New Brunswick, NJ, June 5, 1999, AADC.

77. Emma Warren, "Open Dialogue with Emma Warren '49," Black Alumnae Network, March 31, 2018, AADC.

78. Ibid.

79. Ibid.

80. Ibid.

81. Bureau of the Census, Department of Commerce, *Fifteenth Census of the United States* (1930): Census Place: *Somerville, Somerset, New Jersey*; Roll: *1384*; Page: *8B*; Enumeration District: *0047*; FHL microfilm: *2341119*; Bureau of the Census, Department of Commerce, *Sixteenth Census of the United States* (1940): Census Place: *Somerville, Somerset, New Jersey*; Roll: *T627_2383*; Page: *15A*; Enumeration District: *18-65*.

82. "Oral History Project Interview: Evelyn Field '49," AADC; Warren, "Open Dialogue," AADC.

83. Denda, Hawkesworth, and Perrone, *The Douglass Century*, 83.

84. "Oral History Project Interview: Evelyn Field '49," AADC.

85. "Resigns from Board," *Central New Jersey Home News*, June 16, 1949, 11.

86. "Handbook of Information for Students," 1945, 2.

87. See Jennifer Hillman Helgren, "Inventing American Girlhood: Gender and Citizenship in the Twentieth-Century Camp Fire Girls" (PhD diss., Claremont Graduate University, 2005); Jessica L. Foley, "'Meeting the Needs of Today's Girl': Youth Organizations and the Making of a Modern Girlhood, 1945–1980" (PhD diss., Brown University, 2010).

88. Quoted in Denda, Hawkesworth, and Perrone, *The Douglass Century*, 84.

89. "Oral History Project Interview: Evelyn Field '49," AADC.

90. Carol Elmore, "Enthusiastic about Learning," 3, Folder: Andrews, Emma (1949), AADC.

91. "Oral History Project Interview: Evelyn Field '49," AADC.

92. "Handbook of Information for Students," 1948, 47.

93. Ibid.

94. Perkins, "The African American Female Elite," 735.

95. "Handbook of Information for Students," 1945, 17; "Handbook of Information for Students," 1948, 15.

96. "Oral History Project Interview: Evelyn Field '49," AADC.

97. Ibid.

98. "Emma Andrews, '49," Folder: Andrews, Emma (1949), AADC.

99. Cecelia Avon Rahner, "Douglass Convocation in Voorhees Chapel, June 5, 1999," AADC.

100. Rachel Devlin, *A Girl Stands at the Door: The Generation of Young Women Who Desegregated America's Schools* (New York: Basic Books, 2018); Marisa Chappell, Jenny Hutchinson, and Brian Ward, "Dress modestly, neatly . . . as if you were going to church": Respectability, Class, and Gender in the Montgomery Bus Boycott and the Early Civil Rights Movement," in *Gender and the Civil Rights Movement*, ed. Peter J. Ling and Sharon Monteith (New Brunswick, NJ: Rutgers University Press, 1999), 69–100.

101. Warren, "Open Dialogue," AADC.

102. Beatrice J. Adams, Shaun Armstead, Shari Cunningham, and Tracey Johnson, "The Rutgers Race Man," in *Scarlet and Black*, vol. 2, ed. Kendra Boyd, Marisa Fuentes, and Deborah Gray White (New Brunswick, NJ: Rutgers University Press, forthcoming).

103. "Constance Andrews," *New Jersey College for Women—Alumnae Directory*, Folder: Andrews, Constance (1945), AADC; Elmore, "Enthusiastic about Learning," 3.

104. Devlin, *A Girl Stands at the Door*, xxviii.

105. Ibid., 13.

106. Ibid., xxviii.

107. Patti Verbanas, "Proving the Case for School Desegregation," *Courier News*, May 17, 2016, 7A; "Rutgers Hall of Distinguished Alumni," Julia Baxter, AADC.

108. "Biographical Questionnaire: Maideh Mazda Magee," Folder: Mazda, Maideh (1947), AADC.

109. Denda, Hawkesworth, and Perrone, *The Douglass Century*, 148.

110. Elmore, "Enthusiastic about Learning," 3, AADC.

111. Elmore, "Whatever You Put Your Mind To," 4, AADC.

112. Ibid.

113. Warren, "Open Dialogue," AADC.

114. "Biographical Questionnaire: Anna Carolyn Rice," Folder: Anna Carolyn Rice, AADC.

115. Dean Litt is the tenth dean of Douglass, however, if interim dean Harriet Davidson is counted (2008–2010), Litt is actually the eleventh dean.

116. *1918–2018, Douglass, The Power of 100 Years* (Unpublished Convocation Program, Rutgers, Douglass Residential College), May 12, 2018.

117. Ibid.

CHAPTER 5: Race as Reality and Illusion

1. "The Line Cracker," *Sunday Times*, October 19, 1930, Box 263, Archibald Dunlop folder, Rutgers University Biographical Files: Alumni (Classes of 1923–1939), Special Collections and University Archives, Rutgers University.

2. See Deborah Gray White, *Ar'n't I a Woman? Female Slaves in the Plantation South* (New York: W. W. Norton, 1985), 46–61.

3. Richard P. McCormick, "Archie Williams Dunlop 1933," Box 25, Black Graduates (1892–1968), Folder (1 of 3), Richard P. McCormick Papers, Special Collections and University Archives, Rutgers University.

4. Allyson Hobbs, *A Chosen Exile: A History of Racial Passing in American Life* (Cambridge, MA: Harvard University Press, 2014), 9–11, 30, 31; Lee D. Baker, *From Savage to Negro: Anthropology and the Construction of Race, 1896–1954* (Berkeley: University of California Press, 1998); Glenda Gilmore, *Gender and Jim Crow: Women and the Politics of White Supremacy in North Carolina, 1896–1920* (Chapel Hill: University of North Carolina Press, 1996), 61–63; Gail Bederman, *Manliness and Civilization: A Cultural History of Gender and Race, 1880–1917* (Chicago: University of Chicago Press, 1994), 29; Evelyn Brooks Higginbotham, "African-American Women's History and the Metalanguage of Race," *Signs* 17, no. 2 (Winter 1992): 253–254.

5. For examples of racial ambiguity, see Tera Hunter, *Bound in Wedlock: Slave and Free Black Marriage in the Nineteenth Century* (Cambridge, MA: Harvard University Press,

2017); Kali Gross, *Hannah Mary Tabbs and the Disembodied Torso: A Tale of Race, Sex, and Violence in America* (New York: Oxford University Press, 2016); Shannen Williams, "Confronting Archival Silences and Navigating Spiritual Landmines: Writing a History of Black Catholic Nuns in the Twenty-First Century," lecture at the 40th Annual Susman Graduate Conference, Rutgers University, New Brunswick, NJ, March 30, 2018, manuscript forthcoming; Allyson Hobbs, *A Chosen Exile: A History of Racial Passing in American Life* (Cambridge, MA: Harvard University Press, 2014); Nayan Shah, *Stranger Intimacy: Contesting Race, Sexuality, and the Law in the North American West* (Berkeley: University of California Press, 2012). Also see John Higham, *Strangers in the Land: Patterns of American Nativism, 1860–1925* (New Brunswick, NJ: Rutgers University Press, 1955); Mae Ngai, *Impossible Subjects: Illegal Aliens and the Making of Modern America* (Princeton, NJ: Princeton University Press, 2005); Khalil Gibran Muhammad, *The Condemnation of Blackness: Race, Crime, and the Making of Modern America* (Cambridge, MA: Harvard University Press, 2009); Cheryl D. Hicks, *Talk with You Like a Woman: African American Women, Justice, and Reform in New York, 1890–1935* (Chapel Hill: University of North Carolina Press, 2010).

6. Allen was mentioned in Table 3.1 and Henriksen was discussed in Chapter 4.

7. Bonnie Brewer, "'Empower Ourselves,' Blacks Urged," *Daily Records, Morris County, NJ*, October 25, 1992, A5; Mildred L. Lipscombe, "Grace Baxter Fenderson," in *Past and Promises: The Lives of New Jersey Women*, ed. Joyce N. Burstyn (Syracuse, NY: Syracuse University Press, 1996), 138–139.

8. Bureau of the Census, Department of Commerce, *Fifteenth Census of the United States: 1930 Population Schedule* (April 19, 1930).

9. For more on the history of racial classification, see George Fredrickson, *The Black Image in the White Mind: Debates over Afro-American Character and Destiny, 1817–1914* (New York: Harper & Row, 1971); Baker, *From Savage to Negro*; Ibram X. Kendi, *Stamped from the Beginning: The Definitive History of Racist Ideas in America* (New York: Nation Books, 2016).

10. Tom Perry, "She Broke Barrier, Kept Ego in Check," *Sunday Courier News*, April 14, 1996, A-10.

11. Ibid.

12. Perry, "She Broke Barrier," 1.

13. The Baxters' ownership of a car and ability to afford gasoline to drive back and forth from their home to New Brunswick suggests that the Baxters were more well to do than most Americans caught in the midst of the Great Depression; for more on the history of African Americans during the Great Depression, see Joe William Trotter, *From a Raw Deal to a New Deal: African Americans 1929–1945* (New York: Oxford University Press, 1996); Cheryl Lynn Greenburg, *To Ask for an Equal Chance: African Americans in the Great Depression* (Lanham, MD: Rowman and Littlefield, 2009); Ira Katznelson, *Fear Itself: The New Deal and the Origins of Our Time* (New York: W. W. Norton & Company, 2014); Ira Katznelson, *When Affirmative Action Was White: An Untold History of Racial Inequality in Twentieth Century America* (New York: W. W. Norton, 2006).

14. Dr. Louis Baxter's father, James Miller Baxter, dedicated his career and advocacy toward securing educational opportunities for African Americans after emancipation. Beyond opening a night school for adults, most notably, James Miller Baxter led the campaign to desegregate Newark public schools, a mission he pursued throughout the course of his career. In 1872, with Principal Baxter's assistance, Irene

Pataquam Mulford became the first African American pupil to enroll at Newark (later Barringer) High School. Mulford's enrollment at Newark High School set an important precedent, for that same year, the Newark Board of Education declared that "colored children are entitled [. . .] to admission at all public schools of the city on the same terms and conditions as other children," though Newark schools remained largely segregated. Shortly after Baxter retired as the principal of the Market Street Colored School in 1909, the Newark Board of Education forbade racial segregation in the city's schools, leading to further desegregation. For more on James Miller Baxter's career as a trailblazing race and education activist, see "James M. Baxter (1845–1909)," Villanova University Falvey Memorial Library, https://exhibits.library.villanova.edu/institute-colored-youth/graduates/james-m-baxter-jr-bio/; Kathleen O'Brien, "Black History Month: Newark Project Honors Influential City Educator James Baxter," *NJ.com*, http://www.nj.com/news/index.ssf/2010/02/newark_urban_renewal_project_b.html; Marion T. Wright, "Mr. Baxter's School," *Proceedings of the New Jersey Historical Society* (1941), 131, http://dh.howard.edu/cgi/viewcontent.cgi?article=1009&context=edu_fac; Rudy Johnson, "Last of Segregated Schools in City Abandoned in 1909," *Newark Evening News*, February 12, 1967.

15. Living on campus was a requirement during the initial years of the college. See New Jersey College for Women Announcements for 1919/1920 and 1920/1921. By academic year 1933/1934 the institution advised that "it should be the aim of every . . . student . . . during her four years of college to spend at least a year in dormitory residence." See "A Guide to New Jersey College for Women, New Brunswick, NJ," Bulletin no. 19 (January 1934), 11. Also see *Report of the Dean—New Jersey College for Women, 1935–1936*, Box 1, Records of the Dean of Douglass College (Group 1), 1887–1973, Special Collections and University Archives, Rutgers University.

16. New Jersey College for Women Department of Public Information, "Baxter, Julia Esteve" Folder: Baxter, Julia Esteve (1938), AADC Bio Files, Associate Alumnae of Douglass College (hereafter AADC).

17. Darlene Clark Hine, "Rape and the Inner Lives of Black Women in the Middle West," *Signs* 14, no. 4 (Summer 1989): 912.

18. Deborah Gray White, *Too Heavy a Load: Black Women in Defense of Themselves, 1894–1994* (New York: W. W. Norton, 1999).

19. *Quair* (1934 Douglass College Yearbook), Special Collections and University Archives, Rutgers University, 248, 249.

20. Perry, "She Broke Barrier."

21. See Kali Gross, *Colored Amazons: Crime, Violence, and Black Women in the City of Brotherly Love, 1880–1910* (Durham, NC: Duke University Press, 2006).

22. As mentioned previously, Baxter's grandfather was a pioneering black educator in the Newark public school system. Despite the limited educational opportunities available to African Americans prior to the establishment of schools by the Freedmen's Bureau after the Civil War, James Miller Baxter graduated from Philadelphia's Institute for Colored Youth in May 1864; upon graduation, James relocated to Newark, New Jersey, after accepting a teaching position at State Street Public School in October 1864, the only institution open to African Americans in the city. Shortly thereafter, Baxter was promoted to school principal at the youthful age of nineteen, a position he maintained for forty-five years until his retirement and subsequent death in late 1909. See "James M. Baxter (1845–1909)."

23. See Patti Verbanas, "Julia Baxter Bates: Proving the Scientific Case for Public School Desegregation," *Rutgers Today,* https://news.rutgers.edu/feature/julia-baxter-bates -proving-scientific-case-public-school-desegregation/20160508#.WlvnlZgrJEI; Judith Osborne, "Julia Baxter Bates: A Profile," *Douglass Alumnae Bulletin* (Spring 1989): 5.

24. The Baxter family's commitment to fighting racial injustice dates back to antebellum-era Philadelphia. As the abolitionist fervor swept the nation in the year before the Civil War, Julia and Malcolm Baxter's paternal great-grandparents, James and Elizabeth Baxter, assisted runaway slaves in Philadelphia's Underground Railroad. The couple's son James became a renowned Newark educator and integrationist, while his children J. Leroy, Grace, and Louis participated in various local and national racial uplift initiatives; see Patti Verbanas, "Julia Baxter Bates"; "Baxter Heritage: Negro Left Mark on City," *Newark Evening News,* February 12, 1967; "James M. Baxter (1845–1909)."

25. As quoted in Osbourne, "Julia Baxter Bates," 5.

26. See Verbanas, "Julia Baxter Bates."

27. Osborne, "Julia Baxter Bates," 5.

28. Julia Baxter Bates, "Curriculum Vitae," Folder: Baxter, Julia Esteve (1938), AADC.

29. Bates, "Curriculum Vitae."

30. Julia Baxter Bates, "Speech at Rutgers Hall of Distinguished Alumni Awards," 3, 4, Folder: Baxter, Julia Esteve (1938), AADC.

31. Jennifer Ritterhouse's work explores how African American and white children were socialized to learn race in the South; see Jennifer Ritterhouse, *Growing Up Jim Crow: How Black and White Southern Children Learned Race* (Chapel Hill: University of North Carolina Press, 2006).

32. Malcolm Baxter's alumni autobiography file as well as 1920 U.S. federal census data provide the name of Malcolm's mother as Kate K. Douglass Baxter, who is described as a "29 year-old mulatto" female in the census record. Born on January 16, 1889, in New Bedford, Massachusetts, Kate Baxter died sometime between 1921–1923 from tuberculosis; her certificate of death could not be found; see "Kate K. Douglass Baxter [*sic* Boates]," in Bureau of the Census, *Fourteenth Federal Census of the United States* (1920): Ward 1, Essex County, New Jersey, Ancestry.com, https://www.ancestry .com/interactive/6061/4313340-00668?pid=30279807&backurl=https://search .ancestry.com/cgi-bin/sse.dll?_phsrc%3DlxA50%26_phstart%3DsuccessSource %26usePUBJs%3Dtrue%26indiv%3D1%26db%3D1920usfedcen%26gss%3Dangs-d% 26new%3D1%26rank%3D1%26msT%3D1%26gsfn%3DKate%2520Douglass%26gsfn _x%3D0%26gsln%3DBaxter%26gsln_x%3D0%26msbpn__ftp%3DRhode%2520Island,% 2520USA%26msbpn%3D42%26msrpn__ftp%3DNewark,%2520Essex,%2520New% 2520Jersey,%2520USA%26msrpn%3D7818%26MSAV%3D1%26uidh%3Dq03%26pcat %3D35%26fh%3D0%26h%3D30279807%26recoff%3D%26ml_rpos%3D1&treeid=& personid=&hintid=&usePUB=true&_phsrc=lxA50&_phstart=successSource&use PUBJs=true; "Malcolm Miller Baxter Autobiographical Data Form," Box 306, Malcolm M. Baxter folder, Rutgers University Biographical Files: Alumni (Classes of 1923–1939), Special Collections and University Archives, Rutgers University.

33. Francine Baxter Shea, interview by Shaun Armstead, New Brunswick, New Jersey, January 24, 2018.

34. Quoted from James LeRoy Baxter, interview by Shaun Armstead, New Brunswick, New Jersey, May 25, 2018; Francine Baxter Shea, interview by Shaun Armstead, January 24, 2018.

35. Francine Baxter Shea, interview by Shaun Armstead, January 24, 2018.

36. Quoted from Francine Baxter Shea, interview by Shaun Armstead, January 24, 2018.

37. A review of the housing arrangements for African American students at Rutgers University between the 1930s and 1940s shows that only one student, Walter G. Alexander, lived on campus during the Depression decade.

38. Francine Baxter Shea, interview by Shaun Armstead, January 24, 2018.

39. Malcolm Baxter's service card, filled out and returned to Rutgers University, states that his address as of January 12, 1943, was "Camp Sutton, N.C." See "Malcolm Miller Baxter Service Card," Box 306, Malcolm M. Baxter folder, Rutgers University Biographical Files: Alumni (Classes of 1923–1939), Special Collections and University Archives, Rutgers University.

40. Quoted from James LeRoy Baxter, interview by Shaun Armstead, May 25, 2018.

41. See Richard M. Dalfume, *Desegregation of the United States Armed Forces: Fighting on Two Fronts, 1939–1953* (Columbia: University of Missouri Press, 1969); Rawn James Jr., *The Double V: How Wars, Protest, and Harry Truman Desegregated America's Military* (New York: Bloomsbury, 2014).

42. Hobbs, *A Chosen Exile*, 4, 11, 12.

43. Malcolm and his wife had their first child, Leroy, in France. However, they never intended to stay there. When they brought young Leroy back to the states, he was the youngest traveler to make the transatlantic journey that year. "Youngest Atlantic Flyer," *Rochester Democrat and Chronicle*, June 24, 1946, 9.

44. Francine Baxter Shea, interview by Shaun Armstead, January 24, 2018.

45. James LeRoy Baxter, interview by Shaun Armstead, May 25, 2018.

46. Ibid.

47. Ibid.

48. Ibid.

49. Francine Baxter Shea, interview by Shaun Armstead, January 24, 2018.

50. "Frankenfield-Baxter," *Courier-News (Bridgewater, NJ)*, April 10, 1970, 16.

51. Malcolm "Duke" Baxter III, interview by Shaun Armstead, November 15, 2017.

52. Francine Baxter Shea, interview by Shaun Armstead, January 24, 2018.

53. Ibid.

54. Ibid.

55. Ibid.

56. Malcolm Baxter questionnaire filled out "For the Biographical Files of the Alumni and Alumnae Records Offices Rutgers—The State University," 1972, Box 306, Malcolm Baxter folder, Rutgers Biographical Files (Classes of 1923–1939), Special Collections and University Archives, Rutgers University.

EPILOGUE

1. W.E.B. Du Bois, "The Real Reason Behind Robeson's Persecution," in *W.E.B. Du Bois, A Reader*, ed. David Levering Lewis (New York: Henry Holt, 1995), 798.

2. Editors of *Freedomways, Paul Robeson: The Great Forerunner* (New York: International Publishers, 1998), 287.

3. Ibid., xi.

4. Paul Robeson Jr., "Paul Robeson: Black Warrior," in *The Great Forerunner*, 3

5. The National Football Foundation supports amateur football and oversees the College Football Hall of Fame.

6. *The Great Forerunner*, 317.

7. "Paul Robeson Center? Rutgers Votes Tomorrow," *Central New Jersey Home News*, November 12, 1968, 1; "Rutgers Reports Progress on Host of Negro Demands," *Courier-News*, May 23, 1968, 33; "Rutgers Remembers a Famous Alumnus," *The Record*, February 13, 1972, 8.

8. *The Great Forerunner*, 257.

LIST OF CONTRIBUTORS

BEATRICE J. ADAMS is a doctoral candidate in African American and African diaspora history at Rutgers University–New Brunswick. She received an MA in social sciences from the University of Chicago and a BA in history from Fisk University. In her dissertation, "Standing in the Warmth of Their Own Sun: African Americans Who Stayed in the American South during the Second Great Migration," she examines African Americans' relationship to the American South, focusing on issues of identity, belonging, and migration. Centered on the experiences of African Americans who remained in and returned to the American South during the period commonly associated with the Second Great Migration (1940–1970), her project aims to interrogate the role of migration in both African Americans' quotidian realizations and conceptualizations of freedom.

Archives Visited: Rutgers Special Collections and University Archives

Acknowledgments: I would like to thank the staff at Rutgers's Special Collections and University Archives, Professor Benjamin Justice, and Jerrad Pacatte for his research contributions to chapter one.

SHAUNI ARMSTEAD is a doctoral student in history at Rutgers University–New Brunswick. She works on women's internationalism after the Second World War. Her dissertation, "Toward a Universal Human Family," focuses on how women of color endeavored to create a peaceful and just world free of racism and sexism.

Archives Visited: Rutgers Special Collections, Associate Alumnae of Douglass College

Acknowledgments: Those who were helpful include the entire Rutgers archives staff, but I would like to single out Stephanie Crawford and Fernanda Perrone, who opened the archive for me on a Friday with no notice. Erika Gorder was also helpful with finding information about Edward Lawson Sr. I would also like to thank Malcolm Baxter II's children, Malcolm "Duke" Baxter III and

Renee Baxter, who answered questions about their father and grandfather and put me in contact with their aunt and uncle, Francine Baxter Shea and LeRoy Baxter. I would also like to express gratitude toward Francine Shea and LeRoy Baxter for agreeing to interviews and to Shea for providing the Baxter family photos accompanying the essay. "Race as Reality and Illusion" would be an entirely different chapter without their recollections. Additional thanks to all my Scarlet and Black team members.

MIYA CAREY is a Presidential Diversity Postdoctoral Fellow at Binghamton University. She holds a PhD in African American history from Rutgers University–New Brunswick, and a BA in history from Drew University. Her research interests include childhood, African American women's history, and black citizenship. Her dissertation, "'That charm of all girlhood': Black Girlhood and Girls in Washington, D.C., 1930–1965," examines black girlhood and middle-class women's leadership through the lens of girls' organizations and social clubs in the nation's capital. She has published a portion of this research in an article titled "Becoming 'a force for desegregation': The Girl Scouts and Civil Rights in the Nation's Capital," that appears in the fall 2017 issue of *Washington History.*

Archives Visited: Rutgers Special Collections and University Archives, Douglass Residential College, Associate Alumnae of Douglass College

Acknowledgments: Miya Carey would like to thank Erika Gorder at the Rutgers Special Collections and University Archives, the executive board, staff, and volunteers at the Associate Alumnae of Douglass College, but especially Valerie Anderson and Carol Hamlin, Dean Jacqueline Litt and Maria DePina of the Douglass Residential College, and Kaisha Esty for contributing research to this essay. Carey would also like to thank Drs. Mary Hawkesworth, Fernanda Perrone, and Kayo Denda for sharing their manuscript with us.

SHARI CUNNINGHAM, MS, is a PhD candidate at Rutgers University–New Brunswick in the higher education program at the Graduate School of Education. Previously, Cunningham was the assistant director of financial aid for the Rutgers Biomedical and Health Science programs for the Piscataway campus. She holds master's in business and a bachelor's in American studies with a double minor in history and political science from the College of Saint Elizabeth. Her research explores the socialization of black doctoral students in the humanities and how they make sense of their scholarly journey throughout the phases of doctoral pursuit.

Acknowledgments: Erika Gorder of Rutgers Special Collections, Dr. James Amemasor of the New Jersey Historical Society, who went above and beyond for this project's success, and Beatrice Adams, an amazing team leader and mentor.

TRACEY JOHNSON is a PhD candidate in the history department at Rutgers University–New Brunswick. Her doctoral research investigates how black visual artists created their own institutionalized art spaces in the face of exclusion from mainstream museums and galleries. She places these efforts in conversation with the black power movement.

Archives Visited: Rutgers Special Collections, Gardner A. Sage Library of New Brunswick Theological Seminary, Schomburg Center for Research in Black Culture

Acknowledgments: Dr. John Coakley

ERI KITADA is a doctoral student in the Department of History at Rutgers University–New Brunswick. She studies the links between Southeast and East Asia and the United States, with interests in race, space, gender/sexuality, and empire. Eri holds with a BA in humanities and human sciences from Hokkaido University and an MA from the University of Tokyo.

Archives Visited: Rutgers Special Collections and University Archives

Acknowledgments: Rutgers Special Collections and University Archives: Erika Gorder, Thomas J. Frusciano; New Brunswick Theological Seminary: John W. Coakley, Russell Gasero, Tracey Hunter Hayes, Bethany O'Shea.

JERRAD P. PACATTE is a PhD student in history at Rutgers University–New Brunswick.

Acknowledgments: Erika Gorder, Christine Lutz, Dr. Fernanda Perrone; Cheryl Ferguson and Dana Chandler at Tuskegee University Archives.

BRENANN SUTTER is a doctoral candidate in history at Rutgers University–New Brunswick. She earned a BA from the University of California, San Diego, and an MA from New York University. Her expertise is in American women and gender. Her dissertation, "Consuming the Centerfold: Sexuality and the Fantasy of the American Good Life," explores the myriad ways marginalized groups engaged in consumer and sexual culture in the second half of the twentieth century.

Archives Visited: Rutgers Special Collections and University Archives

Acknowledgments: Erika Gorder

PAMELA WALKER is a doctoral candidate at Rutgers University–New Brunswick specializing in African American history and women and gender history. Her dissertation, "'Everyone Must Think We Really Need Freedom': Black and

White Mothers, The Mississippi Box Project, and the Civil Rights Movement," examines the relationship between rural motherhood, activism, poverty, and political consciousness in 1960s-era social movements. In 2016, she coauthored an article in *Scarlet and Black, Vol. 1: Slavery and Dispossession in Rutgers History* entitled "'And I a Poor Slave Yet': The Precarity of Black Life in New Brunswick, 1766–1835." Walker received a BA in history and journalism from the University of Tennessee at Knoxville and an MA in history from the University of New Orleans.

Archives Visited: Alice Jennings Archibald History Room, Mt. Zion A.M.E. Church, New Brunswick, Rutgers Oral History Archives, Rutgers University (online), New Brunswick Free Public Library Collection

Acknowledgments: I would like to thank Barbara Saunders, historian of the Mount Zion A.M.E. Church in New Brunswick for her invaluable assistance in our research. I would also like to thank Reverend Eric B. Billips and Reverend Myra T. Billips, both of Mt. Zion A.M.E. Church, for allowing me access to the church's private archive.

MEAGAN WIERDA is a PhD candidate who studies American history and the history of science and technology. Broadly conceived, her dissertation project considers the myriad calculations that were impressed in the service of justifying, maintaining, and undermining the institution of slavery during the Early Republic. Meagan received a BA in history from the University of Ottawa in 2012 and an MA in history from Concordia University in 2015.

Archives Visited: Rutgers Special Collections and University Archives

Acknowledgments: A big thanks goes out Erika Gorder for all of her help!

CAITLIN WIESNER is a PhD candidate in the Department of History at Rutgers University–New Brunswick. She specializes in the history of sexual violence, feminist activism, African American women's organizing, and crime control in the late-twentieth-century United States. Her dissertation, "Controlling Rape: Black Women, the Feminist Movement against Sexual Violence, and the State, 1974–1994," examines the antirape activism of African American women in Philadelphia, Chicago, and Washington, DC during the "War on Crime" era of the 1970s and 1980s.

Archives Visited: For the section I wrote for "In the Shadow of Old Queens: African American Life and Labors in New Brunswick," I relied upon local newspapers (*New Brunswick Daily Times, New Brunswick Daily Home News*) held in microform at Alexander Library and the maps and directories held at the Alexander Special Collections. Other authors for the essay made use of the archives of the New Jersey Historical Society, the New Brunswick Free Public Library, and the Mount Zion A.M.E. Church.

Acknowledgments: Special thanks to Jerrad Pacatte for his important contributions on the history of African American men's labor in New Brunswick.

JOSEPH WILLIAMS is a PhD candidate in the Department of History at Rutgers University–New Brunswick. He specializes in late-nineteenth and early-twentieth-century African American and women's and gender history. His research interests include black intellectual history, black women's history, and the history of American religious reform. His dissertation, "Black Club Women's Religious Intellectual Tradition," examines the religious ideas of black women who participated in the club movement in the late nineteenth and early twentieth centuries. Prior to attending Rutgers, he earned an MA in history from DePaul University and a master's in theological studies from Garrett Evangelical Theological Seminary.

Archives Visited: Special Collections and University Archives, Rutgers University Libraries, Gardner A. Sage Library of New Brunswick Theological Seminary

Acknowledgments: Dr. John Coakley

ABOUT THE EDITORS

KENDRA BOYD is an assistant professor of history at York University. Previously she served as the Scarlet and Black Project postdoctoral associate and coauthored "Old Money: Rutgers University and the Political Economy of Slavery in New Jersey" and "His Name Was Will: Remembering Enslaved Individuals in Rutgers History" in *Scarlet and Black: Slavery and Dispossession in Rutgers History*. Boyd has a forthcoming article on black businesswomen in the Detroit Housewives League, and is currently writing a book on black entrepreneurship and racial capitalism in Great Migration era Detroit, Michigan.

MARISA J. FUENTES is the Presidential Term Chair in African American History and associate professor of history and women's and gender studies at Rutgers University–New Brunswick, New Jersey. Fuentes is the author of the multi-award winning book *Dispossessed Lives: Enslaved Women, Violence, and the Archive* (University of Pennsylvania Press, 2016). She has written a number of articles, book chapters, and book reviews, including "Power and Historical Figuring: Rachel Pringle Polgreen's Troubled Archive," which won the Andres Ramos Mattei-Neville Hall Article Prize from the Association of Caribbean Historians. She is also the coeditor of *Scarlet and Black: Slavery and Dispossession in Rutgers History, Volumes 1* through 3 (Rutgers University Press), and a 'Slavery and the Archive' special issue in *History of the Present* (November 2016).

DEBORAH GRAY WHITE is Board of Governors Distinguished Professor of History at Rutgers University–New Brunswick, New Jersey. She is author of *Ar'n't I A Woman? Female Slaves in the Plantation South; Too Heavy a Load: Black Women in Defense of Themselves, 1894-1994;* several K-12 text books on United States history, and *Let My People Go, African Americans 1804-1860* (1999). In 2008, she published an edited work entitled *Telling Histories: Black Women in the Ivory Tower,* a collection of personal narratives written by African American women historians that chronicle the entry of black women into the historical profession and the development of the field of black women's history.

Freedom On My Mind: A History of African Americans, a coauthored college text, is moving into its third edition. As a fellow at the Woodrow Wilson International Center for Scholars in Washington, D.C, and as a John Simon Guggenheim Fellow, White conducted research on her newest book, *Lost in the USA: American Identity from the Promise Keepers to the Million Mom March*. She holds the Carter G. Woodson Medallion and the Frederick Douglass Medal for excellence in African American history, and was also awarded a Doctorate in Humane Letters from her undergraduate alma mater, Binghamton University. She currently codirects the Scarlet and Black Project which investigates Native Americans and African Americans in the history of Rutgers University. With Professor Marisa J. Fuentes she is editor of the 2016 volume: *Scarlet and Black: Slavery and Dispossession in Rutgers History.*